# CITIES IN TRANSITION:
# A GUIDE FOR PRACTICING PLANNERS

Joseph Schilling and Alan Mallach, FAICP

## TABLE OF CONTENTS

# Acknowledgments

 This report is the product of nearly 10 years of fieldwork and policy work with local planners, elected officials, economic and community developers, neighborhood activists, researchers, students, and designers. During our visits to these cities in transition we have heard many inspiring stories and seen dozens of compelling examples, many of which we share here. Our hope is that this compendium of ideas and strategies will help the foot soldiers, whether they are planners or policy makers, in their pursuit of making their cities in transition more resilient and sustainable communities.

We would first like to acknowledge the support of the Ford Foundation that made this report possible. Special thanks to Virginia Tech graduate research assistants Natalie Borecki and Lauren Bulka for conducting and summarizing interviews along with the researching and drafting of different passages of the report. Three external reviewers made time in their hectic holiday schedules to give us critical feedback that reshaped the report and made it more relevant for practitioners: Virginia Tech professor Maggie Cowell, Lead Planner Christina Kelly of the Genesee County Land Bank, and Jennifer Leonard of the Center for Community Progress and former executive director of the National Vacant Properties Campaign that enabled much of our work. At the American Planning Association, Ann F. Dillemuth, AICP, copyedited the manuscript.

As part of our research and writing we gathered insights through a series of practitioner interviews to enhance and amplify our menu of strategies. Excerpts from some of the interviews are included here; the complete set of 17 interviews is posted on the web. (See the Resources for a complete list.) We are extremely grateful for the time and thoughtfulness and extended to us by Anthony Armstrong, Charles Bartsch, Kaid Benfield, Ian Beniston, Teresa Brice, Robert Brown, AICP, Don Chen, Michael Clarke, Deeohn Ferris, Frank Ford, John Gower, Christina Kelly, Phil Kidd, Dan Kildee, Tony Kroeger, Samina Raja, and Bobbi Reichtell.

CHAPTER 1

# Introduction

 Many of America's cities are in states of uncertainty, fighting the challenges of lost population and jobs, shifting demographics, plummeting property values, and shrinking municipal budgets. For many Rust Belt cities, this has been an ongoing struggle that began decades ago with the onset of suburbanization and the loss of manufacturing jobs. Although some of these cities, both large and small, saw recovery in the 1990s and early 2000s, others never shared in that revival and continue to lose population and jobs. For these cities, it is a challenge just to provide basic public services, let alone to find the resources and energy to plan their futures.

For other cities, the crises have erupted more recently. While growth had sustained Sun Belt cities for decades, the collapse of the housing bubble and the onset of the Great Recession in 2006 and 2007 brought falling house prices, widespread foreclosures, and the first signs of systemic disinvestment and abandonment. Other cities saw nascent revivals thwarted, while a growing number of inner-ring suburbs began to realize that they had gradually inherited many of the problems—but often few of the assets—of nearby central cities.

These are all cities in transition. As they look forward, uncertainties loom large. With most observers predicting only a sluggish economic recovery and a housing market that may remain weak for many years, Sun Belt cities may no longer be able to count on growth to revive their local economies, while older cities may find it difficult to capture what little new demand emerges. Immigration is causing dramatic demographic changes in many cities, creating both tensions and opportunities that have yet to be addressed, let alone resolved. Uncertainties about energy costs and long-term climate change raise further questions about many cities' futures and their regional and national roles.

Planners will play critical roles in helping cities find new directions amid these uncertainties. To bring cities back to prosperity and civic health, planners will have to deploy new skills and tools beyond those used to guide growth in the past. They must take on new roles in both framing and executing change strategies, building partnerships, and channeling the allocation of public resources to foster economic regeneration. This PAS Report is designed to introduce new ways of planning for cities in transition and guide the planners who are charged with these responsibilities.

## WHAT ARE CITIES IN TRANSITION?

In one sense, all cities are "in transition": dynamic, changing, constantly confounding planners. As Spiro Kostof has written, "a city has its own mind: it may refuse to go along with what has been prescribed, or find its own mode of obedience that leaves it free to metamorphose without losing track of its idiosyncratic habits"(1992). This PAS Report defines *cities in transition* as those cities facing major challenges of regeneration resulting from fundamental short- or long-term economic, demographic, or physical changes. These cities face critical problems, and they challenge planners to rethink their own missions and roles.

Cities in transition tend to fall into four broad categories:

*Legacy cities:* Sometimes called "shrinking cities," these are older industrial cities such as Detroit; Flint, Michigan; or Buffalo that have been steadily losing population and jobs since the 1950s or 1960s. Located disproportionately in the Midwestern industrial heartland, they have lost the manufacturing bases they were built upon but have yet to find new foundations for economic growth; meanwhile, their population losses have created large inventories of vacant land and buildings.

*Gateway cities:* Predominately located in the Northeast, these older industrial cities are following a different trajectory thanks to new generations of immigrants, whose presence has stabilized or even reversed these cities' population losses. Gateway cities such as Springfield, Massachusetts, or Paterson, New Jersey, suffer from many of the same problems as the legacy cities, but their roles as immigrant gateways offer distinct opportunities as well as challenges.

*Boom-bust cities:* These Sun Belt cities, with economies driven by construction and real estate, were dealt a hard blow by the Great Recession and the collapse of the housing bubble and can no longer count on future growth to resolve their challenges. A legacy of overbuilding in cities such

Cities in transition *are cities facing major challenges of regeneration resulting from fundamental short- or long-term economic, demographic, or physical changes.*

as Phoenix, Arizona; Las Vegas; and San Bernardino, California, coupled with falling house prices and the prevalence of foreclosures, has made the prospect of systemic disinvestment and abandonment in parts of these cities increasingly likely.

*First suburbs:* Almost every older city in the United States is surrounded by a ring of suburbs that grew from the late 19th century through the first wave of 1950s postwar suburbanization (such as Euclid, Ohio; St. Clair Shores, Michigan; and Orange, New Jersey). As the leading edges of suburbia move farther out, many of these "first suburbs" have become heir to the problems of their declining central cities, yet they often lack the assets—such as still-vital downtowns and strong research universities—that offer many central cities hope for the future.

*Housing on hold in Minneapolis*

© iStockphoto.com/Lawrence Sawyer

## THE PLANNER'S ROLE IN CITIES IN TRANSITION

These cities matter. Cities in transition contain a large part of the nation's population and important sectors of the national and global economies, and their recoveries are critical not only to their residents and business owners but to their metro regions, their states, and the country as a whole. But while healthy cities in areas of strong economic growth are likely to prosper with or without the intervention of planning, cities struggling to find a way back will require greater activism in the public sector.

Planners are uniquely suited by training and temperament to help their cities navigate the alternative courses of action that may be available. They bring awareness of both the regional relationships affecting cities and the long time spans needed to bring about sustainable change. To succeed, however, planners will need new ways of thinking about the practice of planning as a whole and specific tools that they can use on the ground.

Traditional planning models provide little guidance for those charged with the responsibility for planning in these cities. Practice and education largely focus on the planner's roles in guiding growth to ensure it addresses the needs of both the natural and human-made environments and helping a community respond to development pressures: what the plan and regulations should permit, what standards should govern development, and what infrastructure changes may be needed to accommodate anticipated growth.

The planner's mission in a city in transition is fundamentally different. Here we introduce five basic principles as a foundation for planning in cities in transition:

### Planning Is Not Necessarily about Growth

Cities in transition must look to a new paradigm of planning oriented to sustainability rather than growth. Most cities in transition have lost and continue to lose population, and many have large expanses of vacant land and numerous abandoned buildings. Such cities need to plan how they can adapt to smaller populations and development footprints without relying on growth. This is not planning *for* shrinkage but planning that recognizes shrinkage as the reality and a starting point for thinking about the future. Even where future growth is possible, planners need different planning strategies to stabilize local economies and create the conditions for that growth. Though for the boom-bust cities of the Sun Belt comparable shrinkage is not an issue, framing a future that does not depend on growth as the engine of prosperity is as important as it is in other cities in transition.

### Planning Is for Activists

Cities in transition are cities that have experienced some degree of market failure. Just as the federal government may have to intervene to address national market failure, as with the near-collapse of the banking system in 2008, local governments may need to help create conditions that can restore a healthy market for housing, jobs, and investment in the city.

The planner's role is to figure out how to do this. What mix of public strategies, investments, incentives, and plans—and what creative partnerships among governments, nonprofits, and the business community—can best restore vitality to the local economy, and which actions are fiscally and socially responsible? The planner must become an activist, advocating for strategies that can change the status quo.

Planners must focus on rebuilding weak markets, stabilizing neighborhoods, and fostering green reuse of vacant land, rather than planning for greenfield growth. They must create a more proactive role for local government in general, and planners in particular, in carrying out strategies for change. Planning must become more strategic and entrepreneurial and less regulatory, with less focus on controlling development and more on how to bring about the change a community needs.

### It's the Economy, Stupid

Planning for cities in transition is more than anything else about creating the economic conditions for a stronger future, yet planners are rarely trained to understand economics and markets in any depth. Planners must learn to better integrate economic factors into their plans and strategies. As the often-dismal history of public initiatives since the urban renewal era shows, plans aimed at reversing urban decline that are not grounded in solid economic premises usually fail.

Every good planner knows that planning is not just about the use of land, but many nonetheless see land use as the center of their work, with social and economic considerations flowing from that center. The situation in cities in transition is reversed. While the planner's mantra in a prosperous growing community might be "adopt the best land-use strategy, and the economics will follow," in a city in transition it might well be "adopt the best economic strategy, and the land uses will follow."

### Planning Is about Engagement

While public and community engagement is at the heart of planning practice, it takes on particular importance in cities in transition, where planning is about changing the status quo. Members of the community may be deeply unhappy or conflicted over the present and future of their city or neighborhood but unsure of what actions to take. The planner must be a good listener as well as advocate, making sure that all voices are heard and all sectors of the community are engaged in the strategies that are ultimately pursued. In some cities, where the civic infrastructure and networks of community-based organizations have deteriorated or no longer exist, traditional civic engagement approaches must be supplemented by institution-building and community-organizing strategies.

*While this block in Baltimore awaits redevelopment, it is temporarily providing green space.*

Joseph Schilling

**Planning Is about Trying New Ideas**

This report offers a new approach for planners tackling the special challenges of cities in transition by focusing on broad-based community regeneration. These challenges demand new ways of thinking, new planning techniques, and new implementation strategies that acknowledge conditions such as population loss, low market values, and large numbers of vacant properties. We use the term *regeneration* in these pages to suggest that these cities may need to go beyond physical rebuilding or economic development and completely rethink their futures using different assumptions and paradigms than in the past. We try to identify areas where different planning approaches are needed and offer specific suggestions to help guide planners who are trying to pursue these approaches.

Planning practice in cities in transition is very much a work in progress. While some of the ideas and strategies that are being pursued in cities in transition are not new, many are. Many, such as sustainable land reuse or the reconfiguration of largely abandoned neighborhoods, are still experimental and largely untested. In these pages we highlight many examples—some tried and true, others new and uncertain—that are emerging from these cities pioneering new strategies for land reuse, market creation, or neighborhood change on the ground.

This is challenging work. Leading change is always more difficult than maintaining the status quo, and playing a proactive role is more difficult than reacting to others' proposals. But in many respects this is the cutting edge of planning practice in the United States. It allows planners to participate in the rebuilding of cities and change the courses of their residents' lives for the better. It is work well worth doing.

**OVERVIEW OF THE REPORT**

After this introduction, Chapter 2 provides some background, defining the universe of cities in transition, the reasons for their current difficulties, and the dimensions of the particular challenges they face.

The next section moves from broad principles and strategies through specific planning approaches and into implementation. Chapter 3 outlines basic planning principles and lays out a framework for strategic policy planning, while Chapter 4 offers specific approaches for developing strategic policy plans for cities in transition. Chapter 5 looks at how planners can adapt traditional planning tools such as zoning to the needs of these cities, while Chapter 6 addresses particular challenges such as vacant land reuse, market building, and neighborhood revitalization. Chapter 7 applies these planning principles to the reuse of individual sites and properties.

We then look at the role of the planner in the context of the political, economic, and organizational challenges found in cities in transition. Chapter 8 explores the central role of community engagement in cities in transition and shows how empowerment and organizing initiatives are helping some cities rebuild their civic infrastructure. Chapter 9 examines the organizational, political, and policy environment in which planners work and explores how a planner can navigate that environment to make planning part of the local decision-making process and link it to implementation actions and successful outcomes. A short conclusion ties together many of the themes in the report.

Adding to the scope and depth of the discussion are four short essays by prominent planning scholars and practitioners, as well as brief case studies or excerpts from interviews with planners practicing in cities in transition. Finally, the Appendix contains four detailed case studies from Allentown, Pennsylvania; Detroit; Orange, New Jersey; and Rialto, California, describing how some of the planning strategies described in the report have been carried out on the ground.

# CHAPTER 2

# Setting the Stage

 In this chapter we take a close look at cities in transition to identify their principal features, challenges, and the reasons for their decline. This information provides the essential framework for discussing the planner's role. We begin by examining the drivers of decline; then we discuss the four categories of cities in transition and the particular factors that had the greatest effect on each type of community. The bulk of the chapter is devoted to a breakdown of the many challenges—economic, social, physical, and institutional—confronting cities in transition. Finally, a short closing section looks at the history of thinking and research on these cities.

## DEFINING THE PROBLEM: DRIVERS OF DECLINE

The current crisis was caused by not just one factor, but rather many different forces that together have transformed the American urban landscape since the end of World War II. While social and economic forces beyond governments' control have been the primary factors fostering urban decline, certain governmental decisions and actions—and in some cases inaction—have exacerbated the effects of these forces.

### Primary Factors

The forces of suburbanization and interregional migration, economic change and deindustrialization, and social and demographic change have been driving decline in older American cities for decades. While many of these first manifested as early as the 1920s, their effects became stronger after World War II as pent-up social and economic pressures emerged with new intensity. More recently, the effects of overbuilding and the housing bubble have led to similar problems in many newer, hitherto fast-growing cities.

*Suburbanization and Regional Migration.* Population loss began in some older cities as early as the 1950s. During that decade Detroit lost 180,000 people, Milwaukee 130,000, and St. Louis more than 100,000. Many older cities lost half or more of their peak populations over the subsequent decades because of two massive migrations—one from the cities to their suburbs and the other from the Northeast and Midwest to the South and West. In 1950, one in 23 Americans lived in Detroit, Philadelphia, Cleveland, or St. Louis; in 2010, only one in 104 Americans did.

Postwar suburbanization was driven by a demand for new homes that had been building since the end of the 1920s. With cities suffering from decades of disinvestment and neglect, the Levittowns and their imitators offered young families a new world. This movement was enabled by the automobile and fueled by public policies favoring suburbanization over urban revival, including widespread access to affordable mortgages for new homes.[1]

At the same time, national population shifts were taking place. Given impetus by significant military-industrial investment during World War II, Sun Belt cities grew rapidly after the war, fueled by diversified, growing economies (often in anti-union right-to-work states), cheap land and lax regulations, and the widespread availability and affordability of automobiles and air-conditioning. While in 1950 New Haven, Connecticut, had a population 1.5 times that of Phoenix, Arizona, by 2010 the population of Phoenix—which went from being the 99th largest to the sixth largest city in the United States—was nearly 11 times that of New Haven. The Sun Belt was a massive growth machine, drawing millions of opportunity-seeking residents from the rest of the country while building local economies increasingly dependent on continued growth.

*Deindustrialization.* The economic expansion of the United States in the second half of the 19th century was fueled by the nation's manufacturing might, which built the country into an unparalleled economic power and created a standard of living that set the pace for the rest of the world. Pittsburgh and Detroit became synonyms for steel making and the automobile industry, and many other cities became known for their manufacturing strengths: major cities like Cleveland and Buffalo, smaller cities like Youngstown, Ohio, with its steel mills, and still smaller places like East Liverpool, Ohio, a hub of the American ceramics industry. Even important financial or business centers like Philadelphia and Baltimore depended on an industrial employment base to offer a decent standard of living to their millions of working-class families. When the factories began to close, key parts of these cities began to die.

The full effects of deindustrialization were not felt until the 1970s. In that decade, Dayton, Ohio, lost 46 percent of its manufacturing jobs, and Detroit lost nearly 40 percent. As plants closed, population loss accelerated. Between 1960 and 1980, Detroit lost nearly half a million people, while Cleveland, Philadelphia, and St. Louis each lost roughly 300,000.

© iStockphoto.com/Tomasz Pietryszek

Since the 1960s and 1970s, three waves of deindustrialization have swept over urban America. In the first, manufacturers often moved from the city to a nearby suburb; in the second, they moved south and west, driven by lower wages, cheap land, and generous financial incentives. More recently, however, deindustrialization has become an international phenomenon, as manufacturing has increasingly relocated not only to China but to many parts of the developing world. Meanwhile, changes in technology have meant that fewer and fewer workers are needed to produce the same amount of goods.

***Social and Demographic Change.*** Population loss is a symptom of the economic transformation of urban areas, but it also drives other symptoms of urban decline. Deterioration of cities' physical fabric and public services, along with rising crime rates, prompted continued middle-class flight, initially made up of white residents but ultimately including much of the middle-class black population as well. As cities hollowed out, they found themselves with weak housing demand, shrinking tax bases that made it progressively more difficult to pay for even basic public services, and increasingly impoverished populations. In the most deeply depressed cities, such as Detroit; Gary, Indiana; and Camden, New Jersey, over one-third of residents are now below the poverty level. As regions have continued to spread, affluent residents have followed the newest growth outward, and older suburbs—including many that grew rapidly in the 1950s and 1960s—have begun to share many of the problems of their central cities.

Race and income are inextricably interwoven in the postwar history of American cities, as large-scale black migration into areas with declining economic opportunities led to conflicts, particularly during the 1960s when many cities exploded in racial violence, speeding the flight of the middle class and urban decline. Today, a new wave of Latino in-migration is transforming neighborhoods and reversing population declines in gateway cities such as Springfield, Massachusetts; Elizabeth, New Jersey; and Allentown, Pennsylvania. While this movement offers opportunities for revival, in the short run the widespread poverty of many newcomers, coupled with ethnic and cultural clashes, has often made these cities' tasks even harder.

***Overbuilding and Collapse of the Housing Bubble.*** Although the fast-growing cities of the Sun Belt long seemed immune from the forces undermining northern cities, that is no longer the case. Beginning in the late 1990s, the largest housing bubble in American history began to grow. This bubble was most pronounced in Arizona, California, Florida, and Nevada, where overbuilding, speculation, and subprime mortgage lending sent house prices to unsustainable levels, creating an explosive situation that blew up in 2006 and 2007 with disastrous consequences. The subsequent collapse of the real estate market and construction industry, coupled with the effects of the Great Recession, has led to an epidemic of foreclosures, sending cities like Phoenix; Las Vegas, Nevada; Fresno, California; and Miami into economic tailspins.

While it is unclear whether growth will someday resume in Sun Belt cities, for the present and near future they will not be able to count on growth to fuel their local economies. Instead, they find themselves forced to confront many of the same problems that cities like Baltimore or Cleveland have been dealing with for decades, including population stagnation or decline, low property values and weak demand, neighborhood destabilization, and property abandonment.

## Contributory Factors

Although these changes in America's cities were driven by broad social and economic forces over which governments may have had little control, public policies have often made matters worse. Urban collapse and uncontrolled sprawl are not inevitable products of postindustrial economic growth; rather, they flow from the interaction of growth forces with public policy. Local government fragmentation, weak land-use regulation that abets sprawl, inadequate public capacity to respond to change, and inconsistent state and federal policy responses have all contributed to the outcomes we see in our cities and regions.

***Governmental Fragmentation.*** While the forces that have driven change in the United States for the past six or more decades are national and regional, the tools that we have to respond to them tend to be narrowly local and highly fragmented. This proliferation of small local governments has not been accidental. Michael Danielson has written, "As the spreading city sorted itself out along income, ethnic and racial lines, political as well as spatial separation from the inner city became increasingly attractive.... Independence promised neighborhood control over taxes and services, a homogeneous local political system responsible to community interests, an end to involvement with the city's complex politics and costly problems, and a more effective means of excluding the lower classes" (1976, 15). By the early 20th century nearly every northern city was "landlocked"—surrounded by separate, incorporated municipalities, each one jealously guarding its power to tax, control its affairs, and regulate the use of land within its borders.

Municipal fragmentation, social pressures to exclude the poor and minorities, and heavy dependence by most municipalities and their school districts on local property taxes created a climate in which regional considerations are a low priority. Suburban officials and civic leaders, many of them self-defined refugees from a central city, were more concerned with protecting themselves from what they saw as the city's ills than helping to remedy them. Competition for ratables led suburban jurisdictions to entice urban employers—though sometimes only to lose them to states and cities elsewhere.

While a few places have built effective regional governance systems, such as the Portland, Oregon, or Minneapolis–St. Paul regions, these are the rare exceptions to the rule. In most parts of the country, regional entities are weak or nonexistent. Although fiscal pressures have in recent years led many local governments to pursue shared services and facilities, the philosophy of "beggar thy neighbor" is still more common than one of cooperation.

*Sprawl and Land-Use Regulation.* Local government fragmentation was not the only force driving wasteful land consumption across an increasingly vast suburban landscape. Over and above the problems inherent in using single-use zoning as a substitute for thoughtful land-use and growth planning, the treatment of land as a commodity or as a means to achieve fiscal goals has diminished its ability to serve as a public resource or as a basis for broader community goals. Both trends lead to outcomes inimical to sound planning and to the creation and support of strong, healthy central cities.

In many areas of the nation, land-use planning is dominated by fiscal considerations. The chase for property-tax revenues alongside social and economic agendas fosters exclusionary zoning, forces up house prices, and pushes growth farther out to the regional periphery. This happens even in areas where little net regional growth is taking place, with growth at the periphery cannibalizing central cities and inner-ring suburbs. For example, between 1970 and 1990, as the Cleveland metro area's population declined by 6 percent, its developed land area increased by 31 percent (Nivola 1998).

In much of the Sun Belt, private developers have historically dictated the terms of land-use regulation to local governments, which then tailored zoning changes and planned community approvals to the developers' land costs. This deeply rooted pattern meant that, whatever the letter of the legal system, no effective will or capacity existed in those areas to control the explosion of speculative building that took place from the late 1990s through the mid-2000s.

*The Equivocal Roles of State and Federal Governments.* As economic and social forces were working to transform the American landscape, state and federal governments played inconsistent and equivocal roles. Though the federal government spent billions on the effort to revive central cities through urban renewal, the premise of that program—that federally funded assembly and clearance of large development sites was the key to urban revitalization—was fatally flawed. After decades of effort and the displacement of more than a million families, "the results were paltry. Many sites, once cleared, lay vacant for years or decades, while much of the redevelopment that did take place was unsuccessful either economically or aesthetically" (Mallach 2011b, 382).

At the same time, even larger federal investments were undermining urban areas. The Interstate Highway System vastly expanded the amount of land accessible to suburban development, prompting shopping malls and office parks to arise near suburban highway interchanges. Simultaneously, ready mortgages for newly built homes—made available through the Federal Housing Administration (FHA) and the growth of Fannie Mae and Freddie Mac—and the difficulty of obtaining financing for older urban properties well into the 1970s combined to fuel suburban development.

While urban initiatives—the War on Poverty, Model Cities, the Community Development Block Grant program—continued to flow from Washington along with housing initiatives such as Section 235 and 236, Section 8, and the Low Income Housing Tax Credit, they did little to change the larger trend. While large-scale construction of urban low-income housing helped many poor families improve their living conditions, it also increased cities' fiscal and economic constraints, further widening the urban-suburban gap. Other federal urban initiatives were undermined by the absence of coherent strategies, lack of coordination among federal agencies or between federal and state agencies, and lack of sustained commitment to the cities and their futures.

Few state governments were any more helpful. Each state sets its ground rules for local-government governance, finance, and land-use regulation—and therefore each must bear ultimate responsibility for fragmented local governments, dysfunctional systems of financing local governments, and the absence of larger regional governance or planning frameworks. While some states mounted urban initiatives, their effect has been minimal compared to the fiscal and governmental status quo of 19th-century systems put in place for a radically different landscape and society.

***Local Capacity and Leadership.*** Despite the larger forces working against them, cities should not be absolved of all responsibility for their difficulties. Many cities took refuge in denial or chased unrealistic or counterproductive strategies, reflected today in the proliferation of failed projects that continue to drain public resources. These can include failed housing projects, dead shopping centers, empty industrial parks, over-subsidized arenas, and other quixotic ventures. Cities' woes have been exacerbated by weak or ineffective political leadership, the tendency to use city resources as ethnic and racial spoils, and the lack of long-term strategies for change.

However, some older cities have had strong and effective political leaders, such as mayors Flynn and Menino in Boston and Clark and Rendell in Philadelphia. Many cities have used sophisticated planning tools to chart their futures and improve their quality of life. In the 1990s, cities such as Boston and Chicago were quick to see how changing market dynamics could be tapped to attract new investment. Today, mayors like Dave Bing in Detroit, Michael Nutter in Philadelphia, and Stephanie Rawlings-Blake in Baltimore and city planners in Cleveland, Philadelphia, and elsewhere are developing creative new strategies for rebuilding their cities.

Still, the picture is at best mixed. Many cities lack strong political leadership or engaged civic and business communities, and many also lack the capacity to turn leadership into solid plans and execution. As cities suffer from increasingly severe fiscal constraints, the pressure to cut back on "frills" such as planning departments, open space maintenance, or capital budgets becomes more intense. Yet it is hard to imagine how a city that is not capable of addressing its future will be able to engage others—whether state or federal governments or the private sector—in that pursuit.

## DEFINING THE UNIVERSE: CITIES IN TRANSITION

In this section, we will flesh out the four distinct categories of cities in transition, with particular focus on the boom-bust cities, which have typically not been considered in this light. The cities in these categories are linked by the challenges they all face in addressing forces of decline, but the categories differ in many important ways.

*Table 2.1. Characteristics of cities in transition*

| Characteristic | Legacy Cities | Gateway Cities | Boom-Bust Cities | First Suburbs |
|---|---|---|---|---|
| | Detroit<br>Youngstown, Ohio<br>St. Louis<br>Trenton, N.J. | Springfield, Mass.<br>Bridgeport, Conn.<br>Paterson, N.J.<br>Reading, Penn. | Las Vegas, Nev.<br>Stockton, Calif.<br>Phoenix, Ariz.<br>Cape Coral, Fla. | Euclid, Ohio<br>St. Clair Shores, Mich.<br>Norwood, Ohio<br>Orange, N.J. |
| Geographic Area | Most heavily concentrated in the older Midwest "Rust Belt" and secondarily in the Northeast but found in all parts of the country | Most heavily concentrated in New England and the Mid-Atlantic states | Concentrated in four states: California, Arizona, Florida, and Nevada | Concentrated around older cities in the Northeast and Midwest |
| Size Distribution | All sizes: from Detroit (713,000) to Highland Park, Mich. (11,000) | Generally between 50,000 and 200,000 population | All sizes, including many large cities like Phoenix and Miami but many smaller cities as well | Generally under 75,000 population |
| Population Trend | Steady loss of population in most decades since 1950 or 1960 | Loss of population between 1950 and 1980 with stability or gain since then. Many have become important immigration destinations. | Steady population growth until 2006 or 2007, loss or stability since then | Varies, but loss of population since 1970s is widespread |
| Economic Base | Historic manufacturing base gone or severely diminished, largely replaced by government and "eds and meds." Larger cities may have downtown economic centers. | Similar to legacy cities, but few have strong downtown economic centers or major national/regional educational or health care institutions | Diversified, but heavily dependent on real estate and construction | Some former industrial suburbs, but many bedroom cities with little indigenous economic base |

Legacy cities are experiencing long-term decline with respect to both jobs and population. Most of these cities have lost population steadily since the 1960s or earlier, and many—such as Detroit or Youngstown, Ohio—have lost more than half of their peak population. For these cities, population and job loss are chronic problems.

But there are many variations on the legacy city theme. Detroit's population loss of 60 percent has fundamentally different effects on neighborhoods, public services, and future prospects than Baltimore's 35 percent population loss. Some city populations have stabilized, as in Philadelphia, while others continue to decline. Similarly, the assets that a large city such as Cleveland offers—major research universities and world-renowned medical centers— are far greater than those available to smaller cities such as Canton, Ohio, or Camden, New Jersey.

Gateway cities experienced substantial population decline but have bounced back in recent years as a result of immigration. Reading, Pennsylvania, for example, lost nearly 30 percent of its residents between 1930 and 1990, but its population grew by 10,000 between 1990 and 2010. With a population of only 88,000, Reading has taken in nearly 37,000 new Latino residents in the past 20 years. These population gains pose new challenges if not paralleled by economic growth; absorbing large numbers of new immigrants is a critical issue for gateway cities.

*Foreclosed homes in North Las Vegas, Nevada*

© iStockphoto/GYI NSEA

Boom-bust cities in the Sun Belt were heavily affected by the past decade's cycles of explosive growth and decline. House prices in the Las Vegas metro area increased by 135 percent between 2000 and 2006 but are now back to where they were in 1998. Tens of thousands of houses have gone into foreclosure, while nearly two-thirds of home owners in the area are underwater on their mortgages (CoreLogic 2011). Home building has dropped to less than 10 percent of its boom level, triggering increased unemployment, while low demand and continued foreclosures have destabilized many neighborhoods. These cities are no longer immune to the problems of population loss, deterioration, and abandonment. In contrast to the legacy cities, however, their problems are acute and not—at least not yet—chronic.

But not all Sun Belt cities are boom-bust cities. Cities in Texas as well as Salt Lake City and Denver have been affected much less than cities in the four states most affected by the boom and the bust: Arizona, California, Florida, and Nevada. Even in those states, however, important distinctions should be made. California's coastal cities, including San Diego, Los Angeles, and San Francisco, although hit hard, have weathered the storm far better than the state's inland cities and counties, such as Stockton, Fresno, or the Inland Empire.

As the edge of suburban development has moved outward, the cities, towns, and villages that were the first suburbs have begun to lose ground. In some cases, like that of Norwood, Ohio, they had manufacturing plants that closed; in others, they had no indigenous economic base. All have been affected by racial and economic changes, decreasing property values and physical deterioration, and increasing difficulties in providing adequate public services and finding clear paths toward better futures. At the same time, many of these communities still have high levels of home ownership and many stable neighborhoods.

As in the other categories, not all older, inner-ring suburbs are experiencing the same difficulties. Many affluent older suburbs like Philadelphia's Main Line communities continue to thrive. Those hardest hit were usually built as modest industrial suburbs or inexpensive postwar developments or are adjacent to cities that have lost the most population and jobs, such as Cleveland and Detroit.

All of these cities face similar challenges in different forms, and though their potential levers of change vary widely, they can all learn from one another. Sun Belt cities like Las Vegas and many first suburbs can learn how to address problems of neighborhood destabilization from Philadelphia or Baltimore, which have been dealing with these issues for decades. Similarly, gateway cities, with their rapid, recent ethnic changes, could learn from the far longer history multicultural communities in the Southwest. In the following section we will dig further into the nature of these challenges.

## DEFINING THE CHALLENGES

Cities in transition face a cluster of interrelated challenges linking social, economic, physical, and operational realities. Loss of economic opportunities and suburban flight have increased the impoverishment of the urban population, which leads to reduced housing market demand, causing reduced property values and abandonment and resulting in diminished municipal resources and less capacity to deal with growing problems. While planners cannot hope to solve every challenge facing their communities, they need a broad overview to understand how issues relate to one another and to better find areas of opportunity or points of leverage.

Not all of these challenges will necessarily be present in every community. And in some cases, a particular issue may affect only parts of a city. Cities are not homogenous entities, nor do they—or their component sections—stay the same over time. The planner must understand the particular dynamics of a community well enough to identify its most urgent challenges, but he or she must keep an open mind, recognizing the magnitude of the problems without being overwhelmed by them.

The following sections look at four different areas: social and human challenges, the challenges of weak market conditions, the challenges of change to the built environment, and, finally, the internal challenges of leadership, information, and capacity that affect cities' abilities to address their challenges.

## Social and Human Challenges

While a city is a governmental entity, as well as a defined geographic area containing buildings and land, it is most fundamentally a social and economic

**WHAT'S IN A NAME?**

Different terms have been used to describe the plight of America's distressed cities: shrinking cities, weak market cities, forgotten cities, cities in transition, and most recently, legacy cities. There is still no consensus on terminology, however. These terms largely apply to older industrial communities that have undergone substantial population losses, but local officials and residents in many of these communities often recoil at the label of shrinking cities, equating shrinkage with failure, perhaps in light of America's historic obsession with growth and development. Commentators such as Kaid Benfield (2009) point out that these cities are not physically shrinking—the jurisdictional boundaries of the city remain static. Further, many of the regions around these cities continue to grow, so that population losses in the urban core are more artifacts of arbitrary municipal boundaries than measurements of regional health.

entity. As such, much of its future will be defined by the social and economic characteristics of its population. This has become a particularly intense long-term challenge for legacy cities, where populations have become poorer, with less educational attainment, fewer skills, and higher unemployment. Though the boom-bust cities still contain diverse populations within their expansive boundaries, many of the inner neighborhoods of these cities are increasingly sharing these challenges.

*Poverty.* Residents of both legacy and gateway cities are significantly more likely than the statewide or national population to be poor, with the percentage of those living in poverty often greater than the national average of 13.5 percent. More telling, though, is the ratio between population below the poverty level and population earning more than double the poverty level. Households earning below the poverty level (about $23,000 for a family of four) are disproportionately likely to be dependent on public assistance—including food stamps, housing vouchers, and Medicaid—and less likely to be paying substantial income or property taxes. Conversely, households earning more than double the poverty level are much more likely to contain employed household members and pay significant amounts in taxes, and they are less likely to rely on subsidized services and transfer payments. "Near poor" households that fall between these two groups can have characteristics of either category. Thus, the ratio between the two reflects the extent to which a community's population is weighted toward being highly service-dependent.

For every person below the poverty level in the United States there are more than five people in households earning more than double the poverty level. As Figure 2.1 shows, in some cities in transition the ratio is more than one to one.

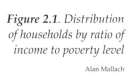

*Figure 2.1*. *Distribution of households by ratio of income to poverty level*

Alan Mallach

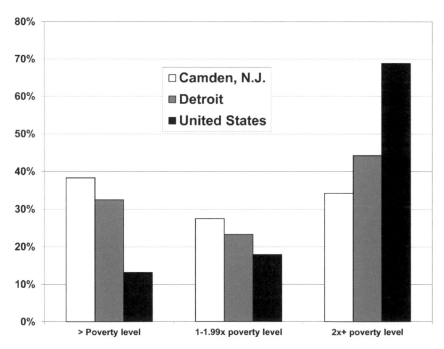

***Educational Attainment and Unemployment.*** The relationship between educational attainment of a population and economic growth has been well documented. As Dan Gilmartin of the Michigan Municipal League has stated, "We know that educational attainment is the biggest predictor of success for cities and metro areas today" (Michigan Municipal League 2011). Especially important is the percentage of adults who hold at least a bachelor's degree (Kodrzycki 2002).

Educational attainment levels are extremely low in some legacy and gateway cities, as residents remaining after middle-class flight and new immigrants tend to have far less formal education than people in the region overall. In most of these cities unemployment is significantly higher than the national average; worse, the official unemployment figures understate the number of idle adults because levels of labor-force attachment—the percentage of adults who are actually in the workforce, whether working or not—are often far lower than in the country as a whole. For example, the labor-force participation rate in Camden, New Jersey, is 82 percent of the statewide rate. The combined effect of labor force participation and unemployment rates means, however, that while in New Jersey as a whole 74.2 percent of all adults ages 20 to 64 had a job, only 53.8 percent of those in Camden were working (American Community Survey 2005–2009).

*Age.* The populations of most cities in transition are younger than that of the nation as a whole, particularly in cities with large and growing Latino communities. Significant exceptions are some of the first suburbs, where large numbers of people who moved to those communities in the 1950s and 1960s are aging in place, forming what have come to be known as "naturally occurring retirement communities" or NORCs.

*Racial and Ethnic Change.* Most legacy cities went through significant racial transitions many decades ago as white households were replaced by African American ones. Some cities, such as Detroit, became overwhelmingly African American, while others, such as St. Louis and Cincinnati, stabilized with populations divided roughly evenly between the two groups.

While such demographics have stayed largely constant in most legacy cities, many gateway cities have recently seen dramatic changes. In Pennsylvania, Reading went from 18 to 58 percent Latino between 1990 and 2010, while Allentown went from 12 to 43 percent. Many first suburbs are also experiencing racial and ethnic turnover as aging white households are replaced by Latino and African-American households from the adjacent central city. Euclid went from less than 20 percent African American in 1990 to over 50 percent in 2010.

Though racial and ethnic changes can ultimately result in positive outcomes, particularly where the alternative is population loss and abandonment, in the short run it can be destabilizing. Addressing rapid racial and ethnic change and integrating newcomers into the city's economic and social fabric are issues that planners in many cities in transition must tackle.

*Crime.* Crime levels are significant measures of social stability and quality of life in communities as well as important factors affecting their potentials for economic growth. As Michael Porter has written, "crime, with its associated fears and costs, is one of the greatest barriers to inner-city economic revitalization" (1997). Most cities in transition—although not all—have crime rates that are higher, and in some cases significantly higher, than national levels.

How crime affects a city's fortunes cannot be captured by a simple equation. Rates of violent crime usually vary widely within a city, and where some neighborhoods are safer and others significantly less so crime can be easily perceived as compartmentalized—especially in sprawling cities where "bad neighborhoods" may be miles away. In these cases, crime may have less of an impact on the redevelopment of the "safer" areas, though it still undermines the quality of life and revitalization potential of areas in which it remains, or is perceived to be, a problem.

### The Challenge of Weak Market Demand

One of the central problems facing cities in transition is low levels of demand for the elements of the city's built environment—principally its housing stock but also its commercial, office, and industrial buildings. While this is seen in its most extreme form in cities such as Detroit or St. Louis with their acres of vacant land where buildings were abandoned and subsequently demolished, the problem of weak demand affects all cities in transition to some extent. Since weak housing demand is at the heart of many of these cities' other problems, it is critical that planners understand it and how it affects the dynamics of their cities.

Weak demand can take many forms. In legacy cities with steady job and population losses, weak demand is a long-term phenomenon, as fewer and fewer people live in cities designed for larger populations. Even with constant demolition of older, abandoned houses, cities cannot keep pace. Detroit has demolished nearly one-third of all of its pre-1950 housing stock, but its vacancy rate and the number of abandoned houses continue to rise. In these cities a significant gap exists between the available supply of buildings and the demand. Many houses in those cities will never find buyers; for those that do, the great majority will be investors, not residents.

In boom-bust cities, weak demand is a more recent phenomenon linked to the overbuilding and speculative mania of the bubble years. Many neighborhoods are starting to see similar effects, with markets driven by speculative investors and properties being increasingly abandoned. It is too soon to tell whether this will become a long-term pattern for these cities, or whether future growth will gradually absorb the excess supply and lead to a more "normal" housing market.

In gateway cities, weak demand is less quantitative than qualitative. While there is sufficient population to absorb the city's housing stock, in-migrants often lack the financial capacities either to buy homes or to pay enough rent to support high-quality rental housing stocks. Weak demand in those cities may lead to a steady decline in home ownership and to a parallel increase in absentee ownership, including many investors more interested in exploiting their properties than in maintaining them. Both are likely to have a destabilizing effect on many of the city's neighborhoods.

A healthy housing market requires three separate elements: first, enough housing demand to absorb properties coming on the market and keep vacancy rates at healthy levels; second, enough home buyer as distinct from investor—demand to maintain healthy home ownership rates; and third, high-enough prices to foster upgrading and replacement of existing housing stocks. Where any one of these elements is absent, the quality of the city's housing and its neighborhoods is likely to suffer. In practice, they are closely linked and often found together.

While an adequate amount of rental housing, which in turn requires a pool of absentee or investor owners, is an important part of any city's housing stock, a strong cohort of home owners is critical. A substantial body of research has linked home ownership—and the resultant stability—to many benefits for both individual households and a neighborhood as a whole (Mallach 2011a). These benefits can include more positive educational outcomes for children, greater self-esteem and life satisfaction, increased maintenance and improvement of property, stronger neighborhood property values, greater neighborhood engagement, and lower tolerance for crime and deviant behavior in the neighborhood.

***The Effect of Low House Prices.*** Even though weak demand may not lead to widespread vacancy and abandonment, it causes house prices to drop, often well below replacement cost (i.e., the cost of constructing a similar new house on the same site or restoring an abandoned house to habitable status through rehabilitation). In Las Vegas, homes in many distressed older neighborhoods (typically 1950s and 1960s vintage) were selling in 2011 for $30,000 to $40,000, while houses in newly built planned communities were selling for little more than $100,000, barely half of what they cost to build fewer than 10 years earlier. In cities like Detroit and Youngstown many houses are selling for less than $20,000.

Low and declining house prices have profoundly negative consequences for a city's housing stock and its neighborhoods. When prices are low, home owners are discouraged from upgrading their homes, and homes that do come on the market are more likely to be bought by investors—often short-term speculators—rather than home buyers. Developers are unlikely to build new houses on available vacant lots since the cost of construction is likely to exceed the potential sales price, and if a vacant house is stripped or vandalized the chances of it being rehabilitated are small, since its final value is likely to be less than the combined cost of acquisition and rehabilitation. These consequences further sap the vitality of the city's neighborhoods and the confidence of its home owners.

Building a stronger housing market by increasing demand and fostering rising house values is critical to building stronger neighborhoods. While great care must be taken to ensure that the needs of lower-income residents—who may be harmed by higher housing costs—are addressed, market building is central to the planner's role in cities in transition. At the same time, planners need to be wary of proposals—especially those requiring public subsidy—to build additional housing in cities where supply exceeds demand. While there may be some cases where this is strategically justified, such as filling a gap in a neighborhood, such activities simply add to the already excessive supply without increasing demand—a recipe for increasing abandonment.

*Neighborhood Variations.* While weak demand is broadly characteristic of cities in transition, housing demand patterns can vary widely from neighborhood to neighborhood and sometimes even from block to block. It is crucial that planners understand these fine-grained variations because the choice of neighborhood strategies will be powerfully driven by an assessment of neighborhood housing market conditions. Figure 2.2 illustrates these varia-

*Figure 2.2.* Small area housing market variations in Saginaw, Michigan

Alan Mallach

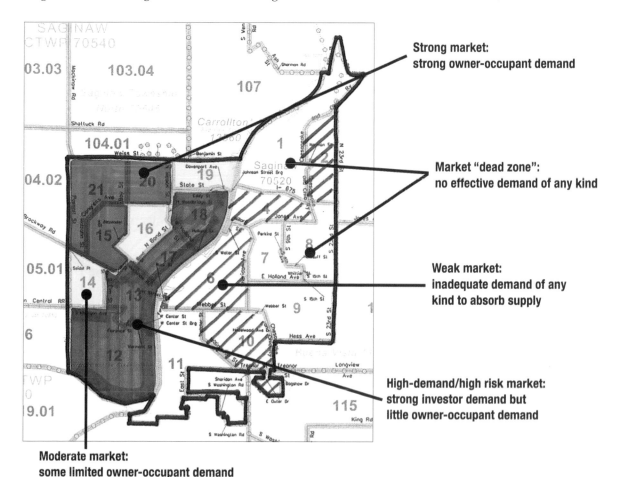

Strong market: strong owner-occupant demand

Market "dead zone": no effective demand of any kind

Weak market: inadequate demand of any kind to absorb supply

High-demand/high risk market: strong investor demand but little owner-occupant demand

Moderate market: some limited owner-occupant demand

tions in Saginaw, Michigan, a legacy city roughly 100 miles north of Detroit. The analysis found five distinct housing market conditions within this city of barely 50,000 residents.

*The Regional Context.* How much a city can stimulate demand for its housing stock, and thus build a stronger housing market and stronger neighborhoods, depends heavily on the level of potential demand in the city's region or housing market area—the area within which prospective buyers might see the city as a possible option. With most older cities containing only a small percentage of their region's households, even a small shift in the number of families who choose to buy in the city rather than in a suburb can make a major difference to the neighborhoods they choose.

Many cities in transition are located in larger regions with little job or population growth. Others, including some gateway cities like Bridgeport, Connecticut, are located in growing, affluent, and economically strong areas. Considering Bridgeport's location, its strong transportation connections, and its amenities, a well-designed market-building effort there should have a high probability of success.

## The Challenges of the Physical Environment

Weak demand leads to physical and social changes that call for the planner's attention. Property owners invest less in their properties, homes shift from owner occupancy to absentee ownership, and increasing numbers of properties become vacant, abandoned, or demolished. A vicious cycle can easily set in as abandonment leads to more abandonment, ending with entire city blocks retaining at most one or two occupied houses. Cities' revenue bases decline as these properties become tax delinquent or end up in tax foreclosure, while at the same time their costs for vacant building cleanup, demolition, and fire fighting increase. Often, a second vicious cycle begins, as financially strapped cities lay off housing inspectors, police officers, and firefighters or cut back on maintaining streets and sidewalks, thus further undermining community confidence and raising the risk of additional disinvestment and abandonment. Addressing these challenges while fostering revitalization and building the city's economic vitality is among the most important tasks facing planners in cities in transition.

*Substandard and Vacant Properties.* Dealing with large and growing numbers of problem properties, particularly vacant ones that have been abandoned by their owners, is a constant challenge for cities in transition. While legacy cities have been grappling with this issue since the 1960s or 1970s, in recent years it has also become a problem in boom-bust cities, as older neighborhoods become dotted with boarded-up houses and shopping centers. Cities need to manage this inventory in ways that minimize harm to adjacent properties and neighborhood vitality. At the same time, they must think about how best to put these properties back to productive use, whether through rehabilitation, redevelopment, or nondevelopment uses such as open space.

One key issue is the extent to which cities should actively gain public control over vacant properties. In their citizens' eyes, cities often "own" the problem whether they have title to these properties or not. The ability to gain title to properties gives them greater control over future redevelopment. Many counties containing cities in transition have created land banks for this purpose, most notably in Michigan and Ohio, where state legislation has created favorable conditions for such entities.

Planners must play central roles in addressing problem property issues in their communities. While much of the day-to-day work falls to building or public works departments, many key issues call for substantial planning input, including where to target limited resources; how to select properties for demolition, rehabilitation, or "mothballing" for future rehabilitation; and how to decide what may be the most appropriate reuse options for vacant land and buildings.

***Foreclosures.*** A particularly complicated issue facing many cities in transition today is the effect of mortgage foreclosures resulting from widespread speculative subprime mortgage lending and overbuilding prior to the collapse of the housing market. While boom-bust cities lead the nation in the frequency of mortgage default and foreclosure, many other cities in transition have similar problems, often caused by subprime lending targeted at minority home owners and home buyers and exacerbated by weak local and regional economic conditions.

While foreclosure itself is nothing more than a legal procedure to collect a debt, its effect on a city's physical environment and economy can be powerful. Properties in foreclosure are often neglected and may be abandoned before title passes to the lender, which can take months or even years. In cities such as Cleveland or Detroit with especially weak markets, lenders may not even bother to take title, letting properties fall into legal limbo. When lenders do take title, they often sell these REO (real estate–owned) properties to investors or speculators, leading to further destabilization. These neglected properties adversely affect property values and quality of life for nearby residents and cast negative stigmas on their neighborhoods, making revitalization that much more difficult.

Although their number is growing, few cities or community development corporations (CDCs) have the combined planning and implementation capacities needed to mount comprehensive revitalization strategies in neighborhoods destabilized by foreclosure. This, too, is an area where planners' skills are needed.

***Brownfields.*** The closing of many of America's older factories has left a bitter legacy of thousands of brownfield sites—sites whose environmental contamination must be remediated before they can be reused—ranging from tiny parcels to tens of acres, often in the middle of still densely populated residential areas. Since the 1990s, public and private efforts and the passage of major state and federal brownfields legislation have led to the reuse of brownfields sites around the country, but many still remain, blighting their surroundings. While the boom years prior to 2006 led to widespread private investment in brownfields reuse, the harder economic times since then have led to a sharp drop in those often high-risk investments, not to mention the collapse of many private firms that had been involved in that work. With many public funding programs cut at the same time, cities are finding it increasingly difficult to tackle their many remaining sites.

*One of Detroit's many areas of disinvestment*

Architecture for Humanity

*Infrastructure.* Cities have elaborate networks of streets, sidewalks, sewers, and water lines, as well as collections of public facilities including school buildings, community centers, libraries, and firehouses. While abandoned buildings and vacant lots are the most visible challenges to the physical environments of cities in transition, the difficulties of maintaining the infrastructure that connects them and enables cities to function are equally great.

As their populations and fiscal resources decline, many cities are struggling just to maintain that infrastructure, let alone upgrade and replace it. In legacy cities, whose infrastructure was designed to serve a far larger population than lives there today, as well as in cities with particularly severe financial problems, this problem is especially acute. Schools, firehouses, and other public facilities have been closed, while streets and sidewalks crumble for lack of maintenance. While closing many facilities may be inevitable, little thought is often given to how particular facility closings will affect future revitalization prospects, either for the city as a whole or for specific neighborhoods.

Cities in transition are often trapped in cycles that are seemingly out of their control. They face continued erosion of their competitive positions and economic vitality if they do not maintain or rebuild their housing stock and infrastructure, yet raising taxes to do so will undermine their ability to compete for businesses, jobs, and middle-class households. The future of many of these cities will depend on their abilities to find paths out of this conundrum.

## The Operational Challenge

The challenges described above are all largely driven by forces beyond the city's control and external to the workings of local government. But how local government operates and allocates its resources, as well as its relationship to its region and to state government, are equal challenges. No city in transition can hope to address external challenges successfully unless it can put its own house in order.

Operational challenges fall into three broad categories. Some have to do with the city's processes and systems: Does the city have a comprehensive plan or a budget-making process adequate to guide key decisions about the use of land or allocation of public funds, and does it have the legal tools and procedures in place to actively address its vacant and problem property issues? Others go to questions of capacity: Does the city have the technical and managerial capacity to execute its plans or to get the greatest benefit out of the limited resources available? Can the city or its CDCs use federal Neighborhood Stabilization Program (NSP) funds in ways that actually stabilize neighborhoods? Are housing inspectors able to spend all their time in the field, or are they spending most of their days in the office filling out paperwork? The rest touch on effective leadership and partnerships: Are city officials truly committed to realistic strategies for rebuilding the city, even at the expense of political capital and long-held practices, and have the public, private, and nonprofit sectors built the relationships that are capable of moving the city forward?

*Processes and Systems.* Cities are complex organisms often managed through fragmented, disorganized collections of processes and systems that have typically accumulated over many decades. Administratively, a city is defined by the way its government is organized, how it performs different governmental functions, the body of ordinances and regulations that govern its actions, and the plans and other documents it has adopted to guide its decisions and allocation of resources.

City governments are often poorly organized to effectively address the problems they are now facing. Responsibilities for problem properties, for example, may be divided among three or more separate agencies or departments, with inadequate lines of communication among them. Problems may fall between departmental cracks, and officials may make decisions without taking key factors into account, such as when a school board closes a school without giving thought to its impact on an at-risk neighborhood, or when a public works department decides to allocate scarce street-improvement resources without considering how those funds can best be used to leverage ongoing neighborhood improvement activities.

Many cities, moreover, lack the guiding documents and legal systems necessary to act effectively. Some older cities may not have prepared a new comprehensive plan since the 1960s or 1970s and lack an overall strategy to guide land-use or neighborhood revitalization decisions. Others may not have the ordinances or regulations in place to mount effective campaigns against problem properties or may be constrained by the absence of state-level enabling legislation. A city must first put tools in place before it can focus on using them effectively.

*Capacity.* Processes and systems, capacity, and leadership are closely linked: capacity is the ability to carry out a strategy or activity, while leadership is the will to carry it out. Without both of these qualities, processes and systems are worthless. A city possesses material capacity in the number of people and dollars it can allocate to tasks; skill capacity in the managerial and technical skill sets and experience of its personnel; and technological capacity in how well it uses the available technology to address its challenges.

Nearly all cities in transition have less material capacity than they need. Cities have cut police officers and firefighters along with housing inspectors and city planners. Discretionary funds for infrastructure improvements, housing subsidies, and brownfields remediation are in short supply and getting scarcer. But as cities make cuts, they risk eliminating positions that are critical for future regeneration. For example, housing inspectors, properly trained and deployed, are critical "first responders" to problem properties and neighborhood decline.

Many cities in transition also face significant skill constraints. Positions may be filled by people who lack the basic technical skills to perform effectively in their roles. Heads of programs and departments may be hired or promoted for their technical skill, longevity, or political connections, none of which ensures that they will be effective managers. These limitations have become critical stumbling blocks in many cities' efforts to tackle their challenges, impeding their abilities to adopt new technology-driven data or management systems.

Planners are often among the few senior staff in local government with the training to identify the specialized skills and technology that a city may need to maximize the value it can derive from its material resources. As such, their roles in helping their organizations build capacity may go well beyond more conventional responsibilities.

*Leadership and Partnerships.* Ultimately, leadership and partnerships are the real tests of whether a local government will be able to address the challenges it faces. By definition, cities in transition are facing an unacceptable status quo. While most political and civic leaders tend to acknowledge that change is needed, it is always more difficult to foster change than to perpetuate the status quo. Leaders are often reluctant to take the steps needed to make change possible.

In this context, leadership is the ability to make decisions and take action that furthers the long-term revitalization of the community, even at the price of

### RESEARCH ON SHRINKING CITIES

Prior to World War II, the problems facing U.S. cities—slums, traffic congestion, public sanitation—were those of rapid growth. Not until the late 1940s was the possibility of population and job loss in the country's large cities taken seriously by urban commentators. Beginning in the 1950s as a consequence of housing shortages, mass suburbanization, the decentralization of manufacturing, racial tensions, and physical deterioration, the manufacturing cities of the Northeast and Midwest regions experienced substantial and sustained depopulation.

Contemporary research on shrinking cities has its origins in this postwar period. Early studies on "urban decline" examined the decentralization of industry and the deconcentration of population to the suburbs (Solomon 1980). Research focused on population and job loss from cities, the identification of slums and assessment of their social consequences, racial change, industrial decline (specifically with respect to manufacturing), and the deterioration of central business districts as retailing followed households to the suburbs. Researchers identified poorly performing schools and high crime rates (or at least the perception of them) along with racial tensions as most influential on the out-migration of residents. Suburbanites became increasingly reluctant to visit the city for culture, leisure, and shopping, which further eroded the centrality of commercial areas. The ways in which cities discouraged visitors and investment became a prominent research topic.

The 1990s witnessed the emergence of a new perspective on urban decline (Billitteri 2010). Relabeling those cities that never recovered their former glory and continued to shed people and businesses as "shrinking cities" reinvigorated research on urban depopulation and neighborhood deterioration. Focus shifted from cities as a whole to distressed neighborhoods and their high levels of vacancies and abandonment. Life-cycle theories and models of housing filtering developed decades earlier became important in understanding the downward spirals of these neighborhoods (Birch 1971). Research into racial discrimination and such activities as blockbusting emphasized the role of landlords, real estate agents, investors, and local governments in exacerbating neighborhood distress.

The shrinking city movement focuses on policy interventions that address the consequences of neighborhood depopulation. At its core is the recognition of the efficacy of bundling various public interventions (e.g., demolition or government foreclosure) with land banking and the "greening" of the resultant vacant land—a relatively new addition to the policy repertoire (Leonard and Schilling 2007). Consequently, while such research often begins with a citywide overview of population loss, it moves quickly to analysis of housing deterioration and disinvestment in distressed neighborhoods.

Researchers today are likely to attend to subsequent uses of the vacant land for personal or community gardens, larger-scale urban agriculture, playgrounds, and open space. Earlier approaches, by contrast, focused on redeveloping these spaces with buildings. In turn, because control over abandoned or derelict properties is key

to solving the problems of shrinking neighborhoods, researchers have looked closely at the mechanisms (e.g., property-tax foreclosure) that local, county, and state governments have created to gain control and move these lands and buildings to useful status.

Much of this research is directed at existing city programs and policies (Dewar 2006). The former include side-lot initiatives, community gardens, government foreclosure procedures, demolition strategies, land banking, urban agriculture, mortgage counseling, code enforcement, relocation assistance, and housing rehabilitation. The intent is to learn what works and what does not. Research has also probed citywide strategic demolition efforts and subsidized reuse of the land, including such prominent examples as the Neighborhood Transformation Initiative launched in Philadelphia in 2001 and programs in Baltimore, Cleveland, and Richmond, Virginia (McGovern 2006).

Among the most extensively studied policy and planning interventions have been the Genesee County Land Bank in Flint and the Youngstown 2010 plan with its pioneering commitment to a smaller, more livable city. As with research on specific programs, the goal is to understand how the problems of distressed neighborhoods—abandoned homes, physically isolated families, illegal land uses, and inefficient public services—can be best addressed.

While knowledge of best practices is central to shrinking city efforts, most researchers, activists, and policy makers recognize that these programs and policies are likely to fail without strong political leadership (Schatz 2012). Many of these programs are not new. What is new is the recognition that they must complement one another and that they need to be backed by a commitment by the city's leadership to rightsize the city. Without political support for the idea that certain neighborhoods and even the city as a whole will never recapture their former scale and metropolitan dominance, these initiatives are likely to be underfunded, uncoordinated, and set in unfair competition with large, catalytic, citywide projects premised on the notion that only such efforts can jump-start the local economy and solve the city's problems. We know little about how such a shrinkage-friendly policy might be crafted and publicly defended. Mayoral leadership seems important along with community support, but more information is needed about issues of cost savings from the downsizing of public infrastructure, how to present and implement relocation, what physical forms these neighborhoods might take, and how public services might be reallocated.

A few studies have placed shrinking cities in national perspective. One approach attempts to create typologies of cities out of a multidimensional analysis of demographic, economic, fiscal, and social variables. In this way, researchers can compare cities to identify which are performing well and which are performing poorly (Vey 2007). Other studies focus on demographic shifts and depopulation or compare city statistics on housing abandonment, a key condition connected to distressed neighborhoods. Still other efforts try to identify the causes of shrinkage (Hill et al. 2012).

*(continued on page 25)*

conflict or political risk. That is a high bar, not only because of the potential need for political leaders to set aside behaviors that got them elected, but because it is often far from easy to know what actions will best further the long-term revitalization of the community. Leadership in an environment where the status quo is clearly unsatisfactory requires purposeful, systematic action. Many of the initiatives that have been pursued in cities in transition have sadly been focused on the short term, poorly thought out, made without engaging key partners and community residents, and in the final analysis unlikely to lead to sustained change.

The ability to form partnerships, to engage all segments of the community, and to share the process of making decisions is equally important. City government alone cannot bring about change. While everyone talks about partnership, however, many mayors and private-sector executives give little more than lip service to the idea, instead making decisions that they expect their so-called partners and the community at large to accede to.

Planners are often in strong positions to address this challenge. As the drafter, and often the public face, of strategies for change, the planner is often the point person for change, not just presenting the city's ideas but eliciting the community's opinions and ensuring that they become part of an open dialogue on the city's future.

## RESEARCH AND THE SHRINKING CITY

What to do about the decline of cities is one of the more perplexing problems that planners, policy makers, and urban commentators have grappled with for decades. In this section we briefly explore the academic foundations of the "shrinking city movement" and how contemporary debates within the planning and urban design fields are reshaping the policy and revitalization landscapes with creative ideas for reimagining cities and neighborhoods experiencing dramatic population losses. The notion of shrinking cities encapsulates many issues of direct concern to all cities in transition, and these discussions have elevated its importance within the planning profession.

For years the question of how to address the impacts of persistent and chronic population loss was a modest research topic for a handful of pioneering academics. Meanwhile, on the ground, public officials, especially local planners, experimented with different economic development and planning strategies, often having to shift with changes in local leadership. In the mid-2000s many voices began to converge across disciplines and bridge the divide between theory and practice. Local initiatives in Cleveland, Flint, and elsewhere offered new models for addressing the challenge of vacant urban land in cities with substantial populations. Policy experts and practitioners came up with the concept of "rightsizing"—repurposing vacant land and surplus abandoned buildings as part of planning strategies to reconfigure neighborhoods around the reality of smaller populations. National efforts such as the National Vacant Properties Campaign and the Brookings Institution's Restoring Prosperity Initiative documented the current state of the field and began to chart new courses for national and local actions around shrinking cities. In recent years, scholars have broadened their understanding of both the causes and effects of population loss, foreclosures, and other phenomena characteristic of cities in transition, while organizations such as the Center for Community Progress, the German Marshall Fund, and others have disseminated their ideas to practitioners throughout the United States.

Scholarly work over the last decade in the United States and Europe has provided a solid underpinning for the proposition that cities in transition, particularly but not limited to legacy or shrinking cities, require different strategies for planning.

*(continued from page 24)*

The Great Recession added the foreclosure issue to this research world, with various studies documenting the scale and geographical incidence of mortgage foreclosures and assessing their social impacts (Kingsley, Smith, and Price 2009).

Finally, the research literature includes numerous reports on shrinking cities in international contexts. Spurring these endeavors was "Shrinking Cities," a three-year German initiative led by Philipp Oswalt that began in 2002. It mounted exhibitions, produced reports and videos, and collaborated with local teams in Detroit, Ivanovo (Russia), Manchester/Liverpool, and Halle/Leipzig. The Shrinking Cities International Research Network (SCiRN), founded at the University of California–Berkeley in 2004, is dedicated to comparative research on shrinking cities and regions. Of particular prominence are the cities of Eastern Europe, with Leipzig in the former East Germany attracting the most attention, particularly for its policy response (Bontje 2004). Cities in Poland, the Ukraine, the United Kingdom (e.g., Manchester), Italy (e.g., Genoa), France (e.g., Marseilles), and natural resource–dependent communities in Australia and Mexico have also drawn the curiosity of shrinking-city researchers. One consequence has been to broaden the perspective to shrinking regions, though in this context the focus on housing abandonment is replaced by concerns about employment and the fate of residents who are unable or have chosen not to migrate to more prosperous places.

Research at the regional, national, and even international levels is important for expanding the policy debate to state and national governments where legislative reach and funding capacities are greater. Shrinking cities are not just losing people; as tax revenues shrink they might well be losing the capacity for governance as well. Consequently, researchers and policy makers need to explore how and where within a community policy is best made and programs best delivered. The key is knowing what might be successful locally, and this is where research on neighborhood change and effective policy is still needed.

*—Robert Beauregard*

## CONCLUSION

Cities in transition are a diverse body of communities, sharing common problems and challenges yet differing in important ways. These challenges, long-standing in legacy cities and more recent in boom-bust cities, are real and deeply rooted in complex economic and social issues. The resulting changes to these cities' built environments pose still further challenges. All of this is rendered more difficult by the limited capacity that many cities have to deal with these issues, which is exacerbated in turn by the fiscal crisis most cities are facing. Though this is a difficult environment for planners, they can play a critical role in building the capacity and framing the strategies that can help bring about their cities' regeneration.

## ENDNOTE

1. The idea, however, that anti-urban federal policies drove this transformation is highly questionable; for a thoughtful analysis of that argument, see Beauregard 2001.

# CHAPTER 3

# The Strategic Framework for Planning in Cities in Transition

In this chapter we examine the critical roles and responsibilities of planners in cities in transition and how they can most effectively work for change. In the first section, we identify the key dimensions of planners' roles and important principles that should guide planners in light of the complex challenges confronting cities in transition. In the second half, we offer a planning framework that strategically links land use and community- or economic-development policies and programs across multiple scales. We call this hybrid planning model a strategic policy plan, as it is rooted in traditional strategic planning and focuses on policy and program integration. Pursuing these approaches requires planners to engage city agencies, nonprofit partners, and neighboring jurisdictions, as well as community residents.

## SAMPLE COMMUNITIES AND THEIR CHALLENGES

Reading, Pennsylvania, has seen its population decline reversed in recent years by significant Latino in-migration. New arrivals are poor, and the regional economy does not offer enough jobs for the growing population. Unemployment is high, and the home ownership rate has dropped sharply, destabilizing many neighborhoods. The city is facing major budget hurdles and has been declared fiscally distressed by the state.

Flint, Michigan, the birthplace of General Motors (GM), is also in deep fiscal distress, and the state has appointed an emergency financial manager to run its affairs. It has lost roughly 50 percent of its population since 1960 and is continuing to shrink, with some neighborhoods largely abandoned. Although much of its population is poor and unemployed, it is also seeing the beginnings of revival in its downtown and has had some success in reusing sites vacated by GM. For its part, GM has increased its workforce in the area slightly in the past year, though the total in the county today is about 7,000, a fraction of what it was at its peak.

Las Vegas has seen growth grind nearly to a halt and house prices decline by 60 percent or more. As property values in planned developments built in the 2000s drop, middle-class families are moving in, abandoning inner neighborhoods built in the 1950s and 1960s. Many of the houses in those older neighborhoods are either being bought by speculators or left empty. With the collapse of construction and contractions in the casino industry, unemployment has skyrocketed.

In Irvington, New Jersey, roughly one out of every seven homes is in foreclosure, and many neighborhoods have been badly destabilized by falling property values, abandonment, and rising crime. While Springfield Avenue, the main shopping street, is still vital, many parts of the city are showing signs of neglect or deterioration. Surrounded by other fully developed towns, and with little vacant land, Irvington suffers from a weak ratable base in a state where local governments have few resources other than property tax revenue. ◀

## THE PLANNER'S WORK: BASIC GUIDING PRINCIPLES

Planners' roles and responsibilities—how planners approach their work, how decisions are made and priorities set—are fundamentally different in cities in transition, despite the common framework of laws and policies that such cities share with others in their states. These differences grow directly out of the fundamental economic, demographic, and physical changes these cities face. These challenges demand different ways of thinking about planning and using the planner's toolkit.

From a narrow perspective, one might ask: Are these planning challenges? Poverty, falling property values, and shrinking government budgets are often not considered as being within the planner's purview. In cities in transition, however, all of these issues are interwoven. Land use, the housing market, the local economy, and fiscal sustainability must be approached in an integrated fashion in order for a city to successfully address its challenges. This framework defines the planner's role.

### Planners as Change Agents

First and foremost, planners in cities in transition need to be change agents. This can be a difficult and lonely role, particularly where the need for change has yet to be recognized by local elected officials or by key private or nonprofit leaders. Even so, for planners in these cities not to advocate for change is to neglect an important part of their professional responsibilities.

All cities in transition are trying to dig themselves out of holes. Planners are often the people in agencies or governments who are best qualified to think through the plans, strategies, and initiatives most likely to be effective in bringing about change at the block, neighborhood, or city level. Furthermore, planners are often well situated to work across scales to develop regional strategies that reflect a city's interests.

The economic condition of any city in transition reflects some degree of market failure, and in most cases it is unlikely that a resurgence of national growth will soon set matters right. In such a setting, local government—in partnership with others at the local, regional, and state levels—must actively intervene to try to change the city's condition.

Most cities in transition already do this to some extent. They use public funds to subsidize housing where market prices will not support the cost of rehabilitation or new construction, provide down-payment assistance to struggling home buyers, and create loan programs to help small start-up firms that cannot qualify for conventional loans. In these cases cities are investing public funds in ways that create stronger communities through better housing, a greater home owner base, or more vital local businesses.

These efforts, though, are usually not driven by any overall strategy or sense of how they contribute to the city and its economy. Planners can make their greatest contributions in framing such strategies and linking the numerous efforts—both those in place and those needed—they entail. To do so requires the ability to put many different pieces together and to recognize that no plan is just about land use or design. Planning in cities in transition needs to integrate economic and social concerns and address issues of resource allocation and implementation.

### Planning Begins with Economics

All land-use and planning decisions should be considered on the basis of how they will make the local economy work better for the city and its residents. That means considering not only "economic development" as conventionally defined but also neighborhood revival and improvements to residents' quality of life. These activities contribute to rebuilding the local economy by enhancing property values and tax revenues and by building a more economically diverse population.

All planning decisions need to be made with economic feasibility constantly in mind. There is little point in zoning land for industrial use if the planner does not also understand the economic conditions under which firms are likely to occupy that zone. Considerations such as the price firms can realistically be expected to pay for land and buildings and the necessity of subsidizing those costs or offering other economic incentives become part of the planning process.

A focus on economic feasibility, however, does not mean that the city should accept everything that private individuals may propose. It is critical to look at how each development proposed will enhance or detract from its surroundings over the long term. A service station in the middle of a pedestrian-oriented commercial district may be economically feasible without public investment, while a multistory mixed use building may require subsidies or tax breaks, but the latter may ultimately yield far more in economic as well as social and aesthetic benefits to the community. The planner's role goes well beyond the conventional role of first identifying the right land uses and standards and then trying to determine what will lead to private development consistent with those standards. The planner will not only develop reuse strategies but help carry them out.

### Planning Is Community Engagement

Few people would argue with the proposition that community engagement is central to the planning process; the image of the omniscient planner making decisions from an ivory tower of rationality is long gone. Community engagement, however, takes on a particularly important role in the planning process in a city in transition, both because of the political dynamics in these cities and because of the nature of the issues that the planning process is seeking to address. Moreover, as we explore in more depth in Chapter 8, engagement strategies and techniques are fundamentally different in cities in transition.

*A community-based effort in Baltimore to reuse vacant land*

Joseph Schilling

The more planning focuses on change, the more it is necessary for planners to work with the people whose lives are going to be affected by the change. In extreme form this can be seen in legacy cities where planners are confronting neighborhoods that have become largely vacant. The remaining residents of these areas are aware that their neighborhoods are in trouble, yet they may understandably resist planners' proposals to rightsize the city—by, for example, gradually emptying these areas of population and replacing them with green land uses.

Community engagement needs to be a two-way street. Planners must be able to listen to a community's needs and preferences and see the city's neighborhoods through residents' eyes. This includes not only understanding how residents see their neighborhoods today but also grasping the neighborhood's history: what it was like and how it has changed over the years. Both that history and today's reality affect how residents will respond to proposals for future change.

At the same time planners should be able to help place residents' knowledge and concerns in larger citywide and regional contexts. Planners can help them understand the economic, physical, and other opportunities and constraints that define the scope of realistic options for their areas, communicating complex information and ideas in language comprehensible to nonprofessionals, with a minimum of technical jargon or terminology.

### Planning Must Address Social Justice

Many cities in transition contain far more than their regional share of minority and lower-income residents and far less than their regional share of resources and opportunities. Therefore, planners working in cities in transition must evaluate strategies and policies with an eye toward social justice—that is, "a just distribution of rights, opportunities and resources" (Barry 2005).

Racial and economic stress, often erupting into open conflict, has long been the central reality in many cities in transition. Racial change, blockbusting, discrimination, and the uprooting of thousands of families of color as a result of highway construction and urban renewal are the ever-present backdrop to today's planning efforts. While the need to foster social justice is always important, this history makes it that much more pressing. When policy advocates and public officials propose rightsizing cities through a process of eliminating public services in heavily depopulated neighborhoods, many residents are reminded of the checkered history of urban renewal.

Social justice in planning does not require that all programs and policies that planners advocate be actively redistributional. Cities in transition need to address many issues if they are to regain prosperity. A strategy to attract a major retail facility to the city or to draw middle-class families into an inner-city neighborhood may not inherently further social justice, yet these strategies serve other purposes that benefit the city. Planners need to maximize opportunities and minimize potential harms, such as by building in programs to provide jobs for city residents in the one case and to prevent displacement in the other.

More than a geographic, governmental, or legal entity, a city is its institutions, organizations, and people.

### Planning Is about Strategic Resource Allocation

If public resources are needed to foster development or other desired outcomes, a critical but difficult question needs to be raised: How can limited resources be most productively allocated? Many public funds can be used only for narrowly defined activities. Low Income Housing Tax Credits (LIHTC), for example, can be used only to build or rehabilitate low-income rental housing, whether or not additional such housing is needed. Other resources, such as Community Development Block Grant (CDBG) funds, may be flexible in theory but limited in practice; although these funds can be used for numerous things, in many cities political pressures, historic allocation practices, and sheer inertia make it difficult to move from the practice of spreading CDBG funds thinly across all eligible neighborhoods to a more targeted approach.

Strategic approaches are often possible. Since 1999 Richmond, Virginia, has directed the lion's share of its CDBG funds to a small number of carefully selected neighborhoods (Accordino et al. 2006). And planners can target tax-credit investment in ways that will most strengthen the city's neighborhoods and enhance the market, whether for rehabilitation or new construction or to buy and fix up scattered single-family houses.

Other funding sources, such as municipal capital budgets, are more flexible. In addition, decisions about allocation of resources—such as where to build or close a school—can create or eliminate other sources of funding. These decisions can be made in silos based on narrow operational criteria, or they can be made in an integrated fashion, taking account of how public investment will leverage private investment. Analyzing how to allocate resources so that each choice about spending or saving furthers the city's regeneration is a planning function.

### Planning Is about Good Design

Ugly or dull buildings, or site planning that violates the logic of the existing fabric of a neighborhood or a downtown, do more than offend aesthetic sensitivities; they devalue their surroundings and impede market revival. Well-designed buildings that are sensitive to their surroundings and careful site planning and treatment can enhance both the economic and social value of their environments.

But design is not just about buildings. The urban environment is permeated with design choices, including how streets, sidewalks, tree plantings, and fencing are handled and how the entire public realm is treated. Good design cannot solve difficult social and economic problems, but it can make neighborhoods and downtowns more attractive to people as they choose where to live, open a business, or spend their leisure dollars. This is true whether the object of design concern is affordable housing, a park, or a major downtown development.

Planners are often the only individuals working for a city or CDC with any design training or expertise; thus, they have a particular responsibility to help enable good design choices. Planners should review local ordinances to ensure that they foster good site planning and site treatment. While land-use approvals may provide only limited scope for design review, many projects in cities in transition also seek discretionary assistance from the municipality, and planners should set design conditions on that assistance beyond what may be possible in the land-use review process.

### Planning Happens in Many Different Ways

Most of the planner's work in a city in transition is not about making a "plan" in the traditional sense but about pursuing activities at various scales and levels of specificity intended to help regenerate the city. Planners should think of themselves as offering menus of strategic options that cut across time and scale, spanning one to 20 years and addressing individual sites, blocks, neighborhoods, or the city as a whole.

Which options are selected is not entirely up to the planner. While planners should advocate for what they consider most appropriate, decisions will reflect the political and financial climate as well as the priorities of the city's political leaders and its partners. The planner's role will often be in-

### THE EVOLVING NATURE OF PUBLIC-SECTOR STRATEGIC PLANNING

Modern concepts of strategic planning originated in private-sector strategic management developed in the 1950s and 1960s in response to rapidly changing and competitive business environments (Bracker 1980). With the expansion of the discipline of organizational development, companies today routinely follow strategic planning processes to craft new mission statements, visions, goals, and objectives. Classic strategic planning helps organizations understand where they are now, where they want to go, what actions they should take to get there, what resources they will need, and how they will know when they get there. By creating a strategic plan an organization hopes to increase overall effectiveness, use resources more efficiently, and facilitate stronger communications within and outside of itself (Bryson 2004).

During the 1990s municipalities began to embrace strategic planning processes and principles and adapt them to their operations, with the support of organizations such as the International City/County Management Association and the American Planning Association. Over the past 20 years the practice and process of public-sector strategic planning has become more sophisticated and complex. John Bryson, the guru of public and nonprofit strategic planning, developed a 10-step model with dozens of actions for each step and complex organizational mapping and diagramming tools (2004).

Most public-sector strategic planning processes indirectly affect policy by improving the operations and direction of organizations and entities. They may establish visions, principles, and goals that guide government officials in budgetary decision making and allocation of resources. However, since these strategic plans typically have no legal standing, they may change with the election of a new city council or mayor or the appointment of a new city/county manager or chief executive officer.

Although strategic policy planning still seems comparatively new in the planning field, Roger L. Kemp's 1992 casebook, *Strategic Planning in Local Government*, includes examples of local governments using strategic planning processes to address a range of planning and policy challenges, such as growth management, program management, long-term fiscal planning, citywide visioning and goal setting, and small-city revitalization. These case studies not only illuminate the political and policy drivers behind these planning efforts but emphasize the importance of strategic planning in an ever-changing political and economic climate. Kemp synthesizes the insights from these cases into a six-phase model. ◄

terjecting a "planning consciousness" into decisions. This can mean preparing data to provide a framework for the decision, evaluating and presenting alternatives, or even asking questions to ensure that issues are put on the table. Though not always an easy role to play, it is an important one.

Poor decisions may still be made. An ambitious plan that exceeds the potential resources available or the city's implementation capacity may be worse than no plan at all, and devoting resources to a neighborhood plan without a capable neighborhood-based entity as a partner may be futile. Conversely, a CDC planner may see developing a neighborhood plan as a way of making the case for a greater share of city resources or for getting the city to change its development policies for the neighborhood.

### A FRAMEWORK FOR STRATEGIC POLICY PLANNING

Finding time and support for strategic planning is difficult. Local officials are constantly reacting to crises such as fiscal instability or the complex socioeconomic problems of homelessness, joblessness, and property abandonment. Orchestrating a planning process, regardless of scale or size, runs afoul of the emergency nature of life within cities in transition. Staff is often consumed with day-to-day operations. Even so, taking a step away from crisis mode and spending energy on strategic thinking will serve a city better in both the short and long terms.

The following section offers a strategic policy planning framework grounded in the realities of cities in transition. This framework borrows from a number of strategic planning models and the experiences of several cities in transition. Various elements of the framework can apply to planning processes of different scales and types, such as revisions to comprehensive plans or the creation of special area or neighborhood plans. Our goal is to provide planners with a flexible framework they can use and adapt to their needs.

While planners familiar with the literature on strategic planning may recognize certain elements of our framework (see sidebar), it covers new territory by establishing the overarching goals of integrating policy and orchestrating action across a spectrum of issues. At its core it seeks to align multiple government and nonprofit players, programs, and policies behind a series of consensus-driven principles and goals. In many respects this hybrid framework resembles policy plans that local governments are now developing as sustainability, climate-action, or community-energy plans. In fact, these emerging sustainability-planning frameworks have important parallels for cities in transition, as many integrate a wide range of policies and programs across multiple departments and agencies in areas such as green buildings, land use, transportation, and energy.

Our framework envisions a much broader role in the planning process for planners and planning departments than is typical, one that extends beyond land use, transportation, housing, and the environment. It proposes that planners or planning departments lead or assist in the design, facilitation, and management of the strategic planning process in collaboration with political leaders, city officials, and community-based organizations to ensure effective implementation. Strategic planning processes rarely follow each of the steps below in sequence; they often weave back and forth among these phases. The sequence of the phases should always remain fluid to accommodate changing conditions.

## Internal Action Plan, Preparation, and Process Design

Before embarking on the strategic planning process, planners should identify stakeholders and build support inside and outside of city hall. A preliminary step is to develop an internal scoping process with planning department core staff and other department and agency directors across the organizational structure, who then vet initial ideas up the chain of command; this scoping process is critical to get input and set the stage for a more formal review and analysis later. It may be important to organize an executive group to manage the initiative, designate its leadership, and identify a spokesperson for the process. A core element of the process design is a communications and outreach strategy to provide feedback loops and opportunities for adjustment throughout the initiative.

## Inventory and Assessment

The first step in any classic planning process is to understand the issues and the environment. For cities in transition this means casting a wide net so that planners understand the interplay among their cities' distinctive physical, social, economic, and environmental characteristics, conditions, and challenges. The inventory and assessment of current conditions should establish an accurate baseline of information for use in the planning process and policy interventions.

In addition to gathering data about the past and the present, planners should explore potential futures through simple forecasting or identification of reliable and relevant forecasts of future trends done by others, using data and visualization techniques to model alternative scenarios. Baseline data should also be used to develop indicators of change and other outcome- or performance-based measurements to enable ongoing feedback. The assessment stage should also focus on the human side of the equation through stakeholder analysis of internal and external partners and qualitative information gathering from focus groups, community meetings, and similar processes.

## A Collective Community Vision

While some cities in transition may need to make only minor revisions or amendments to existing plans, most will need a new vision. This is the case for both older industrial communities that have struggled for decades and boom-bust cities that had planned around a now-obsolete growth model. The new vision must be consistent with the current reality, supported by the data previously gathered and assessed. Acknowledging reality is a critical step in the process of recovery. In Youngstown, Ohio, this took place in 2003 and 2004 at the beginning of the process that led to the Youngstown 2010 plan; through a series of town hall meetings, residents came to the realization that Youngstown would never return to its former size or economic base but could still become a great smaller city.

While the vision may take different forms, strategic planning practice calls for developing a mission statement, goals, and objectives. The goal of any visioning process is to navigate the changes between the past and the present in order to move a community toward a new future—a Zen-like process more often art than science. The vision could be supported by a set of internal principles for guiding the strategic planning process, and it should also enable the articulation of broad community principles and goals that describe a more positive community future.

**PREPARATION**
- Scoping Process
- Internal Action Plan
- Communications Strategy

**INVENTORY AND ASSESSMENT**
- Data and Demographics
- Current and Future Conditions
- Existing Programs and Policies

**COMMUNITY VISION**
- Civic and Engagement Strategy
- Vision Format
- Scenario Planning
- Backcasting

**DIAGNOSIS AND PLACE-BASED POLICY PRESCRIPTIONS**
- Policy/Program Gaps
- Policy Coordination and Integration (Vertical and Horizontal)
- Menu of Policy/Program Interventions

**ADOPTION**
- Formal Adoption by Local Leaders
- Action Plan—Staffing and Budgets

**MILESTONE AND EVALUATION**
- Measurable Targets
- Monitoring and Reporting Process
- Program Evaluation
- Feedback for Policy Revisions

*Figure 3.1. The strategic planning process*

While there are many books and courses on community visioning, one model that may resonate with cities in transition is "backcasting," part of the Integrated Community Sustainability Planning model developed by the Natural Step of Canada (www.naturalstep.org/en/canada/icsp). Backcasting starts with a vision of the future or successful outcome and works back to determine what steps must be taken to get there. In contrast, forecasting builds on existing assumptions and information to identify trends and then projects those trends into the future. Thus, backcasting may work best when a community is searching for a different future, while forecasting is most effective as a continuation of the status quo (Park, Purcell, and Purkis 2009).

### Place-Based Policy Prescriptions

This strategic planning process is set apart from others by its emphasis on policy integration and coordination. We take policy to encompass federal and state economic development programs as well as those within local government that have control over subjects such as land use and development. Although a local plan cannot govern policies and programs beyond its scope, it becomes a blueprint for deploying policies and programs in a more strategic way and incorporates a body of tenets to promote collective action.

In addition to facilitating policy coordination, the strategic policy plan should incorporate a menu of long- and short-term policy and program interventions. At the tactical level, the plan should establish a place-based approach, focusing on adoption of the strategies most appropriate to different market conditions and neighborhood typologies. It should also include an assessment of the city's internal capacity to manage the programs and projects needed to support the policy interventions. These policies and programs should further positive change, improve local conditions, and rebuild civic infrastructure. In addition, it is critical to have contingency plans or alternative policy interventions ready if possible, so the city can respond to changing conditions and circumstances.

### Adoption and Implementation of Strategic Policy Plan and Action Plan

Place-based policies must be turned into a cohesive strategic policy plan. The plan should be subject to an adoption process by the local governing body. This adoption gives weight to the plan, shapes policy, and sends a strong signal of commitment to the plan which will ultimately make the plan and its policies more effective.

After adoption of the strategic policy plan, planners should oversee the creation of a more detailed action plan that assigns responsibility for each program and project and designates target neighborhoods or sites for specific policy interventions. The action plan should detail staff allocations and potential restructuring of city functions as well as partnerships with and roles for regional and local nonprofits, businesses, community-based organizations, universities, and others.

### Setting Milestones, Monitoring Performance, and Evaluating Outcomes

The last step in the strategic policy planning process is to set concrete milestones or measureable targets, regularly track and report on performance, and synthesize and evaluate these performance measures to make midcourse corrections. All three of these steps are necessary; it makes little sense to measure performance if no process exists for sharing this information or determining whether policies and programs need changing.

While local governments have come a long way in developing performance measurement systems, these programs—such as the CitiStat program pioneered in Baltimore (see www.baltimorecity.gov/Government /AgenciesDepartments/CitiStat.aspx)—typically focus on municipal service delivery. Cities in transition need access to data that focus on measuring change in concrete terms at different scales, from the region to the parcel. Examples from recent sustainability plans offer cities in transition good models for setting targets across a wide range of policy issues. Baltimore and Philadelphia's sustainability plans establish a set of sustainability policy principles and goals, such as conserving natural resources, preventing pollution, promoting environmental education and awareness, creating green jobs for city residents, and expanding access to local food systems. Baltimore's plan lists 132 program and policy strategies to help achieve these policy goals along with setting timeframes and identifying potential funding and public and private organizations that might assist with implementation. Philadelphia's plan frames sustainability through five "lenses"—energy, environment, equity, economy, and engagement—and 15 total targets. Each of Philadelphia's five sustainability themes contains an overarching policy goal along with a few measurable targets set for 2015. Each target includes a laundry list of proposed programs and initiatives that could help the city reach its short-term targets and longer-range goals (Schilling 2012).

## INTEGRATING PLANS, PROGRAMS, AND INITIATIVES

The principles and strategic framework outlined above can be translated by planners through different activities working at many different scales and with many different actors. While multiple scales, actors, and strategies are part of the planning reality in any community, the nature of the issues faced by cities in transition—particularly the need for active public-sector intervention in areas such as economic development and neighborhood revitalization—creates special complexities. Planners must give particular attention to integrating these disparate elements into coherent systems to enable cities to use their resources most effectively and focus on the most productive strategies for change.

### Addressing Multiple Scales and Actors

Table 3.1 on page 36 shows the different scales at which planners work in cities in transition. Cities and regions typically contain many different entities engaging in planning activities at different scales and generating a plethora of planning products. Planners may be involved in generating some of these products and also charged with integrating these plans into a coherent whole. To be successful, they must consider multiple levels of integration.

*Integrating Scales.* This ensures that plans and those responsible for preparing them and carrying them out are coordinated at the different geographic scales of planning. Planning products inevitably relate to one another at many different levels and may form a hierarchy of scales; for example, a local economic development plan should be integrated with—and perhaps even be derived from—a regional economic development strategy. As Figure 3.2 on page 37 shows, neighborhood planning follows a logical hierarchy, starting with a citywide assessment of comparative neighborhood conditions—including such key areas as housing market conditions, social engagement, and assets—and continuing through the neighborhood revitalization plan and ultimately down to the individual site level. While smaller-scale planning does not have to follow this sequence, outcomes are likely to be better and resources better used where it does.

*Integrating Actors.* This ensures that the multiple public and nongovernment entities involved in planning are in fact working together. Making sure

| Scale | Principal Planning Entities | Principal Planning Products |
|---|---|---|
| **Region** | County planning agency<br>MPO<br>Regional planning agency<br>Economic development collaborative or partnership | Regional land-use and transportation plans<br>Regional economic-development strategies |
| **City** | City planning agency<br>City community development agency<br>Economic development agency or collaborative | Comprehensive plans (land use, housing, transportation, etc.)<br>Urban design plans<br>Consolidated plan (mandated by HUD)<br>Land-use ordinances<br>Housing market condition/trend assessments<br>Neighborhood assessments<br>Investment/resource allocation strategies<br>Economic development strategies<br>Vacant property strategies |
| **Neighborhood/ subarea** | City planning agency<br>Redevelopment agency<br>CDC<br>Special purpose or special district public entities | Redevelopment plans<br>Neighborhood revitalization/stabilization plans<br>Vacant property–reuse strategies |
| **Block/block group** | City planning agency<br>Redevelopment agency<br>CDC | Target-area strategies in neighborhood plans<br>Block/block group improvement plans<br>Vacant property–reuse strategies |
| **Site** | City planning agency<br>CDC<br>Neighborhood association or block group<br>Developer | Development assemblages<br>Reuse strategies<br>Site plans<br>Building or landscape designs |

*Table 3.1. Planning scales in cities in transition*

that all efforts add up to a coherent strategy is made particularly difficult by the many planning actors working in the typical local environment. These include regional or county planning agencies as well as municipal planning offices and various other entities within city government. In some cities the planning office may be responsible for the comprehensive plan and land-use ordinance, the community development agency for the consolidated plan required for use of CDBG and other HUD funds, an economic development agency or corporation for the city's economic development strategy, and a redevelopment agency for redevelopment area plans. On top of this, many cities contain special-purpose entities such as downtown development agencies or port authorities that may also engage in planning. While all of these efforts are directed at the same goal—the revitalization of the city and its parts—the extent to which they are coordinated or add up to a coherent strategy can vary widely.

*Integrating Plans.* This ensures that planning documents add up to a coherent body of strategies and directions for the community. While planning activities within a city are often poorly coordinated, so are the planning

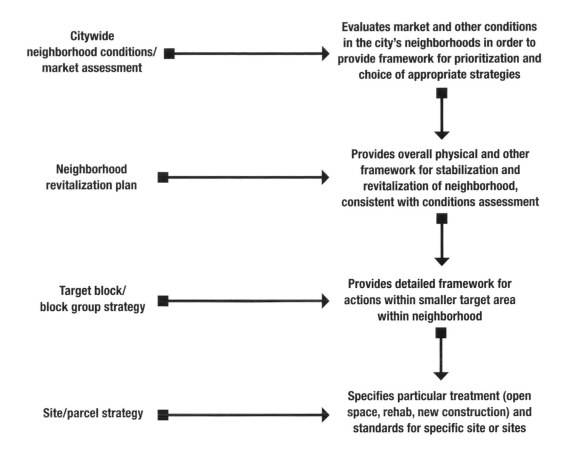

*Figure 3.2. Hierarchical framework of scales for neighborhood planning*

activities conducted by public entities and those carried out by private or quasi-governmental organizations. While some public-sector planners may believe they should have a monopoly on planning activities, such an attitude is shortsighted and unrealistic. Private efforts can enhance and complement public-sector efforts. Economic development organizations often take the lead in economic development planning, while a growing number of CDCs are developing revitalization plans for the geographic areas where they work; in New Jersey, such a plan is required for the CDC to be eligible for certain forms of financial assistance (see sidebar, page 38). Finally, many developers prepare their own plans for sites that they control or would like to obtain from public entities; the closer those plans are linked to an overall citywide strategy or priorities, the more likely it is that their outcomes will be successful. In principle, all planners should recognize the importance of integrating plans and should make sure that their work is linked to that of others, whether they are working for a regional economic development partnership, a municipal government, or a CDC. In practice they often do not, and it is most often the municipal planner who is charged with the responsibility of herding the many cats engaged in planning in a city or region.

### Strategies for Planning Integration

In fostering integration among plans and strategies pursued by different actors at different scales, stronger tools than moral suasion are needed. Useful tools for planners or other key players exist to support effective planning and strategy execution. While these are usually deployed within local government, some can be used by nongovernmental entities.

*Coordinating Local Government Activity.* Coordinating the planning and strategic activity carried out within a local government is perhaps the

### ▶ NEW JERSEY NEIGHBORHOOD REVITALIZATION TAX CREDIT

The New Jersey Neighborhood Revitalization Tax Credit (NRTC) program (P.L.2001, c.415), first enacted in 2001, allows businesses to obtain state tax credits by donating funds to CDCs for neighborhood revitalization activities. In order for a CDC to receive these funds, it must prepare a comprehensive neighborhood revitalization plan, which must be approved by the state Department of Community Affairs. While the plan must be submitted for comment to the municipality, municipal approval is not a requirement of the program. The program provides $10 million per year for revitalization efforts in New Jersey's lower-income neighborhoods. ◀

most important but often the most difficult step. Such coordination can be a function of how the local government is organized (formal structure), what mechanisms exist to ensure coordination across departmental or agency lines (integrative structure), and the extent to which communication takes place among staff of different agencies or departments (informal structure). For example, a growing number of cities with sustainability plans have created sustainability coordinator positions that work across departments to implement the goals and targets set forth in the plans. Many of these coordinators share lessons and insights through the Urban Sustainability Directors Network now facilitated by the National League of Cities. (See www.sustainablecitiesinstitute.org/usdn.) In some small cities where many of the different planning-related functions of city government are combined in a single department, much coordination can take place through internal management systems if the head of that department is a planner or someone sensitive to planning and strategy issues. The coordination of planning with implementation, however, may be another matter, discussed in more detail in Chapter 9.

***Building and Using Data and Information Systems.*** The ability to track a city's or region's economic and housing market trends, foreclosures and real estate–owned properties, tax collections, and other key issues is essential in developing rational strategies to tackle the challenges facing a city in transition. Without this information, decisions are made in a vacuum and often result in wasteful or counterproductive outcomes. Data systems are also critical to guide the operations of cities in transition, particularly those dealing with large numbers of city-owned vacant properties, where understanding the nature of the inventory and tracking the status of properties are both necessary.

Likewise, the ability to build and manage a solid information system and generate reliable data for users within and outside city government can also be a strong tool for integrating planning efforts. While some cities have developed in-house information systems, others have worked with local universities or foundations. For example, the Northeast Ohio Community and Neighborhood Data for Organizing (NEO CANDO) system in Cleveland and northeastern Ohio, run by Case Western Reserve University, has significantly increased the effectiveness of planning efforts in that area (see http://neocando.case.edu/cando/index.jsp).

Data can be used to identify productive strategies; one example is economic cluster analysis, which identifies the industries and interindustry relationships in a city or metropolitan area that have the greatest potential to accelerate value creation, produce revenue, and generate market growth. Data can also be used to assess the feasibility of planning proposals as well as to target resources. A city planning agency that shares solid data on housing market conditions and trends with CDCs and developers can exert a strong influence on the nature of their plans. Data, however, must be interpreted, and potential users may not have the skills or training to translate raw data into usable information. Planners must be able to analyze data, draw sound conclusions and inferences from them, and share those conclusions and inferences with potential users.

***Targeting Resources.*** The most powerful means of integrating planning activities lies in targeting public resources at specific plans and strategies. The degree to which a plan strategically allocates public funds, particularly discretionary resources such as CDBG funds or economic development incentives, largely determines its importance and, in the long term, how effective change efforts are likely to be. Moreover, to be truly effective it is important to strategically align all public resources that have some effect on a city's future, including those for such seemingly unrelated matters as street and sidewalk repairs, park improvements, and school construction or renovation.

In most cities public resources are not effectively targeted around strategic goals and plans. Public entities too often make spending decisions based on internal criteria that may have little or nothing to do with larger strategic concerns. School districts, for example, often operate independently of local governments and do not coordinate their facility decisions—which have a powerful impact on neighborhoods—with simultaneous city- or CDC-led efforts at neighborhood revitalization.

The first step toward effective resource targeting is to establish a consensus around the principle that resources should be targeted strategically. Taking the time and making the effort to build that consensus will make it far easier to later make strategic decisions about the allocation of specific resources. In the end, though, deploying this tool requires leadership at a higher level than that of the city's planning director.

***Building Partnerships and Coalitions.*** Building partnerships among different cities in a region, between a city and its CDCs, and between local government and the business community is an important part of all change strategies and key in fostering planning integration. Often the most important planning partnerships, after those among local government agencies, are between city government and the city's CDCs. With the growth in neighborhood planning activities initiated by CDCs and related organizations, such working partnerships can ensure that individual neighborhood plans are integrated into citywide strategies and that their goals are consistent with one another's, as well as with the city's larger economic and community development goals. Such partnerships can also be effective in linking plans to targeted resource allocation strategies. Where a city has a strong citywide CDC association, as in Philadelphia and Cleveland, the association can become an invaluable partner with city government in supporting the local planning process.

Nongovernmental partners that have become part of the process and that develop a commitment to planning and strategic thinking can also become strong allies for city planners' efforts to foster better planning coordination and more strategic resource allocation. As advocates from outside government, they can often exert influence in ways that planners, as public employees, cannot.

*In most cities public resources are not effectively targeted around strategic goals and plans. Public entities too often make spending decisions based on internal criteria that may have little or nothing to do with larger strategic concerns.*

## CONCLUSION

This chapter outlines the principles and broad strategies to help planners in cities in transition become change agents who actively help their cities rebuild their physical environments and regain economic vitality. To be successful in these environments, planners should facilitate the adoption of strategic policy plans and then focus on integrating planning and building strategies, such as information systems and partnerships, to foster greater coordination of local government, nonprofit, and private bodies working in different ways toward common goals. Within this framework, however, planners must remain constantly aware that their work is about people: community residents must be engaged in the process of change, and social justice must always be part of every important decision and choice that is made. In Chapters 8 and 9 we offer some strategies for how planners might apply these principles and share some examples from the field.

# CHAPTER 4

# Designing a Strategic Policy Planning Framework for Cities in Transition

 As cities in transition reexamine their planning assumptions and chart new courses, existing plans and codes may not reflect current realities or likely trends. The task for planners and policy makers is to devise an overall policy planning framework and then create new plans—or revise and align existing policies and plans—so they are more responsive to contemporary conditions and establish solid foundations for new community visions.

*We suggest three primary planning pathways that planners can adapt for creating the strategic policy plan: amending or updating an existing comprehensive plan; creating a new strategic framework plan; or focusing on a special area or district plan.*

This chapter offers a new policy planning framework for cities in transition—a strategic policy plan—that can serve as the umbrella for a network of plans, policies, programs, and projects. This planning framework we envision would link existing municipal plans and policies, facilitating coordination across city departments, guiding the targeting of city resources, aligning city programs, and creating a stronger organizational culture to improve implementation as well as engaging and building consensus among community groups and local residents. Moreover, a citywide policy framework would also establish linkages with regional entities and neighboring jurisdictions, coordinating policy interventions and building more of a metropolitan approach to regeneration.

We suggest three primary planning pathways that planners can adapt for creating the strategic policy plan: amending or updating an existing comprehensive plan; creating a new strategic framework plan; or focusing on a special area or district plan. Each pathway presents its own set of trade-offs, strengths, and weaknesses. From the perspective of planning theory, a city in transition would ideally adopt a citywide strategic-policy plan by adapting its comprehensive plan or creating a strategic framework plan and nesting within it one or more special area or district plans at the corridor or neighborhood scales. We recognize, however, that some cities may not have sufficient capacity, political will, or community consensus to develop a citywide strategic-policy plan; under these circumstances it might make more sense to test the framework by adopting a special area plan that coordinates multiple policies and programs responding to the challenges of decline and distress at the district or corridor scale.

Within these three planning pathways, this chapter discusses several variations for designing the strategic policy plan, such as amending existing comprehensive plans or embarking on a comprehensive plan overhaul. In Chapter 5 we explore the next level of planning hierarchy by sharing creative ideas for recalibrating and aligning traditional land-use planning strategies and tools, such as zoning codes, capital improvement plans, and growth management plans, with the strategic policy plan.

## HOW IS PLANNING DIFFERENT IN CITIES IN TRANSITION?

A different context demands a different planning approach. Few cities in transition have strategic policy frameworks that offer a systemic planning approach sufficient to address the scope and complexity of their challenges. Many cities in transition lack rich planning cultures or strong planning track records, while shifts in political leadership often undercut positive planning initiatives. These general observations about planning in cities in transition are based on our fieldwork and interviews:

- They have little recent history or experience of planning; planning is becoming a lost art within the local government.

- Their planning focus is narrow and does not reflect the more integrated approach needed to better address the city's interwoven physical, social, and economic challenges.

- Current plans are out of touch with current market conditions, resting on obsolete assumptions of steady growth and development; the plan and its provisions are not geared for managing decline or stabilization.

- Actions and projects have become higher priorities than taking the time to chart more strategic directions; with conditions dire, policy makers demand quick responses.

- Local government planning capacity, resources, and expertise are often insufficient to match the scale of the problems.

- Political support for planning waxes and wanes as elected officials change and their interest fluctuates; those with little grounding in planning may not see its value.

- Insufficient civic infrastructure means that more time and different techniques are needed for engaging residents and building support for planning initiatives.

- There are few successful planning models from similar communities that can be emulated.

## PATHWAYS FOR A STRATEGIC POLICY PLAN

In devising the right planning vehicle, cities in transition have three basic options, as noted: a comprehensive land use plan, a strategic framework plan, and a special area or district plan. Under each of these pathways, planners can experiment with different approaches that will vary depending on local dynamics and current policy priorities. For example, at the citywide scale planners could work on new comprehensive plans or complete overhauls of existing plans, or instead take incremental approaches by developing new elements to plans or stand-alone strategies that guide plan implementation. Alternatively, planners could develop new citywide strategic-framework plans that could serve as broad policy umbrellas by linking the comprehensive plan and special area or neighborhood plans with housing plans, economic development strategies, and capital improvement plans. Finally, planners could create special area plans that coordinate various plans and policies within well-defined districts or corridors experiencing serious decline. Under any of these planning scenarios it is important to clearly define the relationship of these plans to one another and to the overall regeneration strategy. Whichever path a community takes, the outcome should be a cohesive network of plans and policies aligned with a new vision and commitment to regeneration.

More than 15 years ago Edward J. Kaiser and David R. Godschalk created the classic family tree of planning that describes the roots of contemporary comprehensive plans and how they have evolved into hybrid design, policy, and management plans (1995). What we are

### CHRISTINA KELLY: PLAN-MAKING STRATEGIES FOR CITIES IN TRANSITION

As the lead planner for the Genesee County Land Bank Authority (GCLBA), Christina Kelly directs the planning and development team and works on neighborhood and corridor revitalization plans for distressed areas in Flint, Michigan. Kelly acknowledges that planning initiatives have a mixed track record in Flint, which has gone through decades of disinvestment. Flint is now undertaking a complete rewrite of its comprehensive land-use plan in partnership with the GCLBA and community groups, using resources from a HUD Regional Sustainable Communities planning grant.

Reflecting on her experience of how planning is different in cities in transition, Kelly is surprised that prevailing structural assumptions based on growth and development "are so embedded into how planners and policy makers think that we become fooled by the lure of more growth." In light of these inherent growth assumptions, many city plans and policies erroneously apply strategies and tools that were designed for growing communities. As planners we "are using the wrong tools and thereby limiting our ability to effectively plan and respond to challenges confronting cities in transition. . . . We really need to turn our current planning model on its head."

Kelly suggests that when planning for cities in transition, planners first ask which entity is in the best position to manage the planning process and carry out the resulting recommendations—and the answer might not be the local planning department. "Planning in cities in transition requires collaboration with new partners, some who may have more planning expertise and resources than the local government planning department." Kelly's own position in the GCLBA illustrates this new collaborative model. She recently engaged city officials, community organizations, and residents to discuss potential revisions to Flint's comprehensive plan,and she continues to work closely with these groups in the development of neighborhood plans.

Kelly also notes that the elements of comprehensive plans in cities in transition should cover more ground than standard plans. They need to expressly integrate transportation and housing elements with smart growth tools and green-space principles. "Planners should consciously 'unpack' the growth assumptions in existing plans and recalibrate the new plan in light of the structural socioeconomic challenges that cities in transition face," she says. Comprehensive plans tailored to these cities' circumstances must step outside the boundaries of current practice and stretch the prescribed rules of comprehensive planning.

Despite these challenges, Kelly maintains that cities should update their comprehensive plans as long as they are willing to experiment with different models and processes that are more responsive to their dynamics. If full revisions are not feasible in light of resource constraints and limited capacity, cities can instead create framework plans that establish new policy directions by covering wider ranges of planning issues. Either planning approach must still facilitate honest public discussions about the need for real structural changes and provide more opportunities to engage external partners that have planning capacity. While acknowledging that many cities in transition will need state or federal resources to do this type of planning given the fiscal plight of local governments, Kelly contends that supporting long-range planning is well worth the investment. ◀

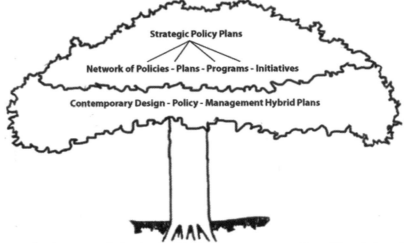

***Figure 4.1.*** *A new family tree*
*of planning*

Freely adapted from Kaiser and Godschalk 1995

suggesting is a somewhat different derivation in which the local comprehensive plan or strategic framework plan serves as a broader planning
canopy that coordinates a network of other plans, policies, and programs
across the governmental, nonprofit, and private sectors. (See Figure 4.1.)
When it comes to practice a community might be best served by having
one citywide strategic-policy plan along with one or more special area
plans that more specifically coordinate programs and policies targeted at
certain problem areas.

In the following section we explore different options for creating the
strategic policy plan and discuss examples slowly emerging from several
cities in transition, ranging from wholesale adoption of new comprehensive
plans to more incremental approaches. Note, however, that these examples
all remain works in progress and may be constrained by various elements
such as political leadership, managerial capacity, or community support. As
of now, none has the breadth of a strategic policy plan, but together they
nevertheless offer insightful lessons for planners to consider and build upon.
Whatever approach a city takes, a good plan should make a clean break from
the past and the present and lay a foundation for a different and hopefully
more prosperous future.

## COMPREHENSIVE PLANS

For most municipalities the local comprehensive plan remains the primary
document for reconciling a community's past and present with its future.
Comprehensive plans offer potential solutions for revamping land-use policy
and revising stale development patterns. However, the comprehensive plans
of many cities in transition are out of date—in some cases decades old—and
disconnected from current conditions, market realities, and growth trends.
Ideally, a city should completely revise its comprehensive plan, even though
this demands a substantial investment of time and resources. This approach
enables local governments to broadly recraft their land-use and other policies
to reflect existing and future market realities and growth constraints.

Essential questions for revising comprehensive plans might include the
following:

- What should the comprehensive plan say about different approaches to
economic development?

- What creative planning strategies can manage change in the context of
little new development?

- What should special area or neighborhood plans say about the reuse of vacant land and abandoned buildings?

- How can regional and local transportation plans better reflect changing mobility patterns caused by extensive job loss and property abandonment?

- What provisions of zoning codes and other regulations may make it difficult to implement urban agriculture and other urban greening strategies?

### Comprehensive Plan Overhauls

A wholesale revision of a comprehensive plan is a huge undertaking that typically takes two to three years with significant investments of staff or consultant resources and time. Youngstown, Ohio, conducted one of the most notable comprehensive-plan revisions for a legacy city; its new plan expressly acknowledges the unlikelihood of future population growth.

In early 2002 Youngstown initiated a multifaceted community-planning process, Youngstown 2010, with the goal of developing a replacement for the city's 1950s-vintage comprehensive plan. The first phase of the process, "Listening and Visioning," culminated in four thematic headlines to further guide the development process. These themes focused on accepting Youngstown as a smaller city and directing the city toward a more sustainable future based on practical and achievable goals. Planning participants then spent three years rewriting the comprehensive plan. During this time, Youngstown 2010 benefited from a branding effort as well as large-scale projects marking the city's forward progress. All in all, 5,000 citizens participated directly in the Youngstown 2010 process. (See www.cityofyoungstownoh .com/about_youngstown/youngstown_2010.)

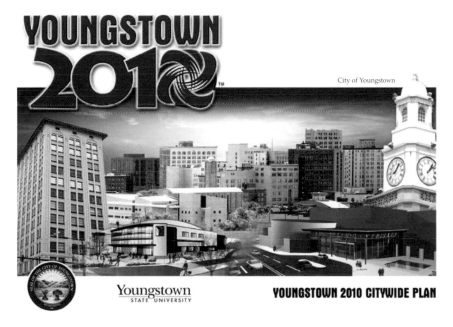

Although it is currently embryonic, a similar comprehensive planning overhaul has begun in Flint, Michigan, funded by a three-year grant from HUD. The process is divided into four phases, with community engagement central to each: (1) information gathering and learning about innovative planning practices; (2) development of an overall planning framework; (3) creating subarea plans for specific neighborhoods or commercial areas; (4) writing and approving the plan. Much as in Youngstown, the guiding principles will flow from community input, although the city is already committed to including social equity and environmental sustainability as two of the guiding principles. In the last stage of the process, a new zoning ordinance, an updated capital improvement plan, and revised maps will be added.

### Comprehensive Plan Revisions and Refinements

While planners should not rule out adopting new comprehensive plans, they should also consider the incremental approach of revising comprehensive plans by adopting new elements or strategies that can guide programs and policies for regenerating the city and revitalizing neighborhoods. The process for a comprehensive plan amendment is less time- and resource-intensive than a complete plan overhaul and so may be more realistic for many cities in transition.

In contrast to Youngstown, which has directly confronted the issue of shrinking population in its Youngstown 2010 process, Cleveland has taken a more subtle policy and planning approach to rightsizing. Facing the loss of over half of its peak population and suffering from high rates of foreclosure and economic decline, the city began to update its comprehensive plan in early 2000 to identify neighborhoods, corridors, and institutional assets where market strength remained in order to channel infill, infrastructure, and capital improvements to these areas. The goal of Connecting Cleveland: 2020 Citywide Plan is to link the city's people, places, and assets with strategic opportunities and resources that can offer residents diverse choices, opportunities, and an improved quality of life and health. (See http://planning .city.cleveland.oh.us/cwp/planIntro.php.)

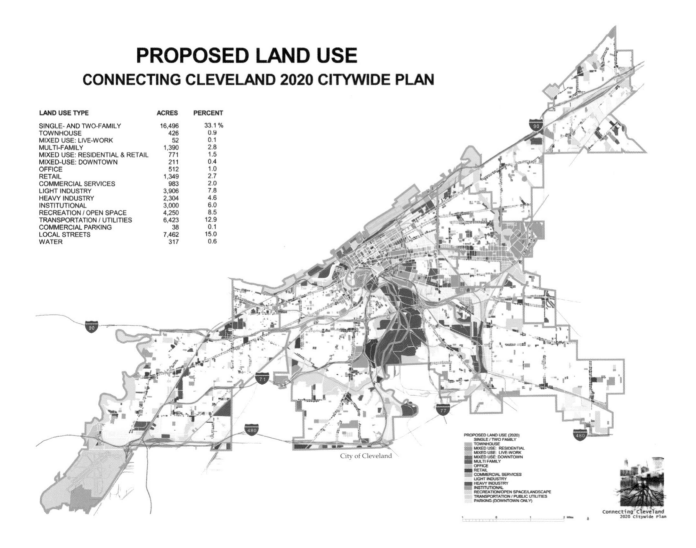

## PROPOSED LAND USE
### CONNECTING CLEVELAND 2020 CITYWIDE PLAN

| LAND USE TYPE | ACRES | PERCENT |
|---|---|---|
| SINGLE- AND TWO-FAMILY | 16,496 | 33.1 % |
| TOWNHOUSE | 426 | 0.9 |
| MIXED USE: LIVE-WORK | 52 | 0.1 |
| MULTI-FAMILY | 1,390 | 2.8 |
| MIXED USE: RESIDENTIAL & RETAIL | 771 | 1.5 |
| MIXED-USE: DOWNTOWN | 211 | 0.4 |
| OFFICE | 512 | 1.0 |
| RETAIL | 1,349 | 2.7 |
| COMMERCIAL SERVICES | 983 | 2.0 |
| LIGHT INDUSTRY | 3,906 | 7.8 |
| HEAVY INDUSTRY | 2,304 | 4.6 |
| INSTITUTIONAL | 3,000 | 6.0 |
| RECREATION / OPEN SPACE | 4,250 | 8.5 |
| TRANSPORTATION / UTILITIES | 6,423 | 12.9 |
| COMMERCIAL PARKING | 38 | 0.1 |
| LOCAL STREETS | 7,462 | 15.0 |
| WATER | 317 | 0.6 |

City of Cleveland

As a result, new partnerships are creating opportunities to leverage resources, solve problems, and advance the city's vision; one example is the city's Urban Agriculture Innovation Zone, a 26.5-acre pilot site for growing local food on previously vacant land. Project funders and partners include the Ohio State University Extension service, the U.S. Department of Agriculture, the Ohio State Department of Agriculture, and the city's Department of Economic Development. Such new initiatives help make Cleveland a greener place to live and link planning with public health initiatives.

According to Cleveland's current planning director, Robert Brown, taking a more incremental approach can help reposition cities in transition toward a more stable future. Brown suggests there is a lot to be optimistic about based on where Cleveland has been, how it is doing now, and where it is headed. The city is seeing growing interest from its residents for convenience in shopping, services, work, and living, as well as a greater propensity of younger people toward urban living with its mix of linked cultural, institutional, recreational, and open space amenities. In the midst of the recession, institutions and developers are investing in Cleveland's priority areas. For example, the Euclid Avenue corridor from downtown's Public Square to University Circle is slated for $4.2 billion worth of real estate development and infrastructure investments between 2000 and 2014 (Litt 2008). In 2008 the city expanded its priority development areas strategy to parts of the city outside its core development areas to better identify ways of reclaiming vacant properties. (See page 48.)

Dayton, Ohio, also provides planners with lessons in how to devise an effective planning framework without a comprehensive plan overhaul. Dayton's last major comprehensive plan update was done in 1996, but over the past 10 years the city has used internal management strategies to ensure its plan can better address the new realities of the marketplace without the need for major rewrites or formal amendments. According to former planning director John Gower, while the old plan was based on the assumption that Dayton would recapture its lost population, these new strategies reflect that the community is going through steps of loss, acceptance, and moving forward. What is emerging from these strategies is a plan that is grounded in a new and reimagined future, one that embraces knowledge and an asset-based community and economy and that also has far less population and density.

More information about both Cleveland and Dayton is available at www.vacantpropertyresearch.com.

## THE STRATEGIC FRAMEWORK PLAN

Cities that do not have the resources, capacity, or commitment to overhaul a comprehensive plan should instead consider developing a strategic framework plan—a short-term programmatic plan to help set policy and budget priorities—that can address pressing challenges such as vacant properties or high unemployment. This approach lays out overarching principles to guide policy and program decisions. A strategic framework plan can also set the stage for subsequent comprehensive plan revisions.

Within the planning family tree, such framework plans were typically long-range state or regional plans that established broad policy goals (Miller 2009). Recently, however, more municipalities have engaged in framework planning at the citywide and even neighborhood scales. We see a trend in planning practice toward these hybrid plans with attributes of strategic framework plans that address regional issues such as watersheds and crosscutting topics such as sustainability and climate change (Godschalk and Anderson 2012). Some of these hybrid plans focus on the revitalization of particular areas or districts. (See sidebar.)

**DAYTON'S GREEN AND GOLD STRATEGY**

In addition to using traditional comprehensive-plan update processes, Dayton's planners and policy makers are beginning to rely on principles set forth in an internal strategy guide—the city's Green and Gold sustainability and investment strategy. According to former planning director and current "reimagining strategist" John Gower, this strategy is an asset- and place-based approach to guiding reinvestment in Dayton that complements the comprehensive plan and offers programs and policies for achieving the city's goals. The "green" portion of the strategy focuses on rebuilding and sustaining an improved quality of life. A central theme is reimagining high-vacancy communities through various means such as strategic demolition, property acquisition, and land banking, coupled with greening schemes such as community gardens and agriculture. The "gold" section focuses on asset-based investments, with strategies linking economic, community, and neighborhood development by melding traditional topics like housing and infrastructure with innovative strategies.

The Green and Gold strategy is not a traditional plan, and it is not yet clear how much influence it will have over actual comprehensive plan updates. Nevertheless, articulations of ideals, strategies, and objectives in whatever form can have great influence over the creation and modification of official city documents, much as strategic frameworks can.

*Cover of a Detroit Works policy audit*

City of Detroit

The overarching principles set forth in a strategic framework plan can serve as a foundation for a new vision for the community and can help planners develop and implement programs and projects consistent with these principles and goals. Like comprehensive plans, strategic framework plans should also involve extensive community engagement. It is especially critical in a city in transition to engage residents and leaders in public discourse to acknowledge the limitations of the current system, recognize the need for structural changes, and set the city on a new course. A strategic framework plan can help build a more collaborative organizational culture for city departments by assigning them roles and responsibilities for implementing the plan. These plans can thus help further internal coordination and provide a vehicle for gaining public support for a new vision of a more sustainable community.

The recent experience of Cleveland demonstrates the promise of using strategic framework plans at the citywide scale. In 2008 the Cleveland City Planning Commission adopted a strategic framework plan, Re-imagining a More Sustainable Cleveland, outlining proactive strategies for remaking vacant land and creating new urban landscapes. (See http://reimagining cleveland.org and http://cudcserver.cudc.kent.edu/shrink/Images /reimagining_final_screen-res.pdf.) The initiative grew from the research and design work of the Cleveland Urban Design Collaborative at Kent State University in partnership with Neighborhood Progress, a citywide community development intermediary. After the completion of the plan, the initiative grew into a collaboration with the planning commission and many other organizations to address land use, environmental planning, parks, brownfields, and agriculture. This framework plan has acted as a catalyst not only for implementing reclamation projects but also for developing complementary policies, such as the urban agriculture ordinance adopted in 2009 that allows the keeping of farm animals and bees within the city.

Another framework plan example comes from Detroit, where in 2010 Mayor Dave Bing introduced Detroit Works as a process to develop a shared and achievable vision of the city's future (http://detroitworksproject.com). The process began with a series of meetings garnering 10,000 responses from community members. With the need for Detroit to act now while planning for the future, in July 2011 the project was split into two tracks: short-term action and long-term planning. The short-term actions are led by city officials and focus on realigning city services and leveraging available resources to make important neighborhood changes based upon current conditions. Simultaneously, long-term planning is being conducted by a technical team of consultants guided by a steering committee. The long-term planning goal is to produce a strategic framework plan by August 2012 that melds community engagement with technical analysis.

In the short term a two-prong approach can make good strategic planning sense where a city's fiscal and organizational challenges demand immediate and different types of policy interventions. A mechanisim to ensure coordination between the two, however, is essential. Much of the short-term work can be driven by revising and reforming internal procedures and organizational structures. At some point, however, these short-term neighborhood scale changes must also align with the principles and visions of long-term planning efforts. As Sam Butler mentions in his Detroit study (see Appendix), the media and community activists reacted strongly to the perceptions and fears around rightsizing that were associated with the launch of Detroit Works' long-range planning efforts. As the dynamic in Detroit illustrates, these types of citywide strategic-planning efforts have to overcome decades of distrust and failed initiatives, so it becomes critical for cities in transition, especially legacy cities, to carefully build momentum and engage the community in new ways.

## SPECIAL AREA OR DISTRICT PLANS

The third pathway for planners to consider is revising or adopting plans that target certain strategic areas such as corridors, districts, or neighborhoods for revitalization and redevelopment. In many cases it may make more sense to identify such discrete areas within a city for special planning and policy interventions before tackling these thorny issues through a citywide comprehensive or strategic framework plan. For the boom-bust and first suburb cities in transition in particular, a special area or district plan may be a more appropriate planning pathway given the concentration of urban decline at the corridor and neighborhood scales.

From a classic planning perspective, small area plans facilitate the implementation of citywide plans. They provide a finer grain of planning detail and the opportunity to respond to the special needs or concerns of a particular neighborhood or district. The small area plan takes many forms that vary from state to state, including district plans, corridor plans, transit-oriented development plans, and, in California, specific area plans (Berke et al. 2006).

In recent years, small area plans have become creative planning tools for managing growth and facilitating new urbanist policies, but few models have been identified that address the challenges of decline and disinvestment. While redevelopment plans might be seen as small area plans for declining neighborhoods, these plans follow strict legal procedures to further redevelopment and do not typically address shrinkage or broader revitalization issues. Many such plans have failed to achieve their goals because they applied a strong market approach in a weak market area or region.

*A community event in the Idora neighborhood*

Sean Posey

One example of a special area plan comes from Youngstown's Idora neighborhood. The neighborhood planning process for Idora began with a stakeholders' meeting in August 2007. In September, the Idora planning team, composed of Youngstown city planning staff and Ohio State University campus planners, hosted a kickoff meeting where it presented background information about the challenges faced by this neighborhood and asked residents to voice their opinions and ideas. From this input, planners drew up a series of priorities that meshed with the four overarching principles of the Youngstown 2010 plan. Based on these priorities, the team prepared a comprehensive neighborhood plan that outlines practical goals and strategies for the community, including a section devoted solely to greening strategies for blighted portions of the neighborhood. (See www.yndc.org/neighborhoods/idora.) A similar example of a special area plan is in Detroit's Lower

Eastside neighborhood, where a citywide association of CDCs facilitated a planning process that led to a community-driven strategic revitalization plan. (See case study in the Appendix.)

Several cities have special area revitalization districts that are experimenting with areawide approaches to brownfields redevelopment and the emerging concept of ecodistricts. Indianapolis, like many cities, has its share of brownfields—former vacant commercial and industrial sites with contamination—but its new Smart Growth Renewal District integrates areawide brownfields actions with principles of transit-oriented development along the 16th Avenue corridor. The new district includes a draft strategic redevelopment plan that involves two CDCs along with a community partnership that together with the city is helping coordinate myriads of federal government resources and technical assistance to transform the neighborhoods surrounding this classic urban arterial into a mixed use, mixed income housing, transit-oriented urban village (Indianapolis Smart Growth Renewal District Partnership n.d.).

In Portland, Oregon, the City and Portland State University's Sustainability Institute are testing the ecodistrict concept in five diverse neighborhoods that could offer a new model for district revitalization (Portland Sustainability Institute n.d.). Through an extensive civic engagement process, the ecodistrict model establishes a series of performance-based standards for how a neighborhood generates and uses its energy, natural resources, and waste as well as how it priorities transportation investments to facilitate a mixed use, mixed income urban village (Brickman 2009/2010). The goal is to not only reduce a neighborhood's carbon footprint but infuse sustainability and smart growth principles into a new revitalization model. The National Capital Planning Commission and the District of Columbia Planning Department are now tailoring the ecodistrict model to a corridor in southwest Washington, D.C. (National Capital Planning Commission n.d.).

## CHOOSING A COURSE OF ACTION

A basic question for cities in transition is whether to undertake a complete overhaul or partial revision of the comprehensive plan, develop a new strategic framework plan, or tackle a smaller special area or district plan. Planners should assess not only the potential scope and content of the plan and its relationship to existing plans but also local planning dynamics—the culture of planning, past and current levels of political and community support, and potential opposition. Several important issues to consider include the following:

- *Timing.* When was the last time the community gave the comprehensive plan a thorough overhaul?

- *Vision.* Is the existing comprehensive plan's vision consistent with current conditions and trends? What are the new problems and potential opportunities?

- *Policy goals.* What does the comprehensive plan say about current policy directions? The plan's policy goals may need a reality check; stabilization may now be the short-term goal in light of place-based policy goals that emphasize neighborhoods, quality of life, and retooling the regional and local economy.

- *Data.* Has the community or region undergone significant changes, making gathering and analyzing new data critical? Is the data readily accessible and available?

- *Land use.* Are the community's development and land-use problems worsening, and what role does the current comprehensive plan play in causing or addressing them?

- *Local planning history.* Does the local government have a history of sound planning? Were the results of the last effort to update the comprehensive plan positive?

- *Internal support.* How would planning staff react to embarking on a major planning initiative?

- *External support.* How would the community and policy makers react to a major planning overhaul? Should new planning initiatives be piggybacked on current political or policy priorities and existing or emerging initiatives, such as energy or transportation plans?

With respect to internal considerations, the municipality's resources and capacity to tackle an intensive planning effort are critical. Cities in transition have limited local revenues and abilities to mount multiyear planning efforts. If the municipality plans to engage consultants to revise the plan and manage the process, it should seek out a firm with experience in planning for cities in transition.

Alternatively, a municipality can take an incremental approach by revising other plans and codes. Dayton appears to have successfully addressed major shifts in population and a declining economy by periodically revising its comprehensive plan and beginning to follow the principles in its Green and Gold strategy. Although more than 15 years have passed since Dayton did a complete overhaul of its comprehensive plan, city officials believe their incremental approach has put them on a sound path.

### Plan-Making Considerations

If a consensus emerges to move forward with a citywide planning effort, planners must make sure the elements of the plan—whether a comprehensive plan or a strategic framework plan—reflect the diverse conditions found in their community. The contents of the plan will vary depending on the city's physical, social, and economic conditions and trends; fiscal health; and the strengths and weaknesses of the existing planning network. Moreover, the plan-making process—from engaging the community and developing the plan to the process of plan adoption and eventual implementation—will have to address the special political, community, and planning dynamics found in many cities in transition.

*Different Assumptions and Goals.* One distinguishing feature of these plans is the acknowledgment of a different trajectory for the community's future. In cities in transition, sustained expansion is not likely to be a reasonable goal or outcome. These plans no longer assume a growth model but instead explore strategies and policies that promote more sustainable existing neighborhoods. For some cities in transition, especially those with long histories of population loss and decline, stabilization itself may be a goal, although one not easily attained. Although Philadelphia and a few other legacy cities appear to have stabilized their populations, many others are still on downward trajectories.

These are some potential goals for planning in cities in transition that could translate into major new policy elements of a comprehensive or strategic framework plan:

- Stabilizing population, jobs, and neighborhood conditions

- Reclaiming and reusing vacant and abandoned properties

- Creating stronger linkages to regional markets and the regional economy

- Integrating economic development and community development

- Building community stewardship and civil society

*The contents of the plan will vary depending on the city's physical, social, and economic conditions and trends; fiscal health; and the strengths and weaknesses of the existing planning network.*

***Data Analysis and Neighborhood Typologies.*** Creating a strategic framework plan with a broad scope and focus on regeneration and revitalization requires collecting and analyzing multiple data sets from many different sources and tracking changes going forward. Collecting data about problem properties and abandonment is essential but poses challenges as the location and conditions of these properties change from day to day. No national or regional databases exist to track the number and location of vacant properties. In some cities, community-based organizations have organized local residents to conduct vacant property surveys in their neighborhoods. The National Neighborhood Indicators Partnership at the Urban Institute has affiliates in 35 cities, often involving local universities, which gather data and identify indicators of change. (See www.neighborhoodindicators.org.)

New methods and technologies for data analysis, mapping, and modeling are steadily emerging that allow cities to explore alternative scenarios, while the emerging field of policy informatics and visualization offers some intriguing opportunities. As Chapter 6 explains in more detail, the more successful planning initiatives in cities in transition have developed data-driven neighborhood typologies to provide policy makers with more fine-grained information about neighborhood conditions and markets as guides to targeting resources. These typologies can also further special area or neighborhood planning efforts.

## URBAN REGENERATION

Most comprehensive plans provide general guidance for the location, type, and scale of development, based on the conventional premise that if the municipality establishes the rules of the development game, private development will come. For cities in transition, establishing the rules alone is not enough to attract private investment; thus, the plan should not only acknowledge these market realities but also strongly link with economic development strategies as well as infrastructure programs and projects.

Cities in transition, especially legacy cities, can strengthen existing planning frameworks by infusing their plans with urban regeneration principles. Urban regeneration has been described as "a comprehensive and integrated vision and action to address urban problems through a lasting improvement in the economic, physical, social, and environmental conditions in an area" (Beswick and Tsenkova 2002). Urban regeneration emphasizes place-based approaches that link the physical transformation of distressed cities and neighborhoods with the social transformation of their residents. It encompasses a wide range of policies and issues, such as community and economic development, education, and social services, at various scales—the region, the city, the neighborhood, and individual sites.

Urban-regeneration policy principles from the United Kingdom, where the term is more widely used, are particularly relevant for distressed American cities. From the 1990s until 2010 the British government adopted a portfolio of national regeneration initiatives that offer intriguing ideas for reshaping planning frameworks for American cities in transition (Tsenkova 2002):

- *Multiagency policy coordination*—coordinating housing, employment, transportation, education, environmental management, planning, health, and community development policies and programs at the regional and local levels

- *Regenerating people, not just places*—connecting social policies that address socioeconomic problems facing low- to moderate-income residents and families with economic and community development policies that focus on revitalizing the physical environment

- *Partnerships and strategic planning process*—formulating partnerships across all levels of government and across all sectors (nonprofit, business, civic, and philanthropic)

- *Capacity building*—creating institutional capacity in the public sector, especially local government leadership and management, to coordinate the requisite regional and local partnerships

- *Community engagement*—involving citizens in all aspects of local regeneration initiatives so individuals and institutions in the community have a strong sense of ownership in the planning process and the outcomes

There are several ways planners can integrate these regeneration principles into their plans. They may infuse relevant regeneration strategies and principles throughout the comprehensive plan, thereby transforming the entire plan into a regeneration plan; alternatively, they may create a regeneration element within the comprehensive plan. Planners may also develop a broad strategic-framework plan based upon these regeneration principles. This policy framework would then act as a coordinating regeneration policy plan that would identify the roles of existing economic development, comprehensive planning, climate action, land use, and environmental plans while establishing implementation protocols.

Whatever planning approach communities take, it should include three core regeneration elements: physical transformation of the built environment, social transformation of people, and capacity building for local governments, nonprofits, and civic infrastructure. Each of these elements should set forth policy interventions, programs, and specific strategies. By incorporating regeneration principles and policies, many cities in transition would for the first time have a comprehensive planning framework that could address the social, economic, environmental, and physical challenges they confront. Within this framework, the community can articulate its own set of urban regeneration principles and goals, supported by specific policies and programs.

## CONCLUSION

Planning in cities in transition can take many forms, but the central guiding theme should be the need for a strategic approach to build and communicate a broad vision and strategy for change in the city's physical, economic, and social conditions. Building a strategic framework can then animate the comprehensive plan as well as neighborhood and special area plans. The particular pathway a city chooses to follow in creating the overall planning framework, however, must depend on local circumstances, needs, and the opportunities offered by specific initiatives or target areas.

CHAPTER 5

# Adapting Traditional Implementation Tools

A comprehensive or strategic framework plan builds a foundation. Translating plans into action requires complementary programs and policy tools. Ensuring that such programs and policies align with the plan's vision and principles is one of the major challenges of planning practice. This chapter offers creative ideas on how planners might adapt traditional planning tools and related development regulations and processes to reflect the social, economic, environmental, and civic challenges found in cities in transition.

Many planning responsibilities within cities in transition are no different than those in other communities. These cities amend and administer zoning codes, process development and building permits, and adopt capital improvement plans. Like most cities they also rely on federal and state government grants for community and economic development programs, transportation, and other infrastructure improvements, many of which require plans to explain how these resources will be used. All of these activities, however, must be aligned with the new directions set forth in the strategic policy plan.

Dwindling local government capacity and resources makes implementing plans more difficult. Planning departments have been drastically cut in many cities in transition, making it hard not only to prepare plans but to manage programs, engage the community, and monitor change. Few models exist, moreover, for revising traditional planning tools to better address the complex challenges confronting cities in transition. Many of our ideas come from conversations with practitioners in different cities; only a few have been adopted or seriously considered.

Despite these limitations, planners and policy makers should explore how to redesign standard planning tools and experiment with new models. While some approaches may require changes to state statutes or local charters, others simply demand a different policy approach or changes to organizational cultures and political commitments. We have identified five major clusters of planning implementation tools as ideal candidates for realignment:

1. Zoning codes and development processes

2. Housing policies and programs

3. Capital improvement, infrastructure, and municipal service–delivery plans

4. Smart growth policies and programs

5. Economic development and redevelopment policies and programs

Some implementation tools fall outside the planning department's typical domain, so planners will need to build strong relationships inside and outside of city hall. These tools guide a network of essential urban systems (such as streets and water and sewer lines) and service institutions (such as libraries and schools) that form the backbone of a community and region (Wachs 2009). In light of fiscal challenges and tough economic conditions, planners and policy makers in cities in transition should pay special attention to coordinating these systems with the strategic policy plan to conserve dwindling municipal resources and improve local government efficiency while stabilizing declining neighborhoods and rebuilding markets.

## ZONING CODES AND LAND DEVELOPMENT PROCESSES

One of the first priorities is aligning the local zoning code with the vision and principles set forth in the strategic policy plan. With the changes in market conditions and land use taking place in cities in transition, particularly legacy cities with large amounts of vacant land, zoning codes and maps need recalibration if not comprehensive overhauls. Below we explore contemporary zoning reform options for our typology of cities in transition, along with zoning code changes in progress in Dayton, Cleveland, and Youngstown, Ohio.

### Recalibrating Zoning Codes

For decades the planning profession has maintained a steady interest in zoning reform. Conventional Euclidean zoning has been criticized for encouraging sprawl through a strict separation of land uses, and in many older cities repeated ad hoc amendments have led to complicated codes that become major hurdles for potential developers and headaches for planners and public officials charged with their administration. Zoning alternatives relevant to cities in transition include form-based codes, zoning codes with an explicit emphasis on sustainability, performance zoning, and special revitalization overlays or districts.

*Form-Based Codes.* Rooted in the work of Andres Duany and others, form-based codes replace use-based zoning with regulations primarily based on the physical form of development. Often these form districts are placed within a rural-to-urban transect that defines zones of transition from low-density agricultural areas to high-density downtown neighborhoods. In contrast to the proscriptive standards of conventional zoning, form-based codes establish prescriptive design standards for the width of lots, size of blocks, building setbacks, building heights, placement of buildings on the lot, and location of parking. Proponents argue this gives the community more control over what actually gets built while taking the guesswork out of design and development review.

Form-based codes receive a disproportionate share of attention in both the planning literature and the popular press, given the relatively small number of cities and counties that have adopted this approach. According to an August 2010 study by Hazel Borys and Emily Talen, the number of communities with form-based codes is still small, and in practice form-based codes seldom apply citywide. Nevertheless, many new zoning codes incorporate some form-based standards, which can help preserve the compact urban form that characterizes many neighborhoods in legacy cities and first suburbs.

*Sustainable Zoning Codes.* The Rocky Mountain Land Use Institute's Sustainable Community Development Code Framework shows how zoning and other development regulations can be used to address sustainability issues such as energy conservation, renewable energy production, climate change mitigation and adaptation, natural resource protection, water conservation, low impact development and green infrastructure, hazard mitigation, mobility and accessibility, affordable housing, and food security (see www .law.du.edu/index.php/rmlui?). While not a model code, this framework does cite numerous examples of code provisions from specific communities to illustrate how sustainability principles can be translated into zoning standards. Both Washington, D.C., and Salt Lake City are using the framework to guide their ongoing zoning reform efforts.

Apart from codes based explicitly on this framework, a number of other communities have used or are in the process of using sustainability as an organizing principle for zoning reform. These include the legacy cities of Philadelphia, Baltimore, and Buffalo and the first suburb of Cleveland Heights, Ohio. In areas with much vacant property and few residents, incorporating sustainability principles into zoning could help facilitate productive reuse of land through urban agriculture, green infrastructure, and decentralized models of renewable energy production.

*Performance Zoning.* Performance zoning establishes goal-based criteria for development projects. Some communities are using performance zoning to infuse existing development regulations and processes with concepts and principles from rating systems such as Leadership in Energy and Environmental Design for Neighborhood Development (LEED-ND). Performance zoning may also help communities encourage "cradle-to-cradle" ecological industrial parks where the waste products of one use become the inputs for another. In addition, performance zoning can be used

### ▶ APPLYING THE TRANSECT TO CITIES IN TRANSITION

In its most familiar form the new urbanist transect depicts a linear continuum of metropolitan density from the countryside (T1) to the urban core (T6). (See the Center for Applied Transect Studies, http://transect.org/rural_img.html.) When applying the transect to legacy cities, the linear progression of densities often breaks down. In many of these cities the urban core may be immediately adjacent to very low density residential neighborhoods that more closely resemble rural (T2) or sub-urban (T3) zones than urban center (T5) or general urban (T4) zones. However, one benefit of applying the transect to cities in transition is that each T-zone is value neutral. If an area is most accurately described as a T3 zone, that does not make it any better or worse than a T2 or T4 zone.

The value-neutral nature of the transect means that cities can use it to frame conversations about both increasing and decreasing density. In other words, an area might move in either direction along the transect. In areas experiencing growth pressures, the city might outline a vision for a general urban (T4) zone to accommodate more density and become an urban center (T5) zone. Alternatively, in areas experiencing depopulation, the city may embrace a future where the T4 zone becomes a sub-urban T3 zone. In *Sunburnt Cities* (2011) Justin Hollander described this as a reverse transect.

In contrast, the rightsizing cities transect proposed by Terry Schwarz and her students in Chapter 6 of *Cities Growing Smaller* (2008) emphasizes the natural changes in land use over time. Instead of focusing on specific T-zones as end states, their rightsizing transect prioritizes the edges between zones, where different uses and densities meet. The goal of the rightsizing transect is to help weave portions of the city together by targeting redesign initiatives in these interfaces. ◀

to encourage green manufacturing or uses that process or distribute food from local urban farms.

*Revitalization Overlays.* In communities where comprehensive zoning reform may be out of reach due to fiscal constraints or political opposition, it may be easier to phase in reform through a special revitalization district or overlay. A city can use this tool to tailor incentives and use or development standards to principles set forth in a neighborhood or special area plan, without changing the regulations for other parts of the community. This approach can help target the right resources and rules to the appropriate neighborhoods.

*Other Zoning Reform Strategies.* As urban commentator Ed McMahon notes, zoning plays a vital role in providing certainty and stability for the real estate development market; despite zoning's shortcomings and the promise of new zoning models, property owners and developers rely on a system they know and trust (2011). Thus, it becomes imperative, especially for cities in transition, to carefully weigh the strengths and weaknesses of zoning alternatives to determine what might work best and where. If implementation proceeds without the involvement of the development community, reform efforts might backfire. The engagement process of reforming zoning codes is as important as the content itself.

Cities in transition can take useful ideas from the above models and tailor them to meet local conditions. For example, Cleveland Urban Design Collaborative director Terry Schwarz and her students devised a transect applicable to older industrial cities that accommodates vacant land conditions and fosters urban experimentation (Schwarz 2008). (See sidebar.) Uses once thought to be incompatible in a dense and highly populated urban environment may be able to coexist peacefully in neighborhoods with high vacancy rates. In order for this to work, conventional approaches to zoning that emphasize a strict separation of uses may have to give way to a more flexible approach.

Perhaps the most significant barrier to zoning reform, especially in cities in transition, is administration of the code once it is in place. Having sufficient staff to administer the code may present a serious challenge. Even with sufficient staff, a new hybrid code may require changes in organizational culture and zoning administration procedures. Zoning officials in cities in transition need to understand their new roles and the outcomes the new codes seek to foster.

Several legacy cities have adopted new zoning codes or are updating existing codes. These reform efforts reflect new strategic land-use priorities that address population decline and disinvestment, such as urban agriculture, green infrastructure, and the consolidation of development. Below we explore the slightly different approaches to zoning reform taken by three Ohio communities on slow-growth or stabilization trajectories: Dayton, Cleveland, and Youngstown.

### Dayton

Shortly following the adoption of a new comprehensive plan, the City of Dayton hired a well-known planning consultant to work with its planning department and plan commission board to update its 1968 zoning code. In the update, the city sought to advance the principles and vision set forth in CitiPlan Dayton (2003) and the 1999 Dayton City Vision by building on Dayton's economic and community assets. At the same time, the city worked to reorganize and update its development strategy to reflect the marketplace, while also investing strategically in areas such as health care and education. After four years of extensive community engagement and feedback, the city officially adopted a shortened and simplified zoning ordinance with some form-based standards in 2006.

Dayton's zoning code offers several intriguing elements and specific provisions that make sense for older industrial cities. It creates a broad and cohesive framework using 27 use districts and five overlay districts that are sensitive to Dayton's diverse urban and suburban fabric. The code references three principal residential neighborhood types throughout: mature neighborhoods developed prior to 1920, which have a traditional urban character with small, dense lots and a gridlike street pattern; suburban neighborhoods generally developed after 1960 and characterized by curvilinear streets, cul-de-sacs, and attached garages; and eclectic neighborhoods that mix mature and suburban features and are often located between the other two neighborhood types. By defining the dominant characteristics of each neighborhood type, the code preserves and strengthens the assets found in each, and it applies these three types in regulating many of the underlying land-use zones. For example, the provisions of the compatible commercial district zones preserve the special characteristics of existing commercial development in each of the three types.

*Dayton, Ohio*

© istockphoto.com/David Liu

The new code encourages the adaptive reuse or conversion of light industrial and warehouse buildings in the urban business district to multistory residential, commercial, and office uses. It also promotes transitional reuse in its two mixed use districts. The transition district focuses on "rehab and redevelopment of underutilized commercially zoned areas, where traditional business district zoning is inappropriate or unsuccessful" (sec. 150.330.1(E)(1)). Permitted uses in this zoning district allow for an appropriate mixture of uses to create live-work units. The mixed use hub district is designed to concentrate development around transit nodes and major intersections, with high-density residential, office, and regional retail as its primary focus.

Dayton continues to amend the code each year to ensure it stays current with evolving interpretations of the 1999 vision and responds to the changing needs and conditions of its residents and their neighborhoods. Recent amendments to conditional and specific use standards acknowledge Dayton's push toward sustainability by tackling the issues of vacant land and renewable energy. The code changes outline standards for installing wind and solar energy systems and enable urban agriculture by allowing small community gardens, larger urban farms ("harvesting" in the parlance of the code), and beekeeping.

## ZONING CODE REFORM PROCESS

Planners should consider the following steps when beginning the zoning code reform process (Mishkovsky and Schilling 2005):

1. *Survey the zoning and land-development territory.* Evaluate the current zoning code's strengths and weaknesses, including its relationship to the comprehensive plan.

2. *Scan the horizon of neighboring communities.* Identify examples of zoning code reform and develop a network of contacts that may offer advice and assistance during the process.

3. *Explore the feasibility of code reform in the community.* Gather support within the local government by forming an internal advisory committee that can draft and oversee a code-reform action plan that sets clear objectives for the reform efforts.

4. *Test and execute a code-reform action plan.* Garner the support of local government officials, community groups, and the development community by convening a code-reform advisory committee and special workshops.

5. *Assemble a technically savvy and expert code-reform team.* Include a blend of top-notch staff and consultants, legal advisors, and an effective facilitation/community involvement group.

6. *Establish a communications and management structure for the code-reform process.* Outline a realistic budget and then establish a formal management strategy and structure.

7. *Engage and educate neighborhood groups, the development community, and elected officials.* Use a menu of mediums and methods, such as illustrations, regular meetings, local success stories, and indicators or milestones to measure performance.

### Cleveland

As in Dayton, Cleveland's desire to improve consistency between its comprehensive plan and its zoning code was an important driver of reform. Adopted in 2006, the Connecting Cleveland 2020 Citywide Plan includes recommendations for updating the zoning map and code and identifies several areas throughout the plan for specific zoning code revisions. But the city is taking an incremental approach. Instead of launching a comprehensive overhaul with a multiyear public engagement process, Cleveland is focusing on priority issues within its neighborhoods, such as the reclamation of vacant and abandoned properties for parks, open space, and urban agriculture.

City of Cleveland

# Connecting Cleveland
## 2020 Citywide Plan

The city has added live-work and mixed use overlay districts that encourage the adaptive reuse of old industrial buildings and promote preservation of compact urban neighborhoods. The Live-Work Overlay exempts converted industrial properties from additional parking requirements, while the Pedestrian Retail Overlay mandates streetside building placement and ground-floor retail uses. In addition to these two overlay districts, the city has created regulations that allow the planning commission to approve the creation of substandard-size lots when the lot is similar in size to adjacent ones.

The city's s first attempt to address vacant land began in 2005 with the adoption of the Open Space and Recreation Zoning District, which permits the city to designate land for parks, recreation facilities, and open space. In 2007 the city added the Urban Garden Zoning District, which permits only agriculture-related uses. Next, the city adopted standards in 2009 allowing residents to keep a variety of animals, the number of which is regulated by zoning district, parcel size, and animal type. Finally, in 2010 the city approved additional standards that allow agriculture as a principal use in residential districts, and it is currently considering adding an urban agriculture overlay district for larger, more intense urban farms.

An intriguing idea from a recent planning commission report, *8 Ideas for Vacant Land Re-use in Cleveland*, is to create special "green overlay zoning districts" that would include stormwater management standards, riparian overlay districts, and green design standards. While the city has yet to adopt this idea, it provides a template that other cities in transition should examine as a possible model.

### Youngstown

To support the implementation of Youngstown 2010, the city is currently revising its zoning and land development codes to address the land-use challenges confronting the city after decades of population loss. With funding through the Ohio Housing Finance Agency, the Youngstown Redevelopment Code will support the plan's land-use, economic development, and quality-of-life goals by addressing issues such as urban agriculture, reforestation, green corridors, and land reuse, while strengthening the neighborhood fabric of stable communities.

During the fall of 2011 Youngstown's code-consulting team finished its diagnosis of existing zoning and land-development procedures and prepared an annotated outline of the new integrated zoning code. The city also worked with local residents and businesses to get their comments on the draft outline. As of early 2012 the city is circulating preliminary draft language for districts, standards, and procedures among neighborhood residents, with the goal of adopting the redevelopment code in the second half of 2012.

Several sections of Youngstown's draft regulations focus on problems common to many legacy cities, such as reclaiming vacant properties and urban agriculture. The draft also includes four new form-based zoning districts—one residential and three mixed use—as well as three new districts oriented to sustainability: an industrial green district focused on new and clean industrial

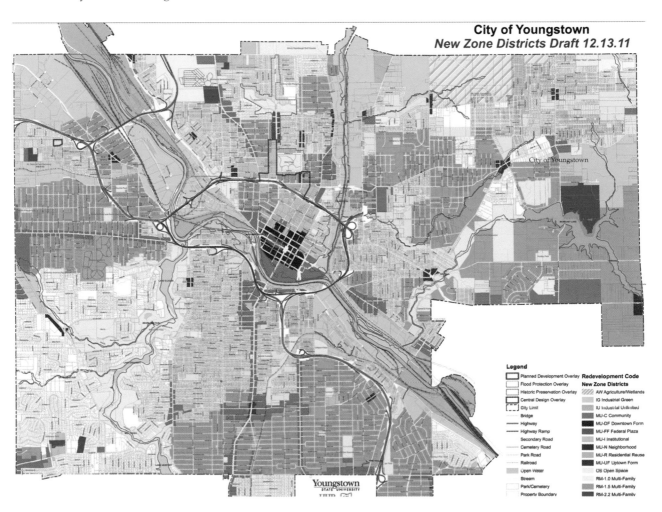

uses; an open space district that looks to protect land for parks, trails, and green corridors; and an agriculture and wetlands district, which places limitations on density and prioritizes agricultural uses or urban wetlands.

Despite the strengths of Youngstown's new code, the city is still grappling with how zoning should implement the core comprehensive plan principles of decreasing the amount of land available for new structures and fostering green reuse. Code revisions that support the former effectively downzone that land, creating potential regulatory takings challenges, although the already diminished value of the land involved may make this unlikely in practice. The issue of urban agriculture is also complex. During the code design process, participants identified related legal and policy issues such as property and owner rights of land used for farming, costs of surveying and replatting contiguous land, soil contamination, and the need to allow freestanding accessory units on vacant land. Until such issues are resolved, the spread of urban agriculture as a method of urban greening may be greatly limited.

### Lessons Learned

Cities can approach zoning reform through a complete overhaul, as in Dayton and Youngstown, or an incremental process, as in Cleveland, that identifies critical issues and amends the zoning code as those topics arise. There are policy trade-offs, issues of timing, and different resource impacts associated with each of these approaches that planners and policy makers must consider. By taking an incremental approach, the zoning code update may not create sufficient citywide traction to address important land-development challenges. Nevertheless, it may make more sense for a community to first tackle a short list of amendments and use this as a springboard to building wider support for a more comprehensive code overhaul. If taking this approach, planners should be careful to watch for and avoid potential conflicts between new and existing code provisions.

Another interesting approach is for a community to adopt a guidance document or a series of principles, such as Cleveland's guidance report on the reuse of vacant land, which serves as a blueprint for where the city may head with respect to future code changes and comprehensive plan amendments. Youngstown's Redevelopment Code contains broad principles that help refine and bring to life the underlying goals of the city's comprehensive plan. Dayton has kept its plan current through creative interpretation and code implementation, enabling the city to synchronize its plans and zoning codes without large-scale rewriting. By building awareness of critical land-development challenges, communities are better prepared to take either course of action.

Youngstown began its code update roughly five years after thorough revisions of its comprehensive plan, and it took Dayton four years to complete its overhaul. Planning theory would suggest overhauling the code sooner so that the synchronization of the code and the plan would be more contemporary and relevant. While this gap may seem like a long time, the zoning reform process requires substantial resources and commitment from political leaders, planning directors, and staff. Creating a meaningful and effective public engagement process also takes time, but it is vital to the ultimate success of the zoning code.

### HOUSING POLICIES AND PROGRAMS

Housing presents one of the greatest challenges for all cities in transition. The mortgage foreclosure crisis and the recession have left many Sun Belt communities with thousands of foreclosed, often vacant homes and even entire half-finished subdivisions. Some communities, such as Clark County, Nevada, and El Paso, Texas, have leveraged federal housing and stimulus funds to upgrade foreclosed homes with energy-efficiency and other green renovations. Many gateway cities confront different housing challenges, such as aging housing stocks that may not meet the needs of recent immigrants and other residents, while the problem in most legacy cities is the oversupply of vacant and often tax-delinquent homes. As Dan Kildee of the Center for Community Progress described it to us, "When the factories closed thousands of people left legacy cities like Flint and Youngstown and forgot to take their homes with them." Some legacy cities have leveraged federal Neighborhood Stabilization Program (NSP) funds to demolish hundreds of abandoned homes and reclaim vacant lots for urban greening projects. Vacant properties pervade all types of communities and will remain a major planning and policy challenge for at least the next decade.

In light of mounting vacant property inventories and other housing problems, cities in transition need to realign traditional housing policies and programs to address the reality of their housing markets and neighborhood characteristics. A good place to start is a simple inventory of existing housing and neighborhood development programs, including those with federal and state support such as CDBG and HOME Investments Partnership Program (known simply as HOME) funds. The local HUD consolidated plan provides information about how the city is using its federal housing resources. Other federal and state grants that address special aspects of neighborhood stabilization, homelessness, and public or social housing should also be examined. Some communities, such as Louisville, Kentucky, have also conducted sophisticated housing market analyses, while cities like Cleveland and Philadelphia have developed data-driven neighborhood typologies. Such local studies and analysis, whether done by consultants, nonprofits, or universities, can provide valuable data for restructuring existing housing programs.

Local housing or community development departments typically administer many subsidized housing programs, as do other public entities, such as public housing authorities and regional planning commissions, as well as nonprofits, such as local housing intermediaries and CDCs working from the neighborhood to the regional scale. At the same time, the housing plan should recognize that the private housing market in these cities not only provides most of the city's affordable housing—with or without public subsidy—but is critical to the long-term vitality of the city as a whole. Market-building strategies and other efforts to engage the private market need to be as much a part of the plan as strategies to use government programs and resources.

After conducting the inventory of local housing policies and programs, the next step is to ensure that the goals and proposed actions of those programs are compatible and consistent with the vision, principles, and elements of the new strategic framework or comprehensive plan. Such an analysis can also identify potential gaps or inconsistencies that might demand legislative amendments or policy changes. By aligning existing programs, policies, and action plans that guide local housing and community development resources, cities in transition can more efficiently target the right resources to the right places. Planners should correlate housing resources (projects and families) with available local and regional housing data on issues such as foreclosures or vacant properties to pinpoint concentrations of housing problems and help identify the appropriate level and type of responses.

Planners should also compare the housing elements in their current comprehensive plans with the new strategic policy plan and ensure the goals in each are compatible and consistent with one another. One example of aligning goals is in Youngstown, where city officials made a policy decision to limit CDBG resources for rehabilitating existing homes to stable neighborhoods rather than neighborhoods with significant concentrations of vacant land and

*In light of mounting vacant property inventories and other housing problems, cities in transition need to realign traditional housing policies and programs to address the reality of their housing markets and neighborhood characteristics.*

abandoned buildings. There may also be other comprehensive plan or zoning and building code provisions, such as a transit-oriented development (TOD) strategy and transportation element or inclusionary housing ordinance, that have important housing implications. Again, the goal is to identify potential gaps or inconsistencies with the new strategic policy plan.

Another goal is to ensure that existing housing policies and programs operate in a more cohesive and collaborative manner. While coordination may be difficult, a number of cities have begun to frame collaborative housing policy initiatives across multiple jurisdictions in response to the foreclosure crisis. For example, the second round of HUD NSP funding prompted many communities to create new multifaceted consortiums of local governments and nonprofits; the winning applications from this competitive funding round included many innovative models that pushed the boundaries of collaborative housing policy.

These new models often rely on support from national intermediaries and foundations. National community development intermediaries such as Enterprise Community Partners, NeighborWorks America, and the Local Initiatives Support Corporation provide technical support and access to capital in many communities and support new entities, such as the National Community Stabilization Trust, that facilitate the acquisition of real estate–owned properties by local governments and CDCs (see www .stabilizationtrust.com). Local housing intermediaries, such as Cleveland's Neighborhood Progress, perform similar roles, providing capital, facilitating strategic housing policy, and building the capacity of local CDCs.

## CAPITAL IMPROVEMENT, INFRASTRUCTURE, AND MUNICIPAL SERVICE DELIVERY PLANS

Investments in public infrastructure, including streets and utilities, and public facilities, such as libraries and schools, are major elements of urban development. Within the overall planning scheme these public and institutional investments should be integrated with the larger regeneration goals of a city's strategic policy plan. Part of the policy challenge is that public infrastructure investments at the state and federal levels still tend to prioritize greenfield growth over infill development and brownfields redevelopment.

Most municipal fiscal tools, such as capital improvement plans and impact fees, were initially designed to facilitate growth and do not address the infrastructure challenges of decline. Cities in transition should carefully examine the legal basis and use of these tools. Allocation of infrastructure dollars should be tied to a typology of neighborhood characteristics and market conditions. Since most cities in transition have aging infrastructure and limited public resources, they should target investments to neighborhoods that have the greatest potential for stabilization and revitalization. A more strategic, place-based capital improvement plan, for example, could direct higher percentages of new and existing resources to the rehabilitation of aging infrastructure that will promote revitalization of existing neighborhoods, as opposed to infrastructure investments that would encourage sprawl or serve little larger purpose.

Some legacy cities are debating decommissioning or reconfiguring infrastructure such as roads, sewers, power lines, and stormwater systems in areas with particularly large amounts of vacant land and abandoned buildings. These discussions raise many questions:

- Can parts of sewer systems be taken offline, and can green infrastructure replace gray infrastructure?

- How can local governments reconfigure the delivery of municipal services such as trash collection, recycling, transit, fire and police, health care, and social services to neighborhoods with few remaining residents?

- Could a network of decentralized utility systems be more efficient and effective than multimillion-dollar centralized utilities for neighborhoods with substantial long-term population loss?
- What policy changes to federal and state infrastructure systems are needed to support a movement to decentralized systems?

We do not have many examples that answer these complex policy questions. The idea of decommissioning runs counter to long-standing engineering principles and practices and might compromise the efficiencies of overall systems. There is little research on the potential short- or long-term cost savings of no longer having to maintain underused infrastructure or of reducing the level of municipal services in underpopulated neighborhoods. Any policy decision not to provide equal services to all segments of a city, moreover, raises difficult issues of equality and social justice.

The current fiscal distress of many cities in transition presents another set of macro policy challenges that directly affect their abilities to provide essential services (Mallach and Scorsone 2011). The State of Michigan has appointed emergency financial managers with near-absolute powers in a number of insolvent cities, including Flint. Reforming existing state laws and local ordinances that govern municipal finance and perhaps even looking at restructuring local government itself raise many complex policy and political challenges well beyond the scope of this report, but planners and policy makers should recognize these structural limitations as they explore innovative ways of using their resources more effectively.

Whether or not they decommission existing infrastructure, cities should make green infrastructure a priority, placing it on an equal footing with traditional gray infrastructure. As concerns about climate change and greenhouse gas emissions grow, green infrastructure can reduce urban heat island effects and become part of a larger stormwater management strategy. One step is to adopt green infrastructure principles and funding allocations within capital improvement plans and annual infrastructure budgets. Local governments could also adopt special green infrastructure plans and strategies as part of their strategic policy plans. Such local policy changes would complement new federal efforts on green infrastructure, such as U.S. EPA's Strategic Agenda to Protect Waters and Build More Livable Communities through Green Infrastructure (http://cfpub.epa.gov/npdes/home.cfm?program_id=298) and the U.S. Forest Service's Urban and Community Forest program (www.fs.fed.us/ucf/about_overview.html).

Communities should also explore ways of recalibrating existing municipal finance tools such as impact fees, utility/user fees, special assessment districts, tax increment financing (TIF), and infrastructure bonds to cover not only the acquisition and development costs but also the maintenance of green infrastructure amenities over time (Young 2011). While many state laws require a supermajority of council or a public referendum to approve new fees or sources of revenue, voters continue to show strong support for state and local land conservation funding initiatives that cover the costs of acquiring, expanding, and maintaining open space, parks, urban forests, and recreational areas (TPL 2011). Cities in transition should tap these funding resources to reclaim vacant properties and expand urban greening initiatives.

## SMART GROWTH POLICIES AND PROGRAMS

Though discussing smart growth may seem out of place in a report about cities in transition, there are two relevant aspects. First, the recent decline of many formerly fast-growing communities is linked to their overreliance on growth as an economic engine and the resulting oversupply of housing units. Second, sprawl development patterns in states such as Michigan and Ohio have been a driver for the population exodus from legacy cities and their first suburbs to more sparsely populated exurban counties and townships in the same region. Had these regions adopted more active or conscious smart growth policies, these cities and suburbs could have better managed the land-use decisions that led to sprawl and perhaps mitigated the severity of the economic difficulties they are currently experiencing.

When it comes to changing current planning policies and programs in cities in transition to encourage smart growth, planners should consider both *defensive* approaches that discourage sprawl, such as removing incentives that support suburban development on greenfields, as well as *offensive* approaches that encourage more compact, infill development in existing neighborhoods, especially those with chronic patterns of decline and disinvestment. Communities should put both policy approaches in place to have an effective "inside-outside" strategy that decreases the push and pull of depopulation, especially in legacy cities. Many such policies require regional as well as local efforts.

Smart growth's core principles support a policy menu for discouraging sprawl and encouraging sustainable regions and livable communities. A major goal of smart growth is to offer more compact and sustainable development alternatives through housing, transportation, and economic development policy choices. Below we discuss a few ideas for reconfiguring some classic smart growth strategies, such as state and local subdivision regulations, transfer of development rights (TDR), urban growth boundaries (UGBs), adequate public facilities ordinances (APFOs), impact fees, and priority funding areas. These proposals may be controversial in some policy and community circles, but dire circumstances often demand radical interventions, especially for those cities where conventional planning and economic development strategies have perpetuated decline and sprawl.

### Citywide or Metropolitan Growth Management Strategies

At citywide or metropolitan scales, smart growth policies offer two models for controlling growth: priority funding areas, as in Maryland's Smart Growth Act, or UGBs, as in Oregon. These models do not translate directly to local action in states that lack similar statutory frameworks, but the insights from these statewide approaches to growth management can be adapted to local land-use policies and plans. For example, the priority-funding-area concept could be used in a strategic framework plan wherein a city, using data and maps, identifies and targets resources to neighborhoods with the greatest promise or potential for stabilization.

Cities in transition should also consider how they might use other smart growth tools to address their land-use and development issues, such as "reverse engineering" APFOs to support the phased decommissioning of infrastructure based on certain thresholds of declining population and service demand or applying phasing concepts to the strategic demolition of thousands of vacant and abandoned buildings. Cities in transition might also recalibrate open space and farmland conservation strategies to address the challenges of acquiring, managing, and maintaining different types of urban green space.

Cities in transition could also use smart growth tools in defensive or regulatory ways to slow or mitigate sprawl, such as changing local subdivision requirements, expanding open space districts, and aligning transportation investments that make it more difficult to develop on the exurban fringes; such strategies may require collaboration with adjacent jurisdictions and regional entities usually beyond the legal and political reach of central cities or inner-ring suburbs. While it is beyond the scope of this report to explore these issues further, it is important to raise them in light of the problems confronting cities in transition.

### Smart Growth Strategies at the Small Area and Property Scales

Several smart growth strategies that work well at the neighborhood, corridor, and parcel scales, such as TOD, overlay zones, and TIF, could effectively apply to many of the revitalization challenges confronting cities in transition. Such areawide approaches to redevelopment typically mix incentives and development regulations synchronized with transportation investments and housing projects. While these strategies might seem more relevant for boom-bust or gateway cities where greater market strength exists, legacy cities are testing them as well: Cleveland's HealthLine, a bus rapid transit route along Euclid Avenue connecting downtown with the Cleveland Clinic and the University Circle anchor institutions, is widely seen as an economic development success.

*The Euclid Corridor Transportation Project, or HealthLine, has brought $4.3 billion in real estate investment.*

Institute for Transportation and Development Policy

In neighborhoods with high levels of property abandonment, cities in transition might rethink a classic smart growth tool—transfer of development rights (TDR)—to encourage the consolidation of property owners and businesses in more stable areas slated for growth. A TDR program could offer residential and commercial property owners in disinvested areas incentives to give their properties to the city in exchange for land in more viable parts of town. The city would then use those lands to support green infrastructure. To that end, a city should consider adopting ordinances that authorize urban conservation subdivisions to encourage the clustering of homes among seas of vacant properties, or explore creating conservation districts that might have special assessment or bonding capacities to support the acquisition and maintenance of urban green spaces. Finally, local governments should consider recalibrating subdivision regulations to make it easier to consolidate lots in former subdivisions—a type of reverse platting—to help promote more productive uses of vacant urban land such as urban agriculture, urban forestry, or other forms of green infrastructure.

### ECONOMIC DEVELOPMENT AND REDEVELOPMENT STRATEGIES AND PLANS

Given that economic conditions drive much of the decline in cities in transition, aligning existing economic development and redevelopment programs and plans becomes an essential task for planners and policy makers. Current economic development practice continues to rely heavily on classic strategies of retaining and attracting existing business types or generating redevelopment projects such as sports stadiums or arenas in the hope of catalytic effects. Where market conditions are often dysfunctional and unstable, as they are in many cities in transition, planning interventions demand a new set of proactive economic development principles.

It is critical for planners and economic developers to understand the complexities of regional and local economies and how to integrate economic development, job training, and workforce development programs into comprehensive approaches to regeneration. In this section we focus on the challenges and opportunities for synchronizing local economic development plans, programs, and projects so that they offer new visions for prosperity as ideally set forth in the principles of the new strategic policy plan. We also highlight a few policies and programs that take a broader approach to economic development, especially those emerging under the umbrella of the green economy.

## The Diverse Worlds of Planning and Economic Development

When thinking about realigning economic and redevelopment policies and programs, two immediate challenges come to mind: first, understanding the historic tension between economic development staff and city planners; second, getting a handle on the proliferation of urban economic development policies, plans, and programs.

Local planners and economic development officials often have competing missions and hence conflicting interests. Planners typically have a longer time horizon and a broader mission within their domain of land use and development, but they often lack the grasp they should have of metropolitan economic issues and the real estate development process. Planners need a better understanding of how markets drive economic and development decision making. On the flip side, economic development officials and staff often focus on the transaction—making specific development projects happen. They understand the time pressures and cyclical nature of local markets and are sensitive to the pressures that banks and businesses place on private developers. Though they may recognize the importance of citywide and special district plans, planning is not their priority, and they rarely operate within the planning domain.

This historic division between planning and economic development is exacerbated by the organizational structures of planning departments and economic development agencies. Economic development agencies are often quasi-independent entities housed outside the formal city government structure; they often generate their revenues and operate as an enterprise function within local budgets, while planning departments rely more on general funds and thus are more vulnerable to the vagaries of city budgets.

Today we see a growing number of collaborations between these two functions, as economic development and planning agencies partner in creating corridor and special area plans for the reuse of former brownfields sites and military bases. A few jurisdictions—such as the cities of Bridgeport, Connecticut; York, Pennsylvania; Minneapolis; and St. Paul, Minnesota—have planning and economic development functions housed in the same umbrella organization. These collaborative structures offer promising models for cities in transition.

## Economic Development Inventory and Policy Scan

As noted, a major challenge in aligning local economic development policies and plans is the sheer number of them. A community may have dozens of grants from federal and state agencies, along with local ordinances, policies, and programs that promote different approaches to economic development, from redeveloping brownfields to workforce development training, and each of these programs may come from different agencies with their own rules and reporting requirements.

An important first step is to inventory existing economic development programs within the jurisdiction. Planners can begin by identifying the departments and agencies responsible for administering these programs and matching them with classic economic-development policy topics, such as incentives, workforce development, manufacturing clusters, high technology, or anchor institutions. Such a scan provides a good snapshot of the economic-development policy landscape and information about resources and programs within a particular community. The policy scan should also include initiatives and projects in which nonprofits, foundations, and institutions are playing pivotal roles. Within the last 10 years a growing number of nonprofits, supported by national and regional foundations, are managing economic development programs and capacity-building efforts as well as their own development areas, including industry clusters, small businesses, green jobs, and especially neighborhood-scale or place-based projects.

*The planner's challenge is finding ways to encourage economic development authorities, especially those independent from the city, to align their work.*

## Gap Analysis and Policy Alignment

After scanning and classifying the landscape of economic development planning and policy, the next step toward synchronization with the visions and principles set forth in the strategic policy plan is assessing whether these programs and projects contain compatible or conflicting goals and outcomes. This could take the form of a gap analysis that evaluates the content of the economic development plans, policies, and programs and fits it within a matrix of principles, goals, and actions derived from the overarching plan. Another approach is to evaluate the content against both vertical and horizontal organizational hierarchies. Vertical integration would examine the relationship of plans, programs, and projects that flow from federal, state, and regional sources to the local plan. Horizontal integration would examine the relationship of local government's own economic development work to its new strategic framework or comprehensive plan, as well as to neighborhood and regional plans. It is useful to lay out what benefits these economic development plans, projects, and programs deliver and the degree to which they address social benefits and equity.

The planner's challenge is finding ways to encourage economic development authorities, especially those independent from the city, to align their work. Systematically adopting urban regeneration principles could foster comprehensive revival, establishing placemaking that includes housing and neighborhood revitalization as a legitimate and successful economic development strategy. In recent years many cities in transition have instituted placemaking strategies that often include anchor institutions, such as universities and hospitals, and have revitalized distressed neighborhoods through community-driven initiatives. One emerging practice is areawide brownfields redevelopment. In 2010, EPA awarded areawide grants to 25 communities to experiment with different models and scales of redeveloping multiple industrial and commercial properties; they have the resources to expand the number of grantees in 2012. These emerging examples show promise in facilitating policy coordination and alignment between economic development and land-use strategies.

## ▶ EMERGING REGIONAL ECONOMIC DEVELOPMENT MODELS

*New York's Regional Economic Development Councils:* In July 2011 the State of New York launched a new regional policy model by consolidating several state and local agencies responsible for economic development while also shifting from a top-down development approach to a more community-driven one. Each of 10 regional councils is responsible for developing its own economic development plan, building on local assets and expertise to best pursue its priorities. The state will assist these regional councils by better aligning state resources and streamlining the delivery of state services and programs. One example is the new Consolidated Funding Application, which combines the resources of several programs and gives the regional councils the opportunity to apply for $1 billion in state funding for projects (see http://esd.ny.gov /ConsolidatedFundingApplication.html). Ultimately, the goal of the transformation is regional empowerment, allowing each area to determine its own economic path and guiding policies.

*The Initiative for a Competitive Greater Reading:* From 2003 to 2009 a coalition of business and civic leaders from metropolitan Reading, Pennsylvania, met to develop the Initiatives for a Competitive Greater Reading (ICGR) plan to spur the revitalization of the area's small cities and towns. In 2009–2010 the chief executives of the Greater Reading Chamber of Commerce and Industry brought together eight economic development organizations to focus the plan on redeveloping smaller parcels, attracting small-to-midsize companies, fostering entrepreneurship and innovation, promoting workforce development, involving the growing Latino community, and providing infrastructure. Many of the plan's recommendations are now overseen by a new regional economic development entity, the Berks Economic Partnership, and its Ride to Prosperity initiative (see http://greaterreading.com and http:// ridetoprosperity.com). ◀

### Program and Project Coordination and Collaboration

Once the content of plans and programs are better aligned, getting managers and staff to collaborate across departments within a local government, with neighboring jurisdictions, or with outside economic development entities presents serious communications and managerial challenges. Each initiative may have its own external stakeholder groups or advisory boards, often narrowly focused on a particular aspect of economic development, while different entities have their own boards of directors, many with local elected officials who have competing policy agendas. New York State is now experimenting with new regional economic-development councils that can facilitate more collaboration around regional economic initiatives through grant conditions and requirements. (See sidebar.)

Several intriguing examples coordinate federal, state, and local assistance at the neighborhood scale, such as the Green Impact Zone in Kansas City, Missouri. While these investments focus on neighborhood revitalization, they are designed to have major economic development impacts. The East Baltimore Revitalization Initiative (see sidebar) has also attracted attention from practitioners and policy makers. EBRI builds on anchor institution redevelopment models (the classic "eds and meds" strategy) by requiring these institutions to make long-term commitments to workforce training, neighborhood schools, and socially equitable relocation programs in their plans and projects.

### Emerging Green Economic Development Initiatives

Our approach to the inventory and analysis of existing economic development policies and programs is intended to facilitate more integrated and equitable models. Economic development initiatives should not only improve private- and public-sector bottom lines but also enhance quality of life for residents who have suffered from decades of disinvestment and decline.

As the green economy emerges, sustainability principles have particular relevance for many cities in transition seeking to devise more integrated economic-development initiatives. In her book *Small, Gritty, and Green*, journalist and historian Catherine Tumber makes a strong case for why and how small legacy cities should play a "central role in a greener, low-carbon, delocalized future"(2011). Visiting planners, city officials, and activists in 25 former manufacturing centers in the Midwest and Northeast, Tumber identifies emerging green collaborations for cities seeking to diversify their economic portfolios to include sustainable agriculture, ecological restoration, renewable-energy harvesting, and advanced manufacturing for low-carbon industries. She also examines how policies designed to curb sprawl and facilitate more independent, wealth-retaining local economies can be particularly beneficial to these cities.

A number of examples exist that illustrate the green economy's potential for cities in transition. The Reinvestment Fund's Pennsylvania Fresh Food Financing initiative provides loans and grants to support entrepreneurs to develop grocery stores, farmers markets, and other healthy food options in low-income neighborhoods throughout the state (see www.trfund.com /stories/supermarkets.html). As of 2010 the program had helped create more than 88 new or expanded food outlets and 5,000 full- and part-time jobs. In Cleveland, the Evergreen Cooperatives, worker-owned firms that supply goods and services to several large anchor institutions in the University Circle area, promote areawide sustainability goals and emerging sustainable business practices in the laundry, solar, and hydroponic food production fields (see Dobb and Warren 2010 and www.evergreencoop.com). And in

Dayton, brownfields redevelopment has led to the transformation of the long-vacant 50-acre National Cash Register campus into the General Electric Electrical Power Integrated Systems (GE EPIS) Research and Development Center. Building on its proximity to the University of Dayton, part of the site is now home to manufacturing facilities, research labs, classrooms, and a charter high school, while another section will see mixed use development under the university's master plan. This joint venture between GE and the university will house GE's aviation power research and development center (a 141,000-square-foot LEED-certified lab and office space complex) and has a targeted completion date of spring 2013. While the project uses traditional brownfields assessment, cleanup, and financing strategies and tools, it illustrates how cities in transition can expand their brownfields redevelopment programs to become catalysts for green development and green jobs (Davis 2012).

Finally, a new wave of regional collaboration encouraged by HUD's regional sustainability grants has significant economic development implications. As part of the Obama administration's Interagency Partnership for Sustainable Communities, HUD has awarded 74 grants since 2009 to coalitions of regional authorities, local governments, universities, and nonprofits to devise diverse sets of regional and local sustainability plans, policies, and programs. Several of the grantees are creating regional sustainability plans with a focus on providing more sustainable transportation systems that can enhance the development of regional economies, while others emphasize green jobs and green businesses. While the recipient coalitions are predominately headed by metropolitan planning organizations and councils of government, the grants require extensive partnerships with local jurisdictions, including subgrants to local governments to revise comprehensive plans, as in Flint (see page 43). Several of the HUD grantees include severely distressed regions, such as northeast Ohio and California's Central Valley.

········································································

### NORTHEAST OHIO'S FUND FOR OUR ECONOMIC FUTURE

As one of the 2010 HUD Regional Sustainability grantees, northeast Ohio's Fund for Our Economic Future works to promote its regional economic competitiveness agenda, Advance Northeast Ohio (see www.futurefundneo.org and Fund for Our Economic Future 2012). Building on America Speaks's extensive northeast Ohio civic engagement initiative in 2007, the fund's agenda reflects the synthesis of priorities expressed by more than 20,000 residents during the engagement activities, along with in-depth economic research. The fund works in collaboration with public, civic, and private-sector organizations, and it developed its Regional Business Plan in partnership with various organizations, including the Brookings Institution. The plan has spurred new initiatives such as the Partnership for Regional Innovation Services to Manufacturers (PRISM), which works to build the product innovation capacity of small and midsized manufacturers. Finally, the fund advocates for federal policies and programs necessary to respond to the specific needs of northeast Ohio's economy. ◄

### EAST BALTIMORE REVITALIZATION INITIATIVE

The East Baltimore neighborhood, adjacent to Johns Hopkins University, has suffered from decades of decay and decline. As part of a new approach to neighborhood revitalization, the university and the city, with support and leadership from the Annie E. Casey Foundation, formed a community-driven redevelopment entity, East Baltimore Development, Inc. (EBDI), to stabilize and revitalize the area (see www.ebdi.org). EBDI is committed to responsible redevelopment combining economic, community, and human development strategies. The ambitious plan for the 88-acre, $1.4 billion project is organized around four major components:

- An inclusive, responsible redevelopment plan that addresses residents' needs while encouraging neighborhood investment

- A comprehensive relocation plan that reflects an ongoing commitment to residents' needs and well-being

- Job training and workforce development programs

- New educational opportunities for residents of all ages

Since 2002 the project has facilitated 300 meetings with residents and stakeholders. EBDI's Housing and Relocation Committee worked with residents to develop a relocation plan and has helped more than 700 displaced East Baltimore residents find new housing (EBRI 2012). Family advocates ensure that families relocate successfully, connecting individuals to jobs, training, credit counseling, and health care.

In addition to a focus on social inclusion and relocation, the initiative seeks to expand job opportunities for East Baltimore residents. Since 2004 EBDI has successfully placed more than 750 East Baltimore residents in jobs, some through the training and workforce development programs established within the redevelopment plan. Another goal was to increase the hiring of minority- and women-owned companies. By December 2010, 40 percent of all contracts were with such businesses (EBRI 2012).

While the recession has slowed development, EBDI has been able to maintain its goal of providing one-third of all its housing units as affordable to low-income households, one-third priced for moderate-income households, and the final third at market rate. In addition, EBDI founded one community school (K–8) by August 2009 and is now developing a new campus location to be completed by 2014. ◄

## CONCLUSION

A wide variety of tools has evolved within the practice of planning with which to implement comprehensive plans and strategies. Zoning is the most well known, but the list includes many tools focusing on specific issues, such as housing, economic development, or sustainability, or on specific geographic areas targeted for special attention. While all of these tools are relevant to cities in transition, planners may need to rethink their traditional uses to better reflect the particular needs and challenges of these cities. For example, zoning codes may become tools to facilitate green reuse or neighborhood stabilization in addition to simply guiding the course of future development. In any case, the design and use of planning tools in cities in transition must engage many actors and organizations beyond planners themselves, and their integration into larger frameworks of regeneration efforts is critical to their success.

# CHAPTER 6

# Designing Strategies to Address the Special Challenges of Cities in Transition

 Cities in transition that have experienced sustained job loss, demographic change, and market decline need planning strategies that aim directly at those challenges. This section will explore how to address a number of those challenges through dealing with the proliferation of vacant and abandoned properties, building market demand, adopting greening strategies, and planning for neighborhood change. While in some cities the framework for such strategies will be laid out in comprehensive plans or other citywide planning documents (such as a strategic framework), in others it may arise from neighborhood planning work or targeted efforts responding to particular conditions in one or more parts of the city.

These strategies must be implemented at the neighborhood level. To generalize that "the city" is suffering from abandoned properties or from weak market conditions is often questionable; most cities contain a wide range of conditions, and both problems and opportunities are unevenly distributed. Even the most distressed cities still have some strong, vital neighborhoods.

The strategies and initiatives discussed here should be integrated with neighborhood-level plans, though their scope may extend to the larger city. They should also be grounded in some form of neighborhood assessment or neighborhood typology, in which neighborhood features are measured, compared, and used to determine which strategies are likely to be most appropriate for each area. Neighborhood planning and assessment are both discussed in detail in this chapter.

## VACANT PROPERTY STRATEGIES

One of the most difficult problems facing many cities in transition is the proliferation of vacant and abandoned properties. They harm their blocks, their neighborhoods, and the city by devaluing neighbors' properties, harboring criminal activity, increasing fire risk, posing health and safety hazards, and undermining vitality. (See Chapter 2.) While endemic in many deeply distressed areas, vacant properties may appear in even the strongest neighborhoods. This issue has challenged legacy cities like Cleveland and Detroit for decades, but in recent years it has become a problem in boom-bust cities like Las Vegas as well.

Putting specific policies and programs in place for reclaiming vacant properties is a precondition for converting these liabilities into assets. The National Vacant Properties Campaign provides useful guidance on vacant property policies; their Buffalo/Erie County (2006) and Youngstown/Mahoning County (2009) assessments are especially relevant from a regeneration perspective. These studies were regional in scope, involving cities, counties, and suburban communities, and they used systems approaches for evaluating existing policies and programs and recommending specific strategies, such as real property information systems and county land banks. These reports also include several recommendations for policy reforms, such as targeting community and economic development resources based on typologies of neighborhood conditions, revamping local code-enforcement programs, and developing neighborhood-based plans that facilitate sustainable reuse of vacant properties. The reports also set forth implementation recommendations, including the establishment of coordinating councils and regional policy frameworks.

Most U.S. cities, however, have yet to institute comprehensive strategies for reclaiming vacant properties. The City of Buffalo, New York, is an exception: its 2006 Queen City Comprehensive Plan included a special facilities and vacant land–management strategy. Even with this vacant property element, however, the plan as a whole still seems to rely on unrealistic assumptions of growth and fails to acknowledge the underlying weakness of its market. Many of its strategies appear to be based on demand that is unlikely to materialize.

The underlying problem of vacant properties is more building supply than demand, but this is exacerbated in many cities by the absence of effective city strategies and systems to gain control over properties and restore them to productive use. Indeed, many local government policies, such as the practice of offering properties to the highest bidder at tax-lien and tax-foreclosure sales or the widespread reluctance of cities to take title to vacant properties, actually make the problem worse. Some cities, though, including New York, Minneapolis, and San Diego, have mounted concerted attacks on their vacant property problems.

There are four areas to address in dealing with vacant properties: developing a vacant property–information base, gaining control over the inventory, reforming systems, and formulating reuse strategies. This section provides only brief sketches of these four elements; references to additional materials are provided at the end of each description. (See Mallach 2010a.)

### Developing a Vacant Property–Information Base

We have stressed the importance—and the frequent shortage—of information for planning in cities in transition. Even city-owned vacant property inventories, which in large cities may contain thousands of properties, are often inadequate. Key questions such as the following are often difficult or impossible to answer:

- How many vacant properties are in the municipality?

- How many of these are the only vacant property on an otherwise fully occupied block?

- How many vacant properties are eligible for tax sale or tax foreclosure?

- Which vacant properties in the municipality are in the process of mortgage foreclosure?

The last is a major issue in states including New York and New Jersey, where the time frame for completing the foreclosure process routinely exceeds two years.

*Vacant properties in Baltimore*

Joseph Schilling

These questions are vital in framing an effective problem-property strategy. Being able to identify privately owned vacant properties alongside a city's vacant property inventory can enable the city to prioritize acquisition efforts, while identifying isolated vacant properties amid otherwise fully occupied blocks can help prioritize rehabilitation activities.

Planners need to evaluate the data systems that currently exist in city government—or in partner organizations such as CDCs or university research centers—and figure out what can be done with the human and financial resources available. While a state-of-the-art system like Cleveland's NEO CANDO (see Chapter 3), which layers multiple information sources in different and creative ways, is likely to be beyond the means of many, most cities today have basic geographic information systems (GIS). A straightforward searchable database that links public records with one another and with the GIS system can be a solid basis for planning. Once the database has been created and linked to management information systems, city staff and others can use it to track the status of properties in the inventory.

Field surveys are usually the only way a city can assemble a vacant property inventory, and these surveys are more easily accomplished than many think. Small cities have organized complete field surveys of their vacant properties by mobilizing neighborhood associations over a single weekend. Once the information is incorporated into the database, it should be updated at least annually.

### Controlling the Inventory

Effectively addressing vacant property problems requires an aggressive approach to taking title to vacant properties. When vacant properties are in private hands, the city's ability to influence their disposition is limited. Many owners live far away or are unwilling or unable to take full responsibility for their properties, and the city often finds itself held accountable for their condition. As Dan Kildee of the Genesee County Land Bank has often told local officials, "If you own the problem, you may as well own the solution."

By taking title to vacant properties a city can control their disposition. Many cities, however, are concerned that this takes properties off the tax rolls and imposes significant burdens and liabilities on the local government. Yet neither objection is insurmountable. Most vacant properties, particularly tax-delinquent ones, contribute little or nothing in revenue, and the city can often hasten the day they return to the tax rolls in responsible hands by taking them into public ownership. And as noted, the burdens and liabilities of maintaining a public vacant-property inventory can be addressed through efficient operating systems and well-designed management protocols and by leveraging private and civic resources.

Some cities and counties have kept problem properties out of the hands of speculators by adopting policies to gain control of properties through tax foreclosure, and they have created land bank entities to centralize acquisition, maintenance, and disposition (Alexander 2011). Depending on the provisions of state law and the circumstances of each community, land banks can operate at the city or county level and function within the general government structure, as separate, quasi-independent authorities, or even as public-purpose nonprofit corporations. In all cases they function as vehicles through which local governments can gain control over vacant properties and make sure their reuse provides the greatest immediate as well as long-term benefits to the community. Successful land banks include those in Genesee County, Michigan, and Cuyahoga County, Ohio.

At the same time, cities need to be more strategic about how they motivate owners to maintain their problem properties more responsibly and bring them back to productive use. The threat of city action can motivate many owners to invest in restoring their properties.

### Reforming Systems

Effective strategies do not exist in a vacuum. They must be grounded in legal and management systems designed to facilitate good results. The planner must be able to evaluate those systems and advocate for changes

*Cities need to be more strategic about how they motivate owners to maintain their problem properties more responsibly and bring them back to productive use.*

needed for successful strategy implementation. In some cases changes to state law may be required; for example, advocates in Michigan had to win major changes to that state's tax foreclosure statute in order to make land banking possible. At the local level, planners can enact change by amending local ordinances, restructuring management systems, or adopting different operating procedures.

Tax foreclosure policies often need reform. Under many state laws or local practices, tax-delinquent properties are auctioned off to the highest bidders in "all comers" open auctions. While this yields immediate revenues for the city or county, many properties end up in the hands of irresponsible or ill-informed owners, leading to a revolving door of tax delinquency and vacancy. A system that enables the county or city to gain control of those properties ends up generating more revenue for the public in the long run and increases the likelihood of stable, sustainable reuse of the properties.

Code enforcement is another important area to address. Many cities do not deploy their personnel efficiently, and the lack of good communication among inspectors, city attorneys, and municipal courts can undermine even the most determined efforts to carry out strategic code enforcement in the field. In the end, the effectiveness of any plan or strategy depends on its ability to be successfully implemented, which depends in turn on whether the necessary conditions for implementation—from a legal and management standpoint—have been put in place.

### Formulating Reuse Strategies

As noted, the purpose of gaining control over the vacant property inventory and going to the trouble and expense of land banking is to control the reuse of those properties and ensure that it furthers long-term goals and maximizes benefits to the community. This subject is discussed in detail in Chapter 7.

### BUILDING STRONGER MARKETS

A central reality of cities in transition is weak market conditions—inadequate overall demand relative to supply and prices too low to support investment in existing homes, new infill development, or reuse of vacant, dilapidated buildings. In legacy cities little development has been seen for decades other than projects subsidized by public funds, while in places such as the Southwest's boom-bust cities markets were strong until the recent collapse of the housing bubble. Fostering a stronger, healthier housing market is required for the regeneration of any city in transition and is likely to be a central element in any planner's work. Without a market capable of stimulating private investment—beginning with individual families deciding where to buy their homes—no city or neighborhood is likely to be sustainable.

Market building is about stimulating consumer demand. Neighborhood housing markets become stronger with the investment of financial and emotional resources by families moving into the area, families already living in the neighborhood who choose to stay when they could afford to move, and builders deciding to buy vacant lots and build new houses on them. Market building capitalizes on the positive features or changes the negative features of a city or neighborhood to increase the likelihood that people will invest their resources there. From the standpoint of a city's vitality, building a stronger residential market and drawing an economically diverse population are arguably far more important than attracting nonresidential ratables or promoting tourism and conventions.

Few cities, however, devote significant resources to building their residential markets, particularly compared to the amounts often spent on other marketing activities. One city that has focused strongly on this area is Baltimore. The LiveBaltimore Home Center, a partnership of city government and local foundations, is perhaps the outstanding model for other cities interested in this work. The center maintains a storefront office in downtown Baltimore and coordinates a wide range of public and private home-buyer incentives and promotional and educational activities, as well as serving as a center for information and referral (www.livebaltimore.com). Another similar initiative is HomeNet, a project supported by the Norfolk, Virginia, Housing and Redevelopment Authority (www.nrha.us/own/homenet).

### Citywide Strategies

Building markets requires two levels of activity: a citywide framework strategy and neighborhood-level implementation steps. The citywide strategy should parallel that of any business seeking to market its product, which in this case is the city and its neighborhoods: identify the opportunities available, the assets that the product has to offer, and the weaknesses or liabilities that must be reduced or eliminated. An asset could be a university or a neighborhood of historic houses, while liabilities often include high levels of crime and poor public schools. Ironically, low house prices are more of a liability than an asset. While they may increase affordability for some, they signal to many prospective buyers that they are at risk of losing their equity if they buy in such an environment. The elements of a citywide market-building strategy are shown in Table 6.1.

| Element | Key Questions |
|---|---|
| Identifying regional opportunities | • What are the key or target populations living in or moving into the larger region that can be attracted into the city? |
| Identifying marketable assets | • What key assets do the city and individual neighborhoods have that can be used to attract people to the city? <br> • How can those assets be made better known or more appealing to the larger region? |
| Identifying liabilities | • What key liabilities affecting the city and individual neighborhoods deter people from investing in the city? |
| Targeting neighborhoods | • Which neighborhoods contain particular assets relevant to the potential target populations living in or moving into the region? <br> • What steps need to be taken to position those neighborhoods to attract those target populations? |
| Building consumer confidence | • How can the city's liabilities be addressed to reduce the problems they represent as well as reduce their impact on consumer choices? <br> • What steps can the city take to make consumers more confident in the future of an investment in the city? |
| Marketing the city and its neighborhoods | • What action steps can the city and individual neighborhoods take to reach target markets and maximize financial and personal investment in the city? |

*Table 6.1. Elements in a citywide market-building strategy*

The market-building process begins with identifying target markets: those populations, defined by household type, age, education, and other features, that are most likely to consider moving into the city or a specific neighborhood. This is critical since the assets that a city or neighborhood offers are likely to be more meaningful to some groups than to others; similarly, different populations will react differently to the city's liabilities. Thus, a city with a strong arts and entertainment scene may be able to attract large numbers of young single people, but problematic public schools may make it unappealing to families with school-age children.

Market building goes beyond marketing in the narrow sense. Marketing a product is likely to be only as successful as the quality of the product. Market building is about actively building on the city's assets and effectively addressing those features of the city that work against its appeal to prospective home buyers and other investors, not about "spinning" or trying to paper over those features.

### Neighborhood Strategies

While there are examples of successful independent neighborhood market-building strategies, a larger citywide framework can better support and reinforce individual neighborhood efforts. Within that framework, neighborhood market-building efforts need to concentrate on three broad areas: the desirability of the neighborhood's housing stock, neighborhood stability, and neighborhood amenity value.

The elements that go into these three areas are shown in Table 6.2. Few neighborhoods can or may need to address all of the areas shown in the table; for each neighborhood the planner should work with residents to identify which elements are most important and develop a strategy that dovetails with ongoing

| Area | Potential Strategy Elements |
|---|---|
| Increasing the desirability of the neighborhood's housing stock | • Creating different housing stock through new construction, rehab, or adaptive reuse<br>• Providing financial incentives to overcome disparity between cost to build/rehab and resulting market value<br>• Providing insurance to protect against loss of equity through neighborhood depreciation<br>• Providing information about quality and availability of housing in neighborhood |
| Increasing neighborhood stability | • Reducing the number of vacant properties<br>• Reducing foreclosures<br>• Encouraging investment in homes and neighborhoods by residents and owners<br>• Reducing poverty concentrations<br>• Carrying out crime-prevention activities<br>• Increasing home ownership rates |
| Increasing neighborhood amenity value | • Improving appearance of neighborhood yards, vacant lots, and other visible features (curb appeal)<br>• Improving quality, use, and safety of parks and open spaces<br>• Increasing job access<br>• Improving public transportation systems<br>• Improving neighborhood shopping and services<br>• Improving neighborhood schools |

***Table 6.2.*** *Elements in a neighborhood market-building strategy*

Adapted from Mallach 2008

citywide efforts. While some activities can be carried out by engaged neighborhood residents and organizations, others, like improving schools or mounting strategic code-enforcement efforts, require the city's active involvement.

### Targeting Neighborhoods

One of the most difficult decisions for many cities is where to focus market-building and revitalization efforts. Not only are public dollars and personnel such as police officers and housing inspectors limited, but in many weak-market cities aggregate housing demand is also severely limited. Where demand is spread thinly over all of the city's neighborhoods, it may not absorb the supply in any of them, leading to decline in all or most of the city's neighborhoods. In other cities where demand is focused in only a few well-established neighborhoods, others that could be stabilized and revitalized might instead fall apart. The same is true for the allocation of public resources.

Difficult as it is for a city government to strategically target resources to certain areas over others, it is a task that a growing number of cities are undertaking. The choice is between fostering transformative change in some areas at the potential expense of others or perpetuating a clearly undesirable status quo.

A successful targeting strategy requires three elements: political commitment, solid data and information, and community engagement. The city government—both the administration and city council—needs to be committed to the strategy as a sustained, ongoing city policy. The strategy needs to be grounded in a solid, data-driven assessment process to ensure that resources and action steps will be directed into the most appropriate locations as well as to protect the process from the whims of either politicians or planners. Finally, the strategy must emerge from a process that broadly engages the community so those who will be affected by the strategy understand not only why it is important for the city's future but how the targeted areas will be selected.

### GREENING, NEIGHBORHOOD RECONFIGURATION, AND SUSTAINABLE REUSE

In cities in transition, certain areas of disinvestment may have long-term redevelopment potential, such as Detroit's Delray neighborhood, which is close to the river and to the relatively strong southwest area of the city. But in other areas there may be no apparent redevelopment potential for the next 10 or 20 years, if not longer, while ongoing demolition of surplus housing and other buildings constantly adds to the inventory of empty land. In many cases the city fabric is changing from a continuous urban pattern to a mixed form in which more densely developed sections are punctuated by large areas of low-density settlement or green space.

*In Detroit, community members work together to allocate resources.*

Joseph Schilling

Vacant land cannot be ignored; at a minimum it must be kept free of debris and periodically mowed or trimmed. Since much of this land has no active private owners, the responsibility often falls on local government. This can represent a significant cost burden for the city, but without upkeep vacant land quickly can blight its surroundings. Planners working in cities or neighborhoods with substantial inventories of surplus vacant land must be able to craft strategies for productive long-term use of these sites that do not involve construction of new buildings. Such strategies are all greening strategies in one form or another and can be integrated into a green infrastructure plan.

A green infrastructure plan offers opportunities for temporary holding strategies, such as community gardens, pocket parks, or open space areas with natural habitat and vegetation, as well as permanent green reuse. Vacant and underused land, especially parcels near existing parks, could enhance and expand parks and open space facilities in cities in transition, providing networks of recreational opportunities for walking and biking that offer health benefits for residents. Green infrastructure can also help manage stormwater, increase biodiversity, restore water quality and soils, and improve air quality. Opportunities may exist for improving local riparian systems through practices such as daylighting streams and for using plants to clean contaminated soils and waters (phytoremediation).

A few legacy cities have become leaders in urban greening. In Philadelphia, the Pennsylvania Horticultural Society's Philadelphia Green program directs an ambitious suite of urban greening and vacant land management projects throughout the city (see www.pennsylvaniahorticulturalsociety.org /phlgreen/index.html). Most urban greening programs focus on the reclamation and maintenance of vacant lots across a variety of neighborhoods, rather than large-scale or long-term reconfiguration of vacant land to meet current population and market demands. More ambitious efforts are emerging, however. In 2009 the City of Rochester, New York, launched Project Green, an urban greening strategy designed to rightsize selected target neighborhoods (see www.cityofrochester.gov/article.aspx?id=8589941695). Similarly, the latest draft of the Saginaw, Michigan, comprehensive plan proposes a 346-acre "green zone" in the city's northeast section, where remaining houses will be demolished as they are vacated and the land returned to a more natural state.

The planner needs to ask a number of definitional questions before deciding on appropriate greening strategies for specific sites. The character of the area in which the vacant land is located is paramount. The potential treatments for a neighborhood with scattered, small vacant lots and some market demand are very different than those for areas with little or no demand and large amounts of vacant land. Important considerations include future redevelopment potential and any need for environmental remediation, which may render some alternatives either infeasible or too expensive. The planner needs to take community preferences and the extent to which individuals and organizations are willing to assume responsibility for properties into account. Ultimately, the goal of all greening strategies is the same: turning surplus land into an asset for the quality of life and future regeneration of the city or neighborhood.

Some green-reuse strategies require a comprehensive framework at either the city or neighborhood level to be successful. The Idora vacant land strategy in Youngstown (see Chapter 4) was part of a comprehensive neighborhood effort; it would have been far less effective if it had been pursued on a site-by-site basis. On a larger scale, some green reuse requires systematic, highly sophisticated planning. For example, Philadelphia has developed a green-infrastructure stormwater management plan to address widespread

## A DESIGN-BASED APPROACH TO URBAN REGENERATION

As cities grow, decline, and change, urban design strategies can help manage periods of transition. Good design can improve a city's appearance and functionality in the current moment and enable a city to adapt to future challenges and opportunities as they emerge. The planning profession traditionally focuses on establishing order, organizing land uses, and imposing limits on the messy and complicated process of urban development, and many planners seem uncomfortable with unpredictability and fluctuation. But for cities struggling with persistent population loss, increased vacancy, and low market demand, the planning process must accommodate uncertainty and experimentation.

encompasses both vacant land (properties awaiting future development) and vacated land (sites that have been abandoned and have little or no development potential). Low-cost greening strategies can maintain appearances and protect surrounding property values from precipitous decline in the event that lots remain vacant for an extended time period. Cities can enact vacant-property regulations that impose minimum maintenance standards to ensure that these sites do not adversely impact surrounding property values or create public nuisances. Cities can also establish stricter design standards for properties that will remain vacant indefinitely, particularly those in high-visibility locations. Fencing, hedges,

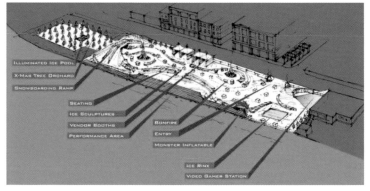

**Figure 6.1.** *(Above) Flats East Bank site, a riverfront parcel in downtown Cleveland where development was stalled for several years*
Adapted from Mallach 2008

**Figure 6.2.** *(Left) This property's developer allowed the site to be used as a temporary public space through the Cleveland Urban Design Collaborative Pop Up City initiative.*
Kent State Cleveland Urban Design Collaborative

Urban design efforts for transitional cities can be immediate, practical, and directly targeted to areas most in need of stabilization. Design thinking can also help planners and policy makers develop broader and more holistic approaches to urban regeneration by understanding the ways that cities respond and adapt to changing economic, ecological, and social conditions. At the most fundamental level, good design makes cities look better and operate more efficiently. Keeping up appearances is especially important during periods of transition. Design interventions can reassure residents and offer a sense of stability in cities coping with disinvestment, demographic shifts, weak real estate markets, increased crime, and other adverse conditions.

Vacancy is a major concern in transitional cities, and flexible standards are needed for land management and reuse. Vacancy

seasonal plantings, and other treatments improve the appearance of a vacant site, particularly along the edges where vacancies abut an intact urban neighborhood. Vacant sites can also accommodate interim public uses, such as sports, passive recreation, or community events, often with modest investments. Although there are costs involved in implementing design treatments, the property owner and the city will benefit from more stable property values and property tax revenues, as well as fewer complaints from neighboring property owners.

Design responses for vacant properties can occur at the parcel, city, and regional levels. Planners must consider the initial cost of design treatments and the long-range challenges of ongoing property maintenance.

*(continued on page 83)*

(continued from page 82)

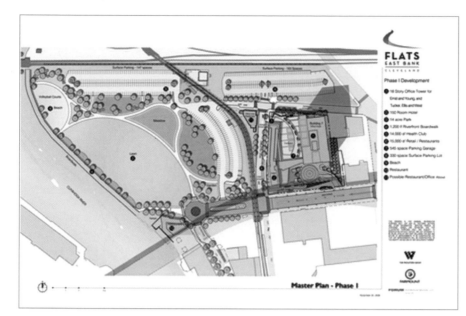

*Figure 6.3.* Phase 1 of the development includes a public lawn along the river; later phases of the project include buildings in this area, although a public walkway along the riverfront will be maintained.

Kent State Cleveland Urban Design Collaborative

At the parcel level, stabilization strategies have to look good and meet community standards. Turfgrass is the most common treatment for vacant parcels since lawns have a high degree of community acceptance and enhance perceptions of neighborhood stability. However, turfgrass requires regular mowing, and when maintenance becomes a city responsibility the costs of upkeep may eventually outpace available resources. The City of Cleveland spends more than $3 million per year mowing lawns; it is exploring lower-maintenance alternatives to turfgrass. Along those lines, the Youngstown Neighborhood Development Corporation's Lots of Green program has introduced native prairie landscapes as a holding strategy for vacant lots. (See www.yndc.org/programs/lots-green.) Flint, Michigan, has a similar approach, combining natural landscapes with three-foot-wide strips of lawn adjacent to public sidewalks. This establishes a visual cue that the property is being maintained while reducing maintenance requirements because the grass requires only a single pass of a lawn mower. A landscape that looks intentional is key to gaining community acceptance.

At the city and regional scales, vacant land provides unprecedented opportunities for restoring urban ecosystems while establishing frameworks for future development that are more resilient, healthy, and equitable. Cities in transition can use surplus real estate and weak market demand to their advantage by making strategic choices about where to target future development and where to conserve or restore natural systems for lasting benefits. Subsequent greening strategies may include expanding the tree canopy, capturing stormwater runoff, expanding urban agriculture, mitigating urban heat islands, promoting ecological diversity, and restoring indigenous waterways within the urban footprint. These cities can become laboratories for urban regeneration and centers of research and innovation that embrace new approaches for integrating natural systems into the built environment.

Some initial design-based responses for managing change in cities in transition include the following:

- Inventory vacant properties and surplus real estate. Categorize these sites as to their physical, ecological, and economic characteristics. Some sites will have high potential for real estate

*Figure 6.4.* Youngstown Neighborhood Development Corporation Lots of Green landscape treatment
YNDC

development, while others will be better used as parks, green infrastructure, urban agriculture, or other nontraditional urban uses. Detailed GIS mapping of vacancy by category and location makes it possible to track changes under way and craft appropriate responses.

- Experiment with temporary uses such as pop-up shops, short-term public spaces, art installations, and events as a way to stabilize and enliven vacant properties and evaluate alternatives for future, permanent development.

- Collaborate with local universities and design practitioners when developing regeneration plans. Complex problems require interdisciplinary solutions; reach out to people with skills that complement and expand the traditional planning toolkit.

Embrace change. All cities grow and decline over time. Some aspects of a city's development cannot be regulated or controlled but simply understood and accommodated.

—*Terry Schwarz, AICP* ◢

problems associated with its combined stormwater and sewer system. The plan has been submitted to U.S. EPA for approval, and if successful, it will eliminate the need for billions of dollars in improvements to the city's sewer system. Site-specific strategies for green reuse are discussed in Chapter 7.

Perhaps the most difficult planning challenge is deciding whether and how a city should reconfigure the built environment in neighborhoods with high levels of abandonment and close to zero demand for the remaining housing. Local officials hesitate to publicly discuss let alone endorse rightsizing strategies—fears that reflect both political considerations as well as the persistent perception that to acknowledge population loss is an admission of defeat.

Most of the creative visualizations of what rightsizing might actually look like in U.S. cities have come from outside of local governments. In the fall of 2008, six national planning and design experts came to Detroit under the auspices of the American Institute of Architects' Sustainable Development Assessment Team (SDAT) program to create a policy and planning framework for a more sustainable city future. The resulting Leaner, Greener Detroit report suggests that the city repurpose its surplus land to create a greener, more sustainable city by promoting high-density, compact, mixed use, mixed-income areas in the urban core and in a network of still viable neighborhoods across the city. These walkable urban villages would have densities designed to facilitate social interaction, offer a variety of transportation options, and be surrounded by green areas that could be either permanent open spaces or interim spaces preserved for future development. The SDAT report argued that a smaller, more compact development pattern emphasizing high-quality planning and urban design would be more efficient in the delivery of city services and better encourage public transit.

Such drastic transformation is not appropriate for all cities in transition, but in places that have lost much of their historic population and in neighborhoods undone by abandonment, planners should at least explore the rightsizing concept.

## NEIGHBORHOOD REVITALIZATION PLANS, STRATEGIES, AND INITIATIVES

While planning in growing suburban and exurban communities tends to take place at either the city or region scale or the parcel or site scale, planning in many cities in transition often takes place at an intermediate neighborhood level. Neighborhoods—distinct, recognized areas smaller than the city yet larger than a block or block cluster—are important features of most older cities large or small.

In cities in transition, neighborhoods are often the geographic level at which challenges to city vitality are played out and where important opportunities to sustain and rebuild that vitality may be found. Cities are far from homogenous in their social, economic, and physical conditions; distinctive assets that can be used to strengthen economic opportunities, housing markets, and social fabric are often found at the neighborhood scale.

Neighborhoods may contain distinctive housing market features, community organizations and institutions, commercial districts, and networks of internal social relationships that distinguish them from adjacent areas. While the impact of these factors may have weakened over the decades, many of them survive, even as neighborhood populations change over time. Areas like Kensington and Mt. Airy in Philadelphia or Pilsen and Wicker Park in Chicago remain strong communities despite profound transformations.

### Planning for Neighborhood Change

In addition to local governments, CDCs and other neighborhood-based organizations have become increasingly engaged in planning neighborhoods, often supported by local intermediaries or statewide CDC associations. Many CDCs have retained planning consultants, hired full-time professional planners, or obtained help from studio programs at graduate planning and architectural schools. A growing body of publications has emerged to assist both planners and citizens in their efforts. (See the References.)

A team at Cleveland State University developed this definition of neighborhood planning:

> Neighborhood planning is a process whereby residents and other stakeholders learn about their neighborhood, envision a shared future, and develop strategies to shape it for the better and sustain it for the long term. The process results in a plan that encourages and directs future social and economic investments toward the development of a healthy neighborhood. (Burkholder et al. 2003)

Neighborhood planning reflects the recognition by the city, a CDC, or a group of neighbors that present trends need to be changed. A plan may focus on neighborhood stabilization, revitalization, or both. While many activities that foster stabilization or revitalization can take place without a plan, actions are likely to be more effective and productive if grounded in an overall strategy that lays out a clear direction for the future. It may be more suitable to call this neighborhood revitalization planning or neighborhood change planning.

In drafting planning guidelines for its Neighborhood Revitalization Zone program, the State of Connecticut boiled the elements of a plan down to four questions: What does the neighborhood look like today? What do we want it to look like? How do we get there? How can we measure our progress? These are the key questions that neighborhood revitalization planning is designed to answer.

It is not simple to move from the present condition of a neighborhood to its desired future condition. A neighborhood revitalization plan should not be simply a list of desirable activities; it must be grounded in a theory of change. The plan must spell out a solid rationalization for why change will occur in the direction of the vision laid out in the plan if the activities it specifies are carried out.

In addition to setting forth a vision for the neighborhood's future and a credible path to getting there, the planning process helps build investment by residents and other stakeholders in the community's future, garners support for the activities called for in the plan, and increases the credibility of the revitalization effort. An in-depth planning process indicates that the revitalization of the neighborhood is not a halfhearted or one-shot effort but rather a long-term commitment, though at the same time a planning process that is too protracted or too focused on abstract goals can easily trigger impatience in residents and others involved.

### Elements of Neighborhood Revitalization Planning

There is no one template for preparing a neighborhood revitalization plan, but Table 6.3 (page 86) describes many common or typical elements. As the list of plan elements suggests, these neighborhood plans are first and foremost strategy plans. While the central issues in some neighborhoods may be addressed through land-use and development strategies, in others they may have little to do with the physical environment. Planners working on neighborhood plans should seek to engage others knowledgeable in areas where they may have little expertise, such as crime prevention, education and youth development, or economic development.

### Assessing Neighborhood Dynamics

The initial assessment of neighborhood conditions forms the foundation of the plan and is essential in helping planners select appropriate strategies for change, as those based on inadequate or erroneous information are unlikely

## TWO NEIGHBORHOOD REVITALIZATION PLANS

Two good models for community-based plans for the revitalization of distressed neighborhoods are the plan developed by the Women's Community Revitalization Project for Eastern North Philadelphia and the Idora Neighborhood Plan developed by the Youngstown Neighborhood Development Corporation.

*Our Community Plan: A Shared Vision for our Neighborhood in Eastern North Philadelphia* (http://files.wcrp phila.com/NeighborhoodStrategicPlan ExecutiveSummary.pdf) blends policy and neighborhood planning. It includes detailed condition maps created through a community-led property condition survey, and it documents the impacts of vacant properties on the neighborhood through powerful photographs and personal stories of residents. The plan's central policy recommendation is that the neighborhood develop its own community land trust rather than wait for the city to overcome the political obstacles to creating a public land bank.

The Idora neighborhood plan (see Chapter 4 and www.yndc.org/neighbor hoods/idora) follows a more traditional planning model, focusing on vacant-property reuse strategies such as urban greening.

Both of these neighborhood plans were developed by local nonprofit organizations in partnership with community residents, citywide nonprofits, and universities and supported by local foundations. While the city's planners were consulted and participated in both processes, they did not take on leadership roles.

| Element | Description |
|---|---|
| Defining the neighborhood | The boundaries of the area that is the subject of the plan and key relationships between the neighborhood and other neighborhoods in the city |
| Assessing neighborhood conditions | A detailed description of conditions in the neighborhood, using both statistical and qualitative information; should identify assets as well as the problems or conditions that have led to the need for stabilization and revitalization |
| Framing a direction or vision for the neighborhood | The overall goals of the revitalization process, as well as specific objectives such as improving housing market conditions or reducing crime; may include a shared vision for what the future neighborhood should be as a result of implementing the plan |
| Identifying strategies for neighborhood revitalization | Specific strategies for change and the rationale for each; that is, what problem conditions does it address and how does it fit into the overall strategy and help realize the goals of the revitalization process? |
| Identifying activities to implement each strategy | Specific activities designed to further each strategy, including achievement measures or targets for each activity where possible |
| Assessing financial requirements and sources to implement the plan | The funds that will be needed for each activity, the nature of those funds (grants, short-term loans, etc.), and potential sources of funds |
| Creating a timetable for action | A timetable for the activities identified, including proposed start and end dates, and, where feasible, benchmarks for measuring progress |
| Establishing criteria and process for ongoing monitoring and evaluation | The manner in which progress will be evaluated and changes made over time as needed |
| Defining the relationship between the plan and other plans | Identification of any other plans (such as master plans, urban renewal plans, etc.) that intersect with areas addressed in the neighborhood revitalization plan, any conflicts or inconsistencies, and how they will be addressed |

**Table 6.3.** *Elements in a neighborhood revitalization plan*

Adapted from Mallach 2010a, 284

to be successful. While housing market conditions are critical, they are not the only area of importance; Table 6.4 outlines the numerous elements required for a thorough neighborhood assessment. The assessment should try to identify trends as well as conditions. Current demographic, housing market, and physical conditions are important, but it is equally important to understand the trends in those areas—how they are changing for better or worse or in ways that may create different resident needs or preferences.

Planners can determine some neighborhood characteristics from statistical data like home sales or crime reports, while other information—such as locations of vacant properties or the conditions of housing, yards, or sidewalks—can be gained through visual surveys. But no neighborhood assessment should rely on statistical or geographic data alone. Planners should conduct formal surveys of neighborhood residents to elicit their attitudes about neighborhood aspects and trends; surveying people outside the neighborhood can help planners understand how the neighborhood is perceived by others. Finally, planners should talk to neighborhood "opinion leaders" and to individuals whose positions give them an opportunity to observe the neighborhood, such as police officers, postal workers, and real estate agents.

| Element | Description |
|---|---|
| Housing market | Dynamics of housing market conditions and trends, including sales volumes, sales prices, home buyer/investor split, rental housing conditions, foreclosure activity, et cetera |
| Physical conditions | Characteristics and condition of housing stock, other buildings, vacant land and public realm (streets, sidewalks, parks, etc.); identification of location and extent of problem properties as well as significant physical assets |
| Demographics | Social and economic conditions of resident population, including key changes taking place with respect to economic or racial/ethnic characteristics |
| Social assets | Presence and strength of neighborhood organizations and institutions (civic associations, block groups, crime watches, churches, clubs) as well as informal networks |
| Attitudes and perceptions | Attitudes about and perceptions of the neighborhood, its features, and its trends held by both residents and outsiders |
| Quality-of-life issues | Significant issues affecting quality of life and neighborhood vitality, including crime, drugs, lack of educational opportunity, et cetera |
| Other assets | Key neighborhood assets (other than those already identified) such as location (proximity to major institutions or employers), transit access, key natural features (rivers, open space), et cetera |

*Table 6.4. Elements in neighborhood assessment*

### Physical Planning

Understanding and reshaping the physical environment plays an important role in neighborhood revitalization planning. Mapping physical and other conditions, such as existing land uses, vacant properties, open spaces, or crime "hot spots," is an essential part of the planning process. Map-based information can help both planners and residents better understand neighborhood conditions and explore which strategies are likely to be most effective in dealing with them. It also enables planners to determine what land-use issues, if any, will be most important in neighborhood revitalization.

Relevant land-use issues that may arise during the planning process or when developing revitalization strategies include the following:

- Eliminating incompatible land uses, such as junkyards or abandoned industrial properties, adjacent to residential areas

- Identifying sites for new housing construction, where appropriate, and determining the most appropriate housing types and configurations for those sites

- Reusing or fostering interim treatment of vacant land parcels

- Identifying the most appropriate treatment of vacant structures (e.g., rehabilitate, mothball for future reuse, or demolish)

- Assembling vacant or underutilized land parcels into larger sites for future redevelopment

- Rezoning areas where current zoning does not reflect economic conditions (such as excessive amounts of land zoned for neighborhood commercial use) or is inconsistent with existing land-use patterns or community goals

- Fostering adaptive reuse of existing structures where the historic use is no longer viable (e.g., industrial buildings, schools, or oversized single-family houses)

- Carrying out street improvements, reconfiguration, or closings

- Identifying locations for new or relocated public or community facilities

Many land-use issues that arise in the course of neighborhood planning are fine-grained, manifesting at individual property, block face, or block group levels. Addressing them successfully requires drawing on the skills of the urban designer, landscape architect, and architect as much as the city planner.

### Resident Engagement and Empowerment

A neighborhood plan should belong to the neighborhood as much as to any public agency or nonprofit organization. The participatory process should be iterative—one in which residents, other stakeholders, planners, and public officials listen to and learn from one another, rather than one in which planners present their ideas for community ratification or rubber-stamp ideas put forth by others. This is not an easy process. Few neighborhoods speak with one voice; even in the smallest neighborhoods there are likely to be strong differences of opinion. In neighborhoods with populations that are highly diverse economically, racially, or ethnically, these differences may be difficult to bridge. Planners must be careful not to defer to the loudest or most insistent of the many voices that need to be heard.

Planners can choose from many different tools to ensure meaningful community engagement. (In Chapter 8 we explore approaches relevant for cities in transition.) One-on-one and small-group activities, such as interviews and focus groups, provide valuable ways of eliciting views on existing neighborhood conditions and trends. Processes to generate community input, such as charrettes and visioning exercises, can be very effective when run well but often require particular skills and training to be successful. Planners who lack those skills may want to seek out universities, firms, or individuals who can assist. Throughout the process, planners must be careful not to influence answers through exercise designs or presentations that betray personal preferences.

While it is important to ensure that the full range of stakeholders is heard in the process, it is equally critical that their good ideas be integrated into the final product. If residents, business owners, and others engaged in the neighborhood are to feel that this is their plan—as distinct from yet another product from city hall—their involvement needs to be real and ongoing. Only in this way does engagement become empowerment.

### Designing Strategies for Neighborhood Revitalization

The heart of any neighborhood plan is the strategies and actions most likely to be effective in implementing necessary change while preserving existing assets. As noted, these strategies must be firmly grounded in the analysis of neighborhood conditions, problems, and resources. Unfortunately, it is easy to let one's perspective be colored by the availability of tools rather than their suitability. Some cities and CDCs have allowed affordable housing production to drive their neighborhood strategies because it was a known, available tool, even though new housing may have been peripheral to the key issues facing the neighborhood or even damaging to its prospects.

A successful neighborhood revitalization strategy must blend three necessary and complementary elements: investment, regulation, and engagement. For example, investments in public park improvements may be wasted unless at the same time officials initiate crime-prevention strategies and organizers encourage neighbors to use parks and monitor their use by others.

*Investment Strategies.* Neighborhood decline often stems from lack of investment, including financial investments, investments in human capital and public services, and the personal investments of residents in their neighborhood. Home owners who lose confidence in their block or neighborhood and put off maintenance and repairs provoke disinvestment as surely as those who just walk away from their buildings. To thrive, a neighborhood must continue to draw financial and personal investment from its residents, new in-migrants, businesses, and the public sector.

A central goal of any neighborhood revitalization strategy is to create a self-sustaining flow of human and financial capital into the neighborhood: home owners investing in their homes, new families choosing to buy houses, contractors rehabbing vacant houses or building new houses on vacant lots, businesses opening, and people participating in civic associations, park cleanups, or crime watch groups. Creating this flow demands an approach that sees public investment not as an end in itself but as a tool to leverage and catalyze private investment.

One example might be public incentives for families willing to buy and rehabilitate vacant houses in neighborhoods where the cost of acquisition and rehab exceeds the resulting market value. The goal here is both to leverage the private investment of those home buyers and to catalyze increased property values so that the value of rehabilitated homes will eventually exceed their cost and the public incentives will no longer be needed.

Catalyzing private investment should be an important, though not the only, criterion used to determine where to invest public funds. In evaluating public investment options, planners can use these questions in selection and prioritization:

- How will this investment make the neighborhood more appealing to its residents and increase their confidence in the future of the neighborhood?

- How will this investment make the neighborhood more attractive to families choosing where to buy a home?

- How will this investment encourage people to invest more of their time and energy as well as money in their neighborhood?

This is very different from the way public investments are often prioritized at present. For example, a school replacement program typically prioritizes the school buildings that are oldest or in the worst physical condition. Instead, those considerations could be balanced against the expected effect of a new school on a neighborhood—as well as the effect of removing an old school that nevertheless helps anchor a neighborhood.

The neighborhood plan is likely to include initiatives from all three investment categories shown in Table 6.5 (page 90). While the latter two categories are largely self-explanatory, neighborhood stability may require clarification. Neighborhood stability is not about reducing mobility or blocking change; it is about creating the conditions that make people—both those living in the neighborhood and those considering moving in—feel that their personal and financial investments are, or will be, secure. Stabilizing a neighborhood is about reducing the incidence of conditions, such as foreclosures or vacant properties, that foster insecurity and enhancing those, such as high levels of home ownership and high standards of property maintenance, that foster a sense of confidence.

| Category | Who Is Most Affected | Illustrative Areas for Public Investment |
|---|---|---|
| Increasing neighborhood stability | Residents and in-movers | • Reducing vacant properties<br>• Increasing property maintenance<br>• Reducing foreclosures<br>• Increasing home ownership<br>• Reducing crime and drug activity |
| Increasing neighborhood quality of life | Residents and in-movers | • Improving parks and open spaces<br>• Reducing crime and drug activity<br>• Improving neighborhood transit connectivity<br>• Improving shopping and services |
| Increasing the desirability of the housing stock | In-movers | • Creating housing that appeals to different target markets<br>• Providing incentives to fill "market gap"<br>• Marketing neighborhood housing opportunities |

*Table 6.5.* *Typology of neighborhood investments*

Adapted from Mallach 2008

*Regulatory Strategies.* Most people obey the law, maintain their proper-ties, and refrain from dumping trash in vacant lots. Some, however, do not, and their actions undermine the health of their communities. Regulatory strategies use governmental powers to penalize behaviors and activities that work against a healthy and thriving neighborhood. Ultimately, as a neighborhood gains strength, people tend to be motivated to improve their properties and respect their surroundings, while resident peer pressure discourages antisocial behavior.

Crime prevention and antidrug initiatives are well-known neighbor-hood regulatory strategies. The other major regulatory area is property, whose regulation can include vacant property strategies, code enforce-ment, nuisance abatement, rental property regulation, and more. Because problem-property issues can significantly contribute to neighborhood de-cline, strategies that focus on property regulation should play an important role in the neighborhood plan. A description of key property-regulation strategies is in Table 6.6.

Regulatory strategies have two parts: the legal mechanism to enforce the regulation and the capacity, allocation of resources, and operating systems needed to enforce the regulation in the field. Without the first, the second is not possible; without the second, the first is academic. Responsibility for regulatory strategies is rarely within the planner's scope of authority. In some cities planning and property regulation are in the same department, but in most cases the planner will have to work closely with other depart-ments within city government to ensure that the necessary ordinances are in place and to frame regulatory strategies.

Limited resources constrain regulatory implementation in many cities in transition. The fiscal crunch has led many cities to lay off code enforce-ment personnel, police officers, and firefighters, reducing their abilities to pursue effective regulations. City officials, CDCs, and neighborhood orga-nizations should explore regulatory partnerships to leverage one another's resources. This can be highly productive as many residents, particularly those engaged in civic associations and block watch groups, are eager to

| Category | Examples |
|---|---|
| Vacant properties | • Vacant property maintenance requirements<br>• Vacant property receivership<br>• Creditor responsibility<br>• Vacant property registration |
| Property maintenance | • Strategic code enforcement<br>• Fire safety inspections<br>• Health inspections<br>• Nuisance abatement |
| Rental properties | • Rental registration<br>• Rental licensing<br>• Good landlord programs<br>• Targeted "bad apple" programs<br>• Rental receivership |
| Public realm | • Antidumping programs<br>• Regulations governing garbage disposal<br>• Sidewalk maintenance requirements |

*Table 6.6. Categories of property regulation*

help the city tackle their neighborhood's problem properties. Cleveland has established such a code-enforcement partnership program. (Frater, Gilson, and O'Leary 2009.)

***Engagement and Empowerment Strategies.*** A neighborhood plan is not about doing things *to* the neighborhood but about doing things *with* the neighborhood. Community participation in the planning process should be the first step in an ongoing effort of engaging residents, businesspeople, and organizations in strengthening and healing their neighborhoods and empowering them to act. For this to happen, city government needs to recognize the neighborhood's residents and their organizations as active partners in that process rather than passive recipients of public largesse. Where the neighborhood contains a strong CDC, this should not be difficult; a strong, capable CDC is a natural partner in neighborhood revitalization and in many cases will already have been involved—or taken the lead—in the planning process. Where no such organization exists, the city can create a neighborhood council and provide it with the staff support it will need to play a strong role in the neighborhood revitalization effort.

The plan should detail an ongoing community engagement strategy, including specific mechanisms that will be used to foster community ownership of the process. Online systems and social media can play important roles; interactive neighborhood websites or Facebook pages can become valuable tools for communication within the neighborhood and among neighborhood residents, organizations, and city agencies. They can also become marketing tools for the neighborhood itself.

## CONCLUSION
Dealing with problem properties, building neighborhood markets, promoting greening strategies, and planning for neighborhood revitalization should all be part of the planner's mission in cities in transition. While the problems arising from large numbers of vacant lots and buildings have long been concerns in legacy cities and many gateway cities and first suburbs,

there is a growing body of evidence to suggest that they will increasingly afflict boom-bust cities in coming years. The need for building markets and for neighborhood revitalization strategies cuts across all cities in transition; regeneration is not possible without healthy housing markets and neighborhoods. All four of the areas discussed here fall directly within the planner's ambit and squarely intersect with the task of framing land use, development, and redevelopment plans for the city and its neighborhoods. All four areas require strategic planning, not a static process of mapping or designating appropriate land uses and development standards.

CHAPTER 7

# Planning for Specific Sites and Properties

Planning frequently comes down to questions of how specific properties and sites are used, what standards will govern those uses, and what criteria guide those decisions. In fast-growing communities with strong private development markets, the planner plays a pre-determined regulatory role based on the city's land-use ordinances and the bounds set by state law, with discretionary decisions largely limited to cases where a developer is seeking an amendment to or variance from the zoning code. In cities in transition the planner's role is very different. With private development activity stalled, many site-specific uses fall into two other categories: uses initiated by a developer or CDC where the developer is seeking some assistance from the municipality, such as city-owned land, tax abatement, or capital subsidy; or uses initiated by the city, particularly vacant-property reuse. In the first category, the city's discretionary role goes well beyond land-use regulation; in the second, the city is initiating the action rather than responding to the private or nonprofit sector.

In both cases the nature of the specific use may be critical to the revitalization of neighborhoods and ultimate regeneration of the community, especially when tied to neighborhood plans or other targeted strategies. Further, individual projects that transform vacant properties or underused spaces can serve as tests for citywide and neighborhood planning efforts. These pilot projects can engage community residents and rebuild civic infrastructure, advancing neighborhood revitalization. In all cases, planners should assess how the proposed use, and the manner in which it will be designed and operated, contributes to both the short- and long-term vitality of the site, its surroundings, and the community as a whole.

Site use or reuse decisions need to factor in many considerations. Market dynamics and ownership complexities often make it difficult to apply traditional community and economic development strategies. While legacy cities contain thousands of abandoned structures, and boom-bust cities like Las Vegas contain many vacant parcels that were "leapfrogged" over during the boom years, market and ownership issues often make sensitive infill development impossible without massive public intervention. Determining when, where, and to what extent such intervention can be justified is a complex but important planning task.

This chapter begins by considering the various reuse options available for specific sites where a local government can control development outcomes—where it holds title to the land or where discretionary municipal action is needed to enable private redevelopment. The next section examines key policy issues underlying reuse decisions, including the tension between short-term objectives and long-term goals and the question of when to demolish and when to preserve vacant or problem buildings. The last part of this chapter describes some of the tools that can help guide reuse decisions.

## CHOOSING REUSE OPTIONS

As described in Chapter 6, a city seeks to gain control over land and buildings to ensure that their reuse furthers the community's long-term goals and maximizes community benefits. In this context, the use and the user are closely connected. Disposition and reuse of city-owned property raises three separate questions: To whom should the property be conveyed? On what terms should property be conveyed? To what use should the property be put, subject to what standards?

Properties should be conveyed to responsible entities that have both the commitment and the capacity to reuse the property consistent with a city or neighborhood plan or strategy, and properties should be conveyed to them on terms that maximize the likelihood that the use will take place as envisioned in the plan. Given the economic constraints affecting redevelopment in cities in transition, revenue will be most likely be modest, perhaps less than what could be realized at an open auction. The city should be prepared to trade off some short-term gain against long-term returns, particularly where the auction process may place the property in the hands of an irresponsible or incapable owner. For privately owned sites, the city should evaluate whether the owner is responsible and capable before offering discretionary financial or other support.

Determining the most appropriate reuse options for a property is a four-step process: understanding the area; evaluating the site; framing goals, strategies, and priorities for the area; and choosing among alternative options. The best use is one that reflects the area's realities while furthering the community's goals for the area. In some cases these goals may need to be tempered by a thoughtful assessment of what is realistic and feasible.

Table 7.1 outlines the principal considerations for these four steps. The use of market factors as a starting point in understanding the context for prop-

| Step | Key Issues | |
|---|---|---|
| Understanding the site | • Physical characteristics (hydrology, topography, etc.) <br> • Environmental characteristics <br> • Spatial characteristics (dimensions, street frontage, configuration, etc.) <br> • Context/adjacent properties <br> • Legal and financial issues | |
| Understanding the area | • Market dynamics and trends <br> • Location factors <br> • Amenities <br> • Community strength and cohesion | |
| Framing goals, strategies, and priorities | • Framing a neighborhood vision <br> • Setting criteria for a stronger neighborhood <br> • Adopting priorities for use of resources <br> • Making connections between property reuse and other strategies | |
| Choosing from alternative reuse options | **Key Options** | **Principal Categories** |
| | Market-driven reuse | • Residential development <br> • Nonresidential development |
| | Nonmarket reuse | • Affordable housing development <br> • Public facilities <br> • Green/nondevelopment reuse |

*Table 7.1. Elements in property reuse planning*

erty reuse is critical and can help planners recognize both the opportunities created and constraints imposed by site location, target limited resources in the most cost-effective manner, and link specific property-reuse decisions to the larger goal of rebuilding the local housing market.

As the table shows, reuse options fall into two broad categories: those that are driven by the market (even if they may require subsidies to make them feasible) and those that are not. While it is important to identify potential market-driven uses that could be made possible through judicious use of public-sector incentives, there are often significant limits—whether on budgets or capacity—on the extent to which cities can do that. Strategies that focus on urban greening rather than conventional redevelopment are likely to play a major role.

### Making Reuse Decisions

Reuse decisions need to be grounded in an analysis of site conditions, the feasibility of the proposed reuse, and its effect on its surroundings and the community as a whole. Some key questions that planners should ask about reuse proposals are shown in Table 7.2 (page 96). This is where the planner's perspective becomes particularly important. It is common for development proposals to be evaluated only in terms of their effects on adjacent properties rather than on the larger area or economic context, even though development decisions for sites both large and small often have ripple effects that go beyond the immediate area.

| Reuse Option | Key Questions |
|---|---|
| Market-driven reuse | • Is the property suitable for the reuse?<br>• Is the use consistent with strategies and plans for the site vicinity?<br>• Who is the target market for the reuse?<br>• What use(s) will the target market support?<br>  o Residential, nonresidential, or mixed uses<br>  o Ownership or rental tenure<br>  o Housing types and sizes<br>  o Nonresidential options (retail, office, etc.)<br>• What price levels will the market support?<br>• What scale is feasible?<br>• What will its effect be on:<br>  o The viability of the private housing or nonresidential market?<br>  o Neighborhood market-building strategies?<br>• What public sector support, if any, will it require?<br>• What short- and long-term fiscal effects will it have on the municipality?<br>**Will it make the neighborhood better?** |
| Affordable housing development | • Is the property suitable for the reuse?<br>• Is the use consistent with strategies and plans for the site vicinity?<br>• What are the unmet needs?<br>• Is the use a cost-effective way of meeting those needs?<br>• What will its effect be on:<br>  o The viability of the private housing stock?<br>  o Neighborhood market-building strategies?<br>**Will it make the neighborhood better?** |
| Nondevelopment reuse | • Is the property suitable for the reuse?<br>• Should the use be short-term or long-term?<br>• Are there significant costs associated with the proposed use?<br>• What is the potential return—direct and indirect—from the use?<br>• How will it affect community- and market-building goals?<br>**Will it make the neighborhood better?** |

*Table 7.2. Key reuse questions*

*Economic Effects.* As discussed, most cities in transition suffer from inadequate demand for housing and nonresidential space; in legacy cities the imbalance between supply and demand is particularly pronounced and has led to widespread abandonment. New development of any kind is potentially in competition with the existing stock of houses, stores, and other buildings. An affordable housing project, if built in an area where private-market housing is inexpensive and oversupplied, may draw tenants out of sound but older buildings, triggering more abandonment. A new shopping center may undermine a viable but shaky neighborhood commercial street.

But this is not necessarily the case. New developments, both affordable and market driven, can target markets not adequately served by existing housing, stimulate demand by enhancing the quality of life in an area, or create new markets. Apartments in Cleveland's Warehouse District, for example, rent for far more than comparable units in other parts of the city yet do not appear to siphon demand from those areas. A new shopping center may strengthen a commercial strip by increasing the critical mass of stores or creating the opportunity for an anchor store such as a super-market. The planner should analyze the economic context for a proposed site reuse and evaluate how that reuse will potentially affect the existing economic environment.

Planners must also evaluate a project's immediate potential effect on public resources. In many cities in transition the cost of building a house often exceeds the potential sales price—or, similarly, the potential rents from tenants in a shopping center cannot cover the development cost—so most development proposals will require some form of direct or indirect public subsidy. The planner should evaluate which projects will provide the greatest overall return—both financially and with respect to social and quality-of-life considerations—to ensure the greatest benefit from scarce public resources.

***Physical Effects.*** When evaluating reuse options, planners must consider the existing visual and physical context of the site (the location and design of buildings and the spaces in-between). Both the use to which a site will be put and the way new uses are designed and sited affect the market potential and the quality of life for the entire block. A cheaply built one-story infill house on a vacant lot between gabled 19th-century houses diminishes the value of those houses as predictably as an empty, boarded-up house does.

Economic realities dictate that many scattered vacant lots, even in viable neighborhoods, will resist infill development. In these instances it is neces-sary to ensure that landscaping and fencing treatments help knit together the fabric of the block.

***Quality-of-Life Effects.*** Since there is no single metric with which to measure quality of life, planners must rely on qualitative assessments of how potential reuses might affect residents' well-being. Some reuse projects improve quality of life by turning highly visible eyesores, such as vacant industrial buildings, into community assets. Other projects may incorporate community-serving features such as green space, plazas, community rooms, or public art.

## Green Reuse Options

As discussed, many vacant properties in cities in transition have no short- or even long-term development potential. These sites are good candidates for green reuse. Table 7.3 presents a list of potential green reuses divided between those that are suitable for small sites located in viable neighborhoods and those most appropriate for larger parcels in failing areas.

In addition to being economically and physically viable, small-lot uses must enhance the quality of life for the people living next door and in the community. The success of some such sites depends on the willingness of neighborhood residents to take responsibility for them. Side-lot programs rely on home owners who can tend or take over the vacant lot next door. Community gardens depend on having gardeners living in the vicinity to take on maintenance responsibilities.

| Vacant Land Type | Potential Green Reuse | Description |
|---|---|---|
| Small- to moderate-size scattered lots in viable neighborhoods | Community gardens | Small gardens supported by residents of neighborhood |
| | Side lots | Sale of lots to adjacent home owners to permit expansion of owner's lot |
| | Mini-parks | Small playgrounds and passive parks for use by neighbors |
| | Park expansion | Adding parcels of land to existing parks and recreation facilities |
| | Stabilization/minimal treatment | Basic treatment and maintenance to provide attractive environment and minimize blighting effects |
| | Pathways | Midblock or multiblock pedestrian and bicycle paths |
| Large parcels in largely disinvested areas | Urban farms | Larger-scale agricultural activities designed to provide commercial products |
| | Low-intensity open space | Re-creation of meadows, woodlands, and other sustainable uses |
| | Park expansion | Adding parcels of land to existing parks and recreation facilities |
| | Greenways | Linear green areas providing for pedestrian and bicycle use |
| | Stream daylighting | Restoring buried natural streams |
| | Stormwater management | Using green space as a natural means of dealing with stormwater flows |
| | Stabilization/minimal treatment | Basic treatment and maintenance to provide attractive environment and minimize blighting effects |
| | Alternative energy production | Using land for renewable energy production such as solar, wind, or geothermal energy |

*Table 7.3. Greening options for vacant land*

Uses for large parcels in disinvested areas are very different. There are few proximate neighbors and even fewer eager to take responsibility for vacant properties. Thus, the uses must not require neighborhood engagement. This may lead to potential uses that might be inappropriate in more heavily settled areas. Two uses shown in Table 7.3 may have particular relevance in legacy cities with large inventories of vacant land: urban farms and renewable energy production.

*Urban Farms.* The primary distinctions between community gardens and urban farms, as discussed here, are scale and function. Urban farms, typically at least an acre, are larger than community gardens, and they produce food for sale or mass donation rather than for individual gardeners and their friends.

Urban farming can address food security issues and create self-sustaining economic activity. At the same time it is far from a panacea for a city's vacant land problems. In addition to the need for capable people to run agricultural operations, successful urban farms require access to distribution and processing networks, which may not exist in all communities. Moreover, many potential sites contain environmental contamination that may render them unsuitable for agriculture without remediation or costly improvements such as raised beds.

The Cleveland Urban Design Collaborative's Cleveland Land Lab has identified the land, water, and resource characteristics necessary to reclaim vacant urban land for agricultural purposes. In light of environmental contamination issues, cities should also consider reuse of vacant land for crops (such as urban forests and biofuel stocks) that could simultaneously support viable businesses enterprises and reduce urban heat island effects. For example, Growth Through Energy and Community Health (GTECH) Strategies grows biofuel crops on Pittsburgh's largest remaining brownfields to remediate the land and produce feedstock. (See http://gtechstrategies.org.)

*Renewable Energy Production.* Emerging solar and wind technologies make it possible to repurpose vacant urban land for renewable energy production. Ground- or building-mounted wind turbines and solar panels are appropriate for brownfield and grayfield sites with insufficient market demand for cleanup or redevelopment. Renewable energy systems on a collection of vacant lots can provide electricity for nearby home owners, and in most utility markets power produced can be sold to the grid through reverse-metering systems. (See, for example, the Steel Winds Wind Farm in Lackawanna, New York; details at www.ci.lackawanna.ny.us/windfarm.html.)

Cities in transition must consider the financial implications of alternative green reuses, starting with initial costs, which can include demolition of existing structures, soil remediation, and more. Even more important is how the ongoing costs of maintaining the use over time will be covered. For that reason major park projects are rarely feasible, even though they might be beneficial to many communities; many cities in transition are hard-pressed to maintain existing parklands and simply lack the financial resources to support additional facilities.

## "Holding" and Permanent Uses

For many years a green use of an urban parcel, such as a community garden, was typically seen as a short-term "holding" use, a way to make a property productive—or at least less of an eyesore—until the site was redeveloped with a permanent use. While this may have been appropriate in settings such as New York's Lower East Side, where it was only a matter of time until once-vacant sites became desirable development opportunities, it is a limited perspective through which to view settings where long-term population and job decline have created long-term imbalances between supply and demand.

In cities in transition, it is important to think of green reuse as a legitimate long-term use of vacant property. It is equally important to be able to distinguish between areas where green reuse is an appropriate long-term use and areas where future redevelopment potential makes green reuse an appropriate holding strategy. An example of the latter might be the Delray section of Detroit. Although heavily vacant and abandoned today, its location along the Detroit River and its proximity to downtown and the improving Southwest area of the city may make it a strong candidate

## REIMAGINING A MORE SUSTAINABLE CLEVELAND

*Re-imagining a More Sustainable Cleveland* shows how innovative urban design and planning can offer city residents a blueprint for sustainability. The creation of this critically acclaimed vacant-properties initiative began in 2007, with a series of studios, community workshops, and meetings led by the Cleveland Urban Design Collaborative's Cleveland Land Lab. In 2008 Neighborhood Progress, Inc. (NPI), a community-development intermediary, and the Land Lab brought together a 30-member working group to explore strategies for reusing vacant land with the goal of making Cleveland a "cleaner, healthier, more beautiful, and economically sound city." With funding from the Surdna Foundation, the group published the results of its yearlong planning effort in *Re-imagining a More Sustainable Cleveland*, which summarizes goals, principles, and strategies for returning vacant properties to sustainable reuse at the city scale. The plan identifies a wide range of vacant land strategies including neighborhood stabilization and holding strategies; green infrastructure strategies to expand recreation opportunities and the green space network, improve ecosystem function, and remediate contaminated properties; and productive landscape strategies (e.g., agriculture and energy generation).

*Re-imagining a More Sustainable Cleveland* outlines criteria for implementing these strategies as well as policy recommendations to support and promote the creative reuse of vacant properties throughout the city. The plan sets forth the following goals:

- *Productive use/public benefit.* Whether vacant properties are developed with buildings and infrastructure, preserved as open space, or put into productive use as agriculture or energy generation sites, they should provide economic returns, community benefits, or enhancements to natural ecosystems.

- *Ecosystem function.* Stormwater management, soil restoration, air quality, carbon sequestration, urban heat island mitigation, biodiversity, and wildlife habitat should be incorporated into future plans for vacant sites in the city.

- *Remediation.* Reuse projects should remove the risks to human health and the environment from pollutants at vacant sites, either with targeted remediation or long-term incremental strategies.

This process led to the Re-imagining Cleveland pilot project in 2009, which provided small grants of $5,000 to $20,000 to more than 50 separate community-initiated projects for green reuse of vacant land. These projects, which are described in the *Re-imagining Cleveland Ideas to Action Resource Book* (2011), include a vineyard, a market garden, neighborhood pathways, pocket parks, and rain gardens. This project, which can be characterized as a "guided bottom-up" approach, could be replicated in any city that has an inventory of vacant, publicly owned land. These projects will be monitored over the coming years to determine how to bring the most successful ones to scale. ◄

## TEMPORARY REUSE

Temporary strategies can be used to reclaim vacated sites for short-term use, enliven transitional neighborhoods, and experiment with alternatives for permanent reuse. Temporary projects provide a valuable means of community engagement for cities in transition. Instead of asking the public to respond to sketches or plans of land-use alternatives, temporary interventions enable people to explore a variety of alternatives and determine their preferences based on actual experiences.

For example, a former gas station in Cleveland's Glenville neighborhood lies vacant, waiting for a previous property owner to clean up environmental contamination from the prior use. Once the site is remediated, ownership will revert to the city, and it will become a small public park. In the meantime the vacant site is being poorly maintained, detracting from surrounding property values and residents' quality of life. One way to address this situation in the short term is through a low-cost, temporary landscape—a holding strategy that will benefit the neighbors while they wait for cleanup to occur (Figure 7.1).

***Figure 7.1.*** *Temporary landscape for Ashbury Avenue and East 105th Street*

Source: Architects for Humanity, Cleveland Chapter and the Kent State University Cleveland Urban Design Collaborative

A temporary landscape on this site provides a mechanism to test different configurations for walkways, planting beds, and seating areas using inexpensive materials and volunteer labor. A design can be created for residents to use and evaluate. Gravel, tires, durable plant materials, and piles of clean fill will be the primary construction materials. If a walkway is in the wrong place, it can be adjusted. If programming and activities on the site disturb adjacent property owners, earth can be moved to create landscape berms and buffers. If plants are trampled or stolen, other surface treatments can be deployed. The landscape can evolve over several years based on residents' preferences. Then, once the site is clean, the neighborhood can invest more substantial funds into permanent park landscaping. That investment will take place with a greater awareness of what works and what does not, so residents will be more likely to get a final product that meets their needs.

*—Terry Schwarz, AICP*

for redevelopment. Certain sites, particularly if close to highways and rail lines, may have long-term potential for industrial uses that can bring valuable jobs. By contrast, given even the most optimistic growth projections for the next few decades, parts of some legacy cities will simply not be needed to accommodate future development demand. In these areas there is little or no downside to making long-term commitments to green uses.

The distinction between holding and long-term green reuse is not as clear-cut as it might appear. An established use may be difficult to undo, as the City of New York found out when it tried to sell its community garden sites for development in the 1990s. In the end, community opposition forced the city to retain more than two-thirds of the sites as gardens, many of which have since been bought by nonprofit entities to ensure that they remain green spaces in perpetuity. Similarly, "permanent" uses are never truly permanent; if there is enough market demand and political support for a change in use 10, 20, or 50 years down the road, it is likely to take place. Indeed, planners and other city officials negotiating sales of public land for green uses should ensure that in the event future demand significantly increases the value of the property, the city will realize a large share of any later gain.

## RESOURCES

Here are a few of the many resources are available for planning and carrying out green reuse projects:

**From the Re-imagining Cleveland project:**
- *Re-imagining Cleveland Ideas to Action Resource Book*. 2011. Cleveland: Kent State University's Cleveland Urban Design Collaborative and Neighborhood Progress. Available at http://reimaginingcleveland.org/files/2011/03/ideas-to-action-white-layout-for-printing.pdf.

**From the American Planning Association:**
- Hodgson, Kimberley, AICP, Marcia Caton Campbell, and Martin Bailkey. 2011. *Urban Agriculture: Growing Healthy, Sustainable Places*. Planning Advisory Service Report no. 563.
- Bonham, Blaine, Jr., Gerri Spilka, and Daryl Rastorfer. 2002. *Old Cities/Green Cities: Communities Transform Unmanaged Land*. Planning Advisory Service Report no. 506/507.

**An excellent guide to stabilization and minimal lot treatment:**
- Haefner, Carl, et al. 2002. *Reclaiming Vacant Lots: A Philadelphia Green Guide*. Philadelphia: Pennsylvania Horticultural Society. Available at www.pennsylvaniahorticulturalsociety.org/garden/vacantmanual.html.

**A guide to the nuts and bolts of urban farming:**
- Partnership for Sustainable Communities. 2011. *Urban Farm Business Plan Handbook*. EPA-905-K-11-00. Chicago: U.S. EPA Region 5. Available at www.epa.gov/brownfields/urbanag/pdf/urban_farm_business_plan.pdf.

## LONG-TERM VERSUS SHORT-TERM CONSIDERATIONS

There is a constant tension in local government between short-term and long-term goals and objectives. This tension is most intense when it comes to making decisions about the use and reuse of parcels of land and buildings:

- Should a city try to maximize the revenue from a land sale today or sell it for less to generate greater benefits in the long run?

- Should a city sell the right to foreclose for back taxes to investors in order to realize an immediate return or take title to the properties in order to use or sell them in the future?

- Should a city approve a minimally acceptable reuse of a site that involves no public financial support or pursue a more substantial reuse that needs public support to succeed?

A related question is whether green reuse should be seen as a long-term permanent use or as a short-term holding activity to keep the site productive until redevelopment is possible.

### Balancing Short- and Long-Term Goals

Among the many people involved in reuse decisions, the planner is most often the advocate for long-term thinking. Most managers and decision makers in local government tend to be preoccupied with immediate concerns, such as how to balance the coming year's budget and avoid furloughs or layoffs. The planner must be able to show that the long-term benefits of one choice may outweigh the short-term benefits of an alternative choice while remaining sensitive to the city's short-term needs.

Comparing alternatives is difficult, and projecting long-term benefits, particularly indirect ones, from a particular project is fraught with uncertainty. For example, imagine a struggling but still viable neighborhood commercial streetfront of late 19th-century three-story buildings in which a corner lot is vacant and available. A private developer proposes to buy the site from the city and build a small convenience store and gas station, offering the city market price for the land and requiring no subsidy or tax abatement. An alternative proposal is to build a new three-story architecturally compatible building on the site. That proposal would require that the city sell the land to the developer for a nominal price and provide tax abatements for five years as well as a small capital subsidy of the development cost. Do the economic benefits of the convenience store outweigh the aesthetic benefits of the alternative?

It is not a simple question. It is easy enough to compare direct costs and returns by calculating the taxes generated by each alternative. In all likelihood, since the larger building will pay more property taxes, its cumulative return will someday exceed that of the convenience store. That point, however, may be too far down the road to be meaningfully weighed against the immediate cost impact. The question of indirect returns then arises: To what extent will each affect the property values and economic activity on the rest of the block? While a strong case can be made that the initially more expensive alternative will lead to significantly greater indirect returns, it is far from certain. Actual outcomes will be affected by forces outside the city's control, such as national economic and demographic trends.

These questions are difficult to answer but must be asked. Reuse decisions made today will affect the site and its surroundings for the next 50 years or more. Despite constant pressure to focus on the immediate and short term, planners must consider and assess long-term effects as best they can.

Econsult Corporation, an economic consulting firm in Philadelphia, conducted a study for the Philadelphia Redevelopment Authority in 2010 and found that "the 40,000 vacant parcels in Philadelphia create a tremendous burden to the city in the form of $3.6 billion in lost property value, more than $20 million in annual maintenance costs and at least $2 million in annual uncollected property taxes" (Econsult et al. 2010). Vacant properties reduced nearby property values by an average of 6.5 percent and up to 20 percent, resulting in an average loss of $8,000 for every household in the city.

## DEMOLITION VERSUS PRESERVATION

Another potentially controversial issue that planners in cities in transition must confront is the choice between demolition and preservation (Mallach 2011b). As properties are vacated in older cities, particularly in distressed inner-city neighborhoods, they may be quickly stripped of fixtures and copper wiring or vandalized. This rapid deterioration increases the blighting influences of these buildings on their surroundings, affecting property values as well as the safety, health, and quality of life of nearby residents. As a result, many cities in transition have demolished hundreds of thousands of old houses, commercial buildings, and factories over the past decades. With continuing abandonment exacerbated in many cities by the effects of foreclosures and with little or no new demand for most abandoned buildings, the rationale to continue demolishing buildings is a powerful one.

At the same time, several arguments can be made against this practice. Aside from its considerable cost, using money that may better be used elsewhere, demolition can lead to the loss of historically and architecturally valuable buildings and can undermine the physical texture of neighborhoods or commercial districts with potentially destructive effects on their vitality and potential for revitalization. These are not minor considerations. Historic buildings and neighborhoods are important community assets, and preserving them can create important opportunities for neighborhood revitalization.

These effects need to be balanced against the costs of not demolishing buildings. In most areas where candidates for demolition are found, rehabilitation or reuse is feasible only with public-sector financial support, a limited resource. While some buildings can be stabilized and secured until rehabilitation is possible, this is itself expensive, particularly if the building must be maintained for an extended period of time. The blighting effects of deteriorating properties must also be taken into account. Finally, reducing the size of the surplus local housing stock can have a positive effect by helping to stabilize the market for the remaining properties.

With their limited financial resources, cities in transition must constantly make choices about which buildings to demolish. Those decisions should not be left to building or construction officials; it is important that planners be at the table so that planning, design, and neighborhood factors are taken into consideration. The process should also allow community residents and historic preservation advocates to be heard. Where a building with historic or architectural value is to be demolished, planners should document the building and where possible encourage practices that minimize waste and that salvage interior and exterior features for future use.

Table 7.4 presents factors that should be evaluated when deciding which properties to demolish and which to preserve. This is a balancing process that cannot be reduced to a simple formula.

## SITE ANALYSIS FOR PRODUCTIVE PROPERTY REUSE

The first step toward productive reuse of vacant properties is the ability to assemble and analyze property data in a cost- and time-efficient fashion. The scope of information to consider for any potential reuse site is shown in Table 7.5 (page 104). To minimize the amount of time needed in the field or searching documents for each parcel being evaluated, the planner should consolidate as much of this information as possible in an accessible and user-friendly database. Certain issues pose particular challenges in cities in transition.

| Demolish ⟵ | | ⟶ Preserve |
|---|---|---|
| The building is obsolete by virtue of its size, physical character, or poor quality of construction. | *Quality of building* | The building is attractive, of high quality, or of architectural or historic value. |
| The building has deteriorated to the point that it cannot be restored, or the cost of restoration would be prohibitive in light of the economic value of the property. | *Condition of building* | The building is largely intact and can be restored at a cost that is reasonable in light of the economic value of the property. |
| The building, by virtue of location and physical character, is not likely to draw the investment needed to bring it back into productive reuse. | *Reuse potential of building* | The building, by virtue of location and physical character, is likely to draw the investment needed to bring it back into productive use. |
| The building is located in an area where the neighborhood fabric has largely been lost through incompatible land uses, abandonment, and demolition. | *Quality of neighborhood fabric* | The building is located in an area that still has a strong neighborhood fabric, and its physical presence contributes to that fabric. |
| Demolition will contribute to the opportunity to carry out a rebuilding or reuse strategy for the area, which may involve rebuilding or green nondevelopment reuses. | *Reuse potential of resulting vacant land* | The demolition of the building will result in a potentially unusable vacant lot, rather than an opportunity for meaningful revitalization or green reuse. |
| In the absence of immediate reuse potential, the nuisance created by the building and the harm that it is doing to the surrounding area in its present condition outweigh the benefits of saving it for possible future reuse. | *Nuisance level of building* | The reuse potential of the building, even if not immediate, outweighs the current harm that the building is doing in its present condition, particularly if enhanced efforts are made to secure or stabilize the property |

*Table 7.4. Considerations for demolishing or preserving vacant buildings*

### Environmental Conditions

In addition to the natural features that all sites contain, such as hydrology and topography, vacant sites in older cities in transition share a key feature: with rare exceptions, they all bear traces of former uses. This is less consistently true in boom-bust cities, where leapfrogging development left behind many vacant parcels that have never been developed.

Many former industrial sites contain environmental contamination that must be identified and often remediated before reuse is possible. Even former residential sites may have soil contamination resulting from lead-based paints, asbestos insulation, or decades of automobile exhaust fumes. In some areas the practice of filling former basements with demolition debris covered by a thin layer of topsoil has resulted in unstable subsurface conditions. While all of these conditions can be corrected with sufficient financial resources, monetary constraints make them severe obstacles to many reuse options.

| Site Feature | Elements |
|---|---|
| Physical characteristics | • Hydrology<br>• Plant growth<br>• Topography |
| Environmental characteristics | • Natural constraints (wetlands, floodplains, etc.)<br>• Environmental contamination<br>• Subsurface conditions |
| Spatial characteristics | • Area<br>• Dimensions<br>• Configuration (shape)<br>• Street/sidewalk frontage and condition |
| Context/adjacent properties | • Utility service<br>• Transit service<br>• Surrounding land uses<br>• Contiguous/proximate vacant or underutilized parcels<br>• Characteristics (condition, value, distinctive design, or other features) of adjacent properties<br>• Characteristics of surrounding area |
| Legal and financial issues | • Ownership and title problems<br>• Liens and other financial issues<br>• Public ownership/ability of government to gain title |

*Table 7.5.* Site analysis information elements

### Assembling Parcels

Consolidating multiple parcels of land can offer cities an expanded menu of reuse possibilities. This is particularly important in older cities in transition, where individual parcels are often as small as 25 by 100 feet if not smaller. For many reuse options to be feasible, multiple lots must be consolidated to create a single larger lot. Sites that may not be reusable by themselves may become potentially attractive to developers if consolidated into multiacre parcels.

Site assembly can be difficult in practice because few cities have a single database that integrates all relevant information. Public land data are rarely in the same database as general parcel data, while critical information such as which privately owned properties are currently facing tax foreclosure is likely to be in a separate file held by the treasurer or tax collector. Although many cities have GIS-based parcel-data systems, most of these systems lack accurate or timely information about vacancies or the condition of occupied properties.

Where public land is held by many separate entities that may be subject to varying laws, policies, and practices governing parcel use or disposition, it may be necessary to develop a process that facilitates effective cooperation and agreement on common procedures or objectives for property reuse. This can be difficult due to competing agendas or priorities of the different actors and is likely to require leadership from the top. Where ownership is split among multiple agencies across different levels of government, the problem is exacerbated. Resolving this problem should be a priority, however, if the city is to mount an effective strategic-reuse effort.

### Legal and Financial Concerns

Urban land parcels often have tangled ownership histories and may be subject to unresolved financial obligations. In many states, when properties are taken by the city or county for tax foreclosure, the process leaves the title defective and uninsurable. While most liens and judgments against parcels are eliminated through property-tax foreclosure, they may still be on the books if the county or city has provided inadequate notice.

The legal ability of a city to gain control of vacant or troubled property varies widely from state to state. In some states municipalities can choose which properties they take through tax foreclosure, while in others they can take only those properties scorned by third-party bidders. A number of states permit cities to use "spot blight" eminent domain, under which a city can take control of scattered vacant, blighting parcels without designating a redevelopment area or adopting a redevelopment plan. New Jersey's spot blight statute also mandates a process for determining fair market value that, if properly applied, bases the determination on market conditions in the immediate area rather than an appraiser's guess.[1] If site reuse depends on the city gaining control of the property, the site-assessment process should include an evaluation of the likely time and cost to acquire it.

### PATTERN BOOKS AND DESIGN GUIDELINES

Pattern books and design guidelines can be very helpful in generating ideas for reuse and setting standards for quality in specific reuse projects. Architectural pattern books—collections of ideas or plans for buildings—have been in use for many years, and widespread use of such books in the United States during the 18th and 19th centuries explains why stock building types that initially emerged in one part of the country can be found in so many other areas. Recently, a number of architectural firms, such as Urban Design Associates of Pittsburgh, have begun using pattern books as tools for neighborhood revitalization.

The Cleveland Urban Design Collaborative has published *Ideas to Action,* a pattern book for the reuse of vacant land parcels in Cleveland linked to the Re-imagining Cleveland pilot projects (http://reimaginingcleveland .org/files/2011/03/IdeastoActionResourceBook.pdf). This book describes, illustrates, and provides cost estimates for different use options including pathways, pocket parks, and rain gardens. (See Figure 7.2, page 106.) While an architectural pattern book suggests what can be built on a site, the vacant land–reuse pattern book helps answer the broader question of what can be done with a site and shows community residents and others the possibilities that reside in neglected vacant lots.

In cases where site reuse is likely to involve infill development, urban design guidelines may be more appropriate than pattern books. Local architectural schools may be willing to develop guidelines for a particular neighborhood as a studio project. An excellent example is the guidebook created by students at the University at Buffalo, State University of New York, in support of a neighborhood stabilization project for Buffalo's Lower West Side neighborhood (2002). (See Figure 7.3, page 106.)

Planners should attempt to build a library of patterns and guidelines for use and reuse of vacant sites in their communities. Potential sources include the examples illustrated here as well as locally specific works developed in partnership with local universities or chapters or divisions of APA or AIA. Building such a library not only serves as an educational resource but reduces the guesswork and uncertainty in both development and green reuse of the community's vacant lands.

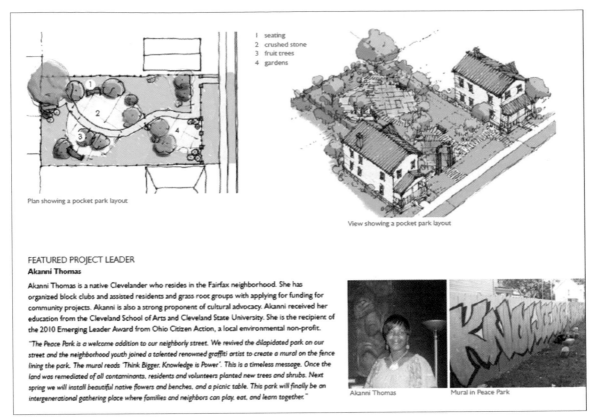

1 seating
2 crushed stone
3 fruit trees
4 gardens

Plan showing a pocket park layout

View showing a pocket park layout

FEATURED PROJECT LEADER

**Akanni Thomas**

Akanni Thomas is a native Clevelander who resides in the Fairfax neighborhood. She has organized block clubs and assisted residents and grass root groups with applying for funding for community projects. Akanni is also a strong proponent of cultural advocacy. Akanni received her education from the Cleveland School of Arts and Cleveland State University. She is the recipient of the 2010 Emerging Leader Award from Ohio Citizen Action, a local environmental non-profit.

"The Peace Park is a welcome addition to our neighborly street. We revived the dilapidated park on our street and the neighborhood youth joined a talented renowned graffiti artist to create a mural on the fence lining the park. The mural reads 'Think Bigger. Knowledge is Power'. This is a timeless message. Once the land was remediated of all contaminants, residents and volunteers planted new trees and shrubs. Next spring we will install beautiful native flowers and benches, and a picnic table. This park will finally be an intergenerational gathering place where families and neighbors can play, eat, and learn together."

Akanni Thomas

Mural in Peace Park

**Figure 7.2.** *(above) Illustrative pages from* Re-imagining Cleveland: Ideas in Action

Kent State University Cleveland Urban Design Collaborative

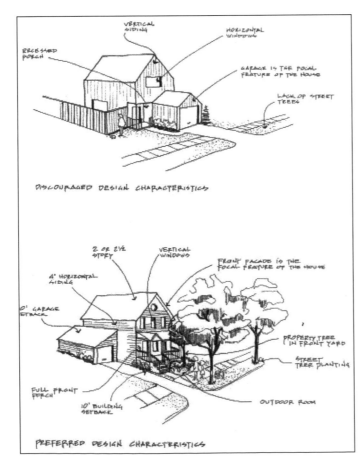

DISCOURAGED DESIGN CHARACTERISTICS

PREFERRED DESIGN CHARACTERISTICS

**Figure 7.3.** *(left) Sketches from* The Lower West Side Neighborhood Stabilization Project: Housing Design Review Guidelines, *developed by The Urban Design Project, School of Architecture and Planning, University at Buffalo, for the Mayor's Housing Design Advisory Board in Buffalo, New York (2nd ed., January 2002)*

The Urban Design Project

## CONCLUSION

The ultimate test of the planner's effectiveness takes place at the individual site or parcel level, where plans and strategies must meet the manifold tests of economic feasibility, site suitability, and community acceptability. In contrast to other communities where most development is developer-driven, in cities in transition most development is driven by the public sector, either explicitly through public decisions about uses and projects or implicitly through decisions about property sales and the use of subsidy funds and tax abatements. In thinking about the development of individual parcels, cities in transition need to balance the trade-offs between short-term and long-term outcomes. Planners often find themselves in the middle of these discussions and need to bring their perspective to a process often otherwise dominated by short-term fiscal, political, or other concerns.

## ENDNOTE

1. New Jersey Statutes Annotated, 55:19-56(c) and 55:19-102. For a detailed discussion of the valuation method set forth in the statute, see Mallach 2005, 33–36. Conventional appraisal methods are reasonably reliable in areas where a large volume of truly comparable market sales exists but are far less reliable in determining realistic market values in distressed urban areas.

CHAPTER 8

# Engaging the Community

 Planners can learn about community engagement strategies and techniques from dozens of guidebooks and articles and innumerable workshops and seminars. Our goal here is to offer insights into how planners can most effectively address community dynamics within cities in transition.

▶ **VOICES FROM FORGOTTEN CITIES**

In a nine-month oral history project, nearly 100 practitioners, political leaders, and experts gathered at the Massachusetts Institute of Technology to share their stories of revitalizing older small American industrial cities. Synthesizing these interviews and the data from these "forgotten cities" with populations ranging from 15,000 to 150,000, Lorlene Hoyt and André Leroux identified common stages of dominance and decline (2007). During the era of past dominance these cities and their leaders shared a common history the authors call the "Five Pillars of Dominance"—infrastructure, industry, in-migration, institutions, and identity— followed by the "Five Slides of Decline": shock, slippage, self-destruction, stigmatization, and shame. Using the participants' words, Hoyt and Leroux describe common community dynamics and collective attitudes in these cities today: fragmented civic capacity, low governing capacity, increased crime and corruption, large minority or immigrant populations, isolated racial and ethnic groups, and struggling schools and poverty.

For more details, see http://sap.mit .edu/resources/portfolio/forgotten _cities. ◀

The discussions and insights found throughout this chapter have been informed by our work with dozens of communities. This chapter also highlights a series of conversations with practitioners in Flint, Youngstown, and Phoenix. Many of them are trained planners who work for nonprofits and CDCs. They have experimented with new approaches and adapted older techniques as they attempt to rebuild their communities. They understand the DNA of distressed communities and recognize that engagement in those settings requires a proactive approach to rebuild and reenergize often dormant civic infrastructure. The complete versions of their comments and additional interviews with other practitioners working in or with cities in transition can be found at www.vacantpropertyresearch.com.

## UNDERSTANDING THE DYNAMICS OF DISTRESS

Appropriate approaches to engagement are not only vital but fundamentally different in most cities in transition. Understanding the present and past struggles of these communities is essential to building trust and ensuring the credibility of any engagement effort. While there are many parallels, each community and each neighborhood has its own narrative based upon local geography, culture, and history. Understanding this local narrative is central to the engagement process.

Legacy cities share an arc of growth, strength, and decline, with deindustrialization representing not only the loss of their economic foundations but the loss of community identity. The narrative for boom-bust cities is less clear. Cycles of boom and bust have been a constant part of these cities' histories, but every previous decline has been accompanied by the conviction that it was no more than a temporary bump in the road. The potential for long-term slow growth or decline is a new and deeply unsettling prospect.

Planners working to engage residents, neighborhood groups, and civic leaders in cities in transition should recognize common community dynamics and collective attitudes. The cumulative weight of these and similar factors leads many local residents to disengage from existing and future civic affairs.

- *Racial inequalities and socioeconomic disparities*: Given demographic shifts, sprawl, and out-migration patterns in many cities in transition, remaining residents are often people of color confronting long-standing problems of lower standards of living, poor housing conditions, higher levels of unemployment, and less educational attainment (Vey 2007). For cities experiencing new waves of immigrants in search of affordable housing and jobs, overcoming language barriers and helping newcomers sink roots in their community are critical issues.

- *Lack of trust*: Many cities in transition, especially legacy cities, have long-standing histories of inequality, discrimination, and indifference that have engendered deep-rooted general distrust of government and authority. Neighborhood residents often feel that local governments have ignored them or instituted policies and programs, such as urban renewal, that were actively inimical to their needs and interests.

- *Sense of despair, hopelessness, and shock*: The physical deterioration of some neighborhoods has continued so long without improvement that the remaining residents may feel despair about their area's future and a sense that effort is hopeless. In some areas, this deterioration may have few precedents and may have come on relatively quickly, heightening the impact.

• *Weakened networks of civic groups and civic capacity*: After decades of decline, the social and civic infrastructure of many cities in transition has become weak and fragmentary. Many of the city's elderly and poor residents do not actively participate in public processes, nor do they have the resources or equipment to engage in the world of social networking and electronic communication.

Successful community engagement is always a dynamic process that varies from neighborhood to neighborhood and evolves over time. Thus, planners should adopt a flexible approach that is responsive to subtle shifts of opinions and attitudes, with constant opportunities for input, feedback, and tactical changes.

For cities in transition, planners should pursue two approaches to community engagement: capacity building and outreach (both discussed below). Depending on community dynamics, these two approaches may happen simultaneously or in different phases and may be led by the same or different organizations. Community organizers working for a CDC may focus on capacity building, while the local government planner takes the lead with outreach. Either way, the two approaches will intersect and should be knit together into a cohesive and collaborative community-engagement strategy.

## REBUILDING CIVIC INFRASTRUCTURE

Many cities in transition may need to rebuild the capacity of existing civic and neighborhood groups or develop new entities and vehicles to empower and engage residents. Community-organizing strategies can sometime cause conflicts between neighborhood organizations and city hall, and some local policy makers and planners may hesitate to support or work with organizations that have a strong advocacy mission. The value of organizing and empowering neighborhood residents, however, should outweigh the occasional tensions that may arise.

*Youngstown, Ohio*

**PHOENIX AT THE CROSSROADS**

"Right now the Phoenix metropolitan region is struggling to recover from decades of growth and overbuilding," says Teresa Brice, executive director of the Phoenix office of the national community-development intermediary Local Initiatives Support Corporation (LISC). According to reports from the Morrison Institute at Arizona State University, Phoenix has a record number of vacant homes and skyrocketing foreclosure rates accompanied by high unemployment, particularly in real estate and construction. The Phoenix region is going through a critical transition.

"A few business and government leaders continue to believe this is just another temporary plateau, yet there are other voices that contend Phoenix can no longer rely on the construction and development sectors as the prime economic engine—they argue the housing market will not return to the same pre-2007 levels," says Brice. "From our vantage point at Phoenix LISC, the current downturn presents us with an opportunity to transform our development-driven economy toward a more sustainable model."

Phoenix is a young city that owes much of its growth to the national economic changes and policy choices of the postwar period. (See Chapter 2.) After decades of near-constant growth, especially in the 1980s and 1990s, Brice explains, the city "became dependent on growth for growth's sake."

When the housing, financial, and construction markets collapsed in 2007–2008, the Phoenix region fell fast and hard. With less home-building activity, local governments had less permit revenue, and with less revenue cities became cash strapped and had to cut staff, especially those in planning and building departments. Without new home construction, real estate agents had fewer houses to sell, banks had less demand for their loans, local government had less sales-tax revenue to fund programs and services, and thousands of households no longer had disposable income for goods and services.

According to Brice, cities like Phoenix do not have a history of philanthropic support for housing and community development. "Moreover, for years it has been hard for the community development field here to compete with robust and often politically powerful private home builders," Brice adds.

In addition, Brice observes that fast-growth Sun Belt cities cannot be judged by the same standards as older industrial cities. Older industrial cities often have a more compact urban form that helped immigrant communities bond, while Sun Belt cities typically follow a classic suburban development pattern with large lots and wide streets, which does not foster the same degree of social cohesion. As a result, residents of boom-bust cities think about their neighborhoods differently than people who live in legacy cities.

### REBUILDING YOUNGSTOWN'S CIVIC CAPACITY THROUGH COMMUNITY ORGANIZING

Youngstown is experimenting with a number of creative community-organizing approaches thanks to the work of Ian Beniston, AICP, deputy director of the Youngstown Neighborhood Development Corporation (YNDC), and Phil Kidd of the Mahoning Valley Organizing Collaborative (MVOC). Both have deep roots in the city and are committed to making the vision of the Youngstown 2010 plan a reality.

Community organizing and engagement are very different in a legacy city than in areas with stronger markets. They have far fewer resources and often lack the capacity to provide basic services that meet community needs. Beniston and Kidd observe that hope and community confidence are often missing in the neighborhoods in which they work, so community organizing activities must create new momentum. They suggest investing modest resources in small projects that reap quick results so that that people can see and experience positive change in their neighborhoods. They say that nothing works better than to get local residents to roll up their sleeves and work alongside one another. "Holding the typical public meeting is not going to stir the confidence of residents or significantly transform a distressed neighborhood."

Beniston calls for an "evolved engagement process" that offers a plethora of options for people to get involved. As part of this process, Kidd adds, achievements "no matter how small get celebrated and communicated." This organizing strategy calls for grassroots publicity and media campaigns, including video and social networking, along with low-cost but resource-intensive planning approaches. Beniston says, "The goal is to reignite neighborhood capacity and then strategically build upon it, developing it to the point where they no longer need you." Kidd notes that "what ultimately creates more hope is having an intentional approach and place-making process."

Community-level or grassroots organizations like neighborhood associations and block clubs can develop their own capacity and become self-sustaining if members learn how to be proactive, work well in groups, prioritize problems, and make progress on action items. Community organizing requires meeting people in their homes and, most important, involves an intensely personal style of communication. Both Beniston and Kidd have seen this type of time and investment pay off in Youngstown, with growing numbers of people becoming involved with the activities their two organizations offer. They have concluded that what works best in places like Youngstown is a hybrid community organizing/engagement approach that relies not only on e-mail, public meetings, and websites but, more important, on good old-fashioned community-organizing strategies.

Beniston offers the following basic neighborhood management activities for community groups in distressed areas:

- Conduct a property condition survey, emphasizing problem properties

- Identify distressed properties and desired outcomes

- Organize to address basic problems such as cutting weeds and boarding properties instead of waiting for the city

- Install welcome signs to convey neighborhood pride and identity

- Organize teams of volunteers to paint and repair neglected houses

- Hold street, park, and neighborhood cleanups to tackle signs of neighborhood neglect

- Employ reuse and greening strategies for vacant properties, including community uses as interim uses

- Build relationships with neighborhood merchants and people connected to small businesses

- Build from strength—don't start on the neighborhood's worst blocks

- Foster a sense of urgency

- Have fun and create multiple ways for the community to have fun

- Create opportunities for people of all ages to get involved

- Seek small grassroots grant opportunities

- Develop a collective voice

Foundations in Cleveland (the Cleveland Foundation and the George Gund Foundation), Detroit (the Kresge Foundation), and Flint (the Charles Stewart Mott Foundation) have supported many neighborhood revitalization projects and initiatives that are driven by local residents and community groups. Local foundations now play important roles in fostering engagement and empowerment in many communities. In Youngstown, the Raymond John Wean Foundation supported the creation of the Mahoning Valley Organizing Collaborative (MVOC; www.mvorganizing.org), which hired community organizers to work in that city and two others nearby. The MVOC addresses neighborhood problem-properties at different scales, engaging with federal policy through a network of national organizing groups as well as with state and local policies on topics such as land banking and code enforcement. While local governments can partner with and support community-based organizations, organizations like MVOC can often better lead community-building efforts than can city hall.

## DEVELOPING AN OUTREACH AND ENGAGEMENT STRATEGY

An explicit, well-designed outreach and engagement strategy should be part of any strategic policy planning process or neighborhood revitalization initiative. The outreach strategy should at a minimum address three fundamental process questions: Who is the community? What are the issues that matter to them? And how do planners engage community members, build momentum, and sustain support and involvement?

### Who Is the Community?

Defined traditionally, communities comprise supportive relationships of individuals and institutions that often share common goals, interests, and common spaces or places. In recent decades, however, the sense of community in many legendary cities has weakened, and the traditional foundations for community cohesion such as shared ethnic or economic identities have largely disappeared. Many people have stronger attachments to regions or to virtual networks than to traditional communities. In some cases the concept of community is contested; a neighborhood space may be shared by people of different ethnicities, economic levels, age groups, or social interests, each defining the community differently. Where a neighborhood contains such diverse groups, the planner is faced with the difficult task of reconciling multiple interests to create a cohesive neighborhood identity.

Community identity can exist at different scales. Some people may think of themselves as residents of a city or even region and have little sense of connection to a smaller area, while others may identify with a small area and not with any larger agglomeration. Many legacy cities have clearly defined neighborhoods, while boom-bust cities tend to have fuzzier neighborhood boundaries and large areas that lack clear identities.

It is important to look for the lines of neighborhood demarcation that are most meaningful to residents. At the same time, it is possible for planners to create a neighborhood identity where none previously existed; for example, the small industrial city of Geneva in New York State's Finger Lakes region used a participatory process to delineate and name new neighborhoods as the basis for building resident identification with those areas.

A deeper understanding of community dynamics can help in designing the scale and type of engagement strategies to make them relevant to residents. Defining physical boundaries is critical to ensure that community engagement takes place at the most appropriate level. In legacy cities the sense of community has been under stress for decades due to dramatic demographic changes and out-migration. Still, many remaining residents have strong connections to their cities or neighborhoods, as evidenced by an extensive network of blogs written by Rust Belt expatriates with emotional attachments to their former homes. (See, for example, the website of Flint Club, http://flintclub.wordpress.com.)

**What Are the Issues?**
Any successful plan should reflect residents' perceptions of the nature of the problems they face, the priorities for change, and the outcomes that would represent success for the city or neighborhood. In some cases there is consensus on such matters; more often, consensus needs to be laboriously built. In Youngstown, the core of the planning effort was a citywide visioning initiative designed to change people's perspectives on the realities and the future prospects of their community. Other efforts may focus on more immediate concerns such as vacant properties or neighborhood crime. Determining desired outcomes to defined problems may be even more difficult; for example, some people may see demolition as the best strategy for dealing with problem properties, while others may want to see the same buildings rehabilitated.

Planners should go beyond the issues and identify the underlying interests of the different groups in the community. It can be valuable to elicit why people care about particular issues. Do their interests relate to fundamental concepts such as the quality of life, the quality of space, and public safety, or do they reflect intergroup

**BUILDING NEIGHBORHOOD POWER IN FLINT**

Cities and nonprofit organizations often have multiple engagement activities going on in different neighborhoods, resulting in sporadic and inconsistent participation. In Flint, Christina Kelly notes that community partners came to realize that they were all doing similar work but in different neighborhoods, spurring them to explore how they could coordinate their neighborhood engagement efforts. In an environment where each community has a different starting point, the groups decided to organize a series of capacity-building workshops under the umbrella of Building Neighborhood Power (BNP), a partnership of public and community organizations that includes the Genesee County Land Bank Authority, the Flint Police Department, the Ruth Mott Outreach Center, and Salem Housing CDC, with other organizations participating as necessary.

BNP, says Kelly, saw itself as "a local response to local concerns [that] strives to create positive change by creating opportunities for empowerment of the residents of the City of Flint." Currently, it focuses on giving residents the opportunity to learn and explore issues related to the city's master-planning process and other local initiatives. By sharing the organizational capital and skills of the various partners, BNP responds to resident requests to support neighborhood organizing and planning. The resulting training sessions focus on building the skills necessary to form functional neighborhood groups and foster a stronger community.

"The structure that guides BNP's work is meant to ensure direction, foster creativity, and allow for adaptation," says Kelly. BNP tailors the content, format, and length of its workshops and training sessions to match the needs of the neighborhood and its residents, thus providing the partners with a menu of engagement options. BNP actively reaches out to elicit participation in these programs, contacting neighborhood organizations and making 300 to 400 phone calls for each event. Between 20 and 75 residents participated in each of 12 workshops and trainings offered in 2010. In all cases, BNP helps initiate and facilitate community engagement processes while building residents' capacity to sustain these efforts.

Building Neighborhood Power has faced challenges. These include securing funding for its efforts as an independent entity, as well as maintaining accountability and developing the ability to measure its impact in concrete terms. Despite these challenges, BNP continues to work to build resident capacity and support Flint's master-planning process.

## STRATEGIES FOR ENGAGING A DISTRESSED COMMUNITY

According to Christina Kelly, lead planner for the Genesee County Land Bank Authority in Michigan, gender, race, class, and the ability of the planner can all have positive or negative influences on the community-engagement process and its outcomes. "Planners need to understand the privilege they bring to the [planning] process, which can work against or for setting the stage in building trust and credibility within the community," Kelly observes.

Although it may not be an easy task, such introspection on the part of the planner is necessary given the racial and social tensions in many highly distressed neighborhoods. In Kelly's view, "starting from a very honest place becomes crucial in building trust with community residents." She also recommends that stakeholders take key leadership positions on the planning or facilitation team.

Many planners in cities in transition have trouble connecting residents with the plan and its process. Transparency, Kelly says, is critical. For example, residents of Flint, which is in Genesee County, had no knowledge that the majority of planning and decision-making efforts had been funded through foundations; some planning processes were done by students or led by consultants who were working under severe time contraints or lacked the capacity to facilitate meetings. Kelly notes, "Most of the community was not connected to past planning efforts either through its development or its content."

Kelly points to Youngstown's recent work empowering residents through neighborhood-based planning efforts. "Part of Youngstown's success rests with nonprofits that focus on building relationships with the community and building the capacity of neighborhood residents." Kelly emphasizes that it is important when working at the neighborhood level to slow down the planning process and not push the plan through too quickly. In her view, too many planners spend too much time building GIS maps or creating PowerPoint presentations when they should be talking to people. While these maps and presentations may help jump-start conversations, Kelly thinks building relationships is more critical to the long-term success of the planning effort.

"Planners need a certain level of humility when doing this work," says Kelly. She offers the following checklist of requisites for public meetings:

• Be culturally sensitive

• Build a multicultural planning team

• Have the facilitation skills necessary for public meetings

• Design and customize each meeting around the audience

• If using consultants, make sure they are prepared to field questions about what they can bring to the community

• Do design work as a collaborative problem-solving process, where designers really listen to the community.

• Create a process for continuous feedback

or intergenerational conflicts? Planners should consider doing a stakeholder assessment that inventories key organizations, institutions, and opinion leaders; identifies their underlying interests and ranges of influence; and maps their relationships to one another. The goal is to develop a profile of participants' worldviews through a community lens.

### How Do Planners Engage Community Members?

Social media has become all but obligatory in community-engagement practice. Almost every comprehensive plan or zoning code update has a website, a Facebook or Twitter account, and virtual town-hall meetings. (See PAS Report no. 564, *E-Government*.) These online community-engagement techniques should not be discounted, but the dynamics in many cities in transition demand a more "high-touch" approach in order to build trust and commitment on the part of a discouraged and disinvested public. If coming from outside of the community, planners need to think about how they will likely be viewed by residents. In order to lay a foundation for open dialogue they may need to acknowledge issues of privilege, past and present social or racial tensions, and legacies of failed policy or planning initiatives.

It is important to include existing community-based organizations in the engagement process. Although their strength and credibility can vary widely, many organizations contain individuals with the skills and relationships that can help reach a broad audience and build engagement in a community. Additionally, informal associations and networks of individuals, including social clubs, churches, and the like, may be more connected to some parts of the neighborhood than formal neighborhood organizations. Planners should take the time to acknowledge, understand, and connect these networks or, if they do not exist, work with organizers to try to build them. A vital civic infrastructure is critical to the success of a regeneration planning effort.

Many techniques have evolved for fostering greater community engagement, both generally and in a planning context. Informal, self-organized gatherings, such as study circles, neighborhood coffees, and potluck dinners, can bring people together to discuss issues and build stronger links among neighbors. Planners can engage young people by providing them with the tools to make photo essays and YouTube videos, for example, focusing on the strengths and weaknesses of their neighborhoods.

Other techniques are specific to the design and planning process. Most planners are familiar with charrettes—intensive participatory design exercises—which are a highly effective way of both engaging residents and generating valuable design ideas for a site or neighborhood. Students and faculty from planning or architecture programs at nearby universities can often be enlisted to work on neighborhood issues through design studios or student competitions. However, great care must be taken in all such processes to make sure that the product is useful to the community and reflects the goals and concerns of the area's residents. Many architects and planners, as well as graduate students, lack the training or inclination to work effectively with nonprofessionals in a truly participatory environment and, for all their goodwill, end up trying to impose their ideas on the community.

## CREATING A CULTURE OF ONGOING ENGAGEMENT

Community engagement should not end once a plan has been adopted or a program launched. Planners should think beyond a particular plan or project to ask how to instill a community and organizational culture that supports meaningful ongoing civic engagement. The process of maintaining engagement and recruiting and training new leaders is an ongoing and difficult one, as leaders move on and energy dissipates. Much of these efforts are better suited for organizations outside city hall, such as CDCs and other community-based organizations. Local governments can support such efforts by creating positions such as neighborhood coordinators, who provide staff support for community-based engagement efforts, and by integrating regular neighborhood meetings to discuss progress, evaluate changes in conditions, and get feedback with the basic fabric of the city planning function. Engagement is not just an element in a specific planning project but an ongoing part of the planning process itself.

## CONCLUSION

Throughout our conversations with practitioners, they consistently made the point that the process of engaging people can be more important than the specific elements and strategies in the plan itself. A meaningful, transparent, and equitable process is a precursor to developing effective strategies. Moreover, it can provide communities with the opportunity to let go of the past and confront the present, as their members come together to forge new visions for the future.

# CHAPTER 9

# Organizing for Successful
# Planning and Implementation

 The ability of the planner to engage the community, coordinate efforts across city departments, and build strong partnerships is likely to determine whether any citywide plan or neighborhood initiative will ultimately succeed or fail. Cities in transition typically have dozens of programs and policies already in place to address various facets of the social and economic challenges they confront.

Most cities have access to federal and state programs—among them Community Development Block Grants (CDBG), the Neighborhood Stabilization Program (NSP), and the HOME Investments Partnerships Program (HOME)—and many supplement funds with community or foundation resources. These programs and policies are often fragmented, however, with little strategic focus. By harnessing these resources within a strategic policy planning framework, cities can more efficiently and effectively move toward more stable and sustainable futures.

Orchestrating the many players involved, each with its own interests and cultures and with little history of working collaboratively, is a complex and difficult endeavor. Programs often have legal and policy mandates that restrict a city's ability to redirect or coordinate resources. Many of the agencies, departments, and institutions responsible for spending resources or directing programs fall outside of the planner's traditional domain. Thus, planners must better understand the dynamics of these stakeholders to build trust and communication among the many players.

This chapter explores the operational and organizational dimensions of planning practice within cities in transition—the so-called inside game. It examines the organizational framework for planning in a community, including the role that planning plays in city government, the financing of planning activities, and partnerships with other stakeholders in the planning process. The chapter ends with a discussion of how the planner can help mold the policy climate of the city as well as play a role in policy advocacy beyond the city's boundaries.

## BUILDING THE ENVIRONMENT FOR PLANNING IN CITY HALL

While planners work for many different agencies and organizations from neighborhood-based CDCs to regional planning agencies, the focal point for most planning activities in the United States is still local government. For this reason, planners in cities in transition must understand how the organizational structures of their city governments affect both planning processes and the abilities of cities to carry out their plans. The effectiveness of both planning and implementation in a city will depend heavily on how well aligned the responsibilities of different local agencies and departments are with the goals, strategies, and implementation steps of any strategic planning effort. This section will explore some of the issues associated with bringing about that alignment and creating a supportive environment for planning and implementation.

Many city department activities intersect with planning. (See Table 9.1.) While the mayor or city council makes final or official decisions, these departments typically initiate the actions leading to those decisions, and their directors or commissioners often make specific recommendations about those decisions to the mayor and council.

Agencies in city hall are not the only ones whose activities affect the planner's work. In many states tax foreclosure is in the hands of county rather than city government; therefore, reuse of tax-foreclosed properties by the city must be coordinated with county government. Cities also contain many semiautonomous or independent agencies, authorities, and quasi-governmental corporations that, depending on state statutes and local custom, may or may not be subject to municipal control or influence. These can include urban redevelopment agencies, housing authorities, sewer and water districts, park districts, port authorities, parking authorities, economic development agencies or corporations, downtown development corporations, and special-improvement districts. Navigating this organizational jungle, let alone bringing it into alignment, can be a daunting task.

| Department* | Key Roles |
|---|---|
| Housing and Community Development | • Controls discretionary funds, such as HOME and CDBG<br>• May be responsible for preparing HUD-mandated consolidated plan<br>• Key city partner with CDCs and other neighborhood-based organizations |
| Economic Development | • May control discretionary funds, including project financing and tax incentives<br>• Key decision maker for nonresidential development proposals<br>• Key decision maker for use and reuse of nonresidential parcels, including brownfields sites<br>• May be responsible for preparing economic development plans and strategies<br>• May be key liaison with regional planning and economic development organizations |
| Public Works | • May be responsible for maintenance and disposition of city-owned surplus land<br>• Allocates resources for installation, maintenance, and repair of streets, sidewalks, street lighting, and other public features<br>• Responsible for maintaining streets<br>• May be responsible for maintaining and improving public facilities such as senior centers and police substations |
| Buildings and Inspections | • Responsible (with law department) for enforcing codes and other laws for vacant and other problem properties<br>• Responsible for reviewing and approving building plans<br>• May be responsible for zoning review<br>• May be responsible for demolishing properties |
| Parks and Recreation | • Responsible for maintaining and improving city's open spaces and recreation facilities<br>• Makes decisions to create new facilities and expand or close existing ones |
| Finance | • Responsible for allocating city fiscal resources |
| Law | • Responsible (with inspection department) for enforcing codes and other laws for vacant and other problem properties<br>• Responsible for acquisition and disposition of public property<br>• Responsible for approving the legality of city agency actions |

* Cities vary widely in how they divide up their functions and what names they give their various departments and agencies.

**Table 9.1.** *City departments and their roles in planning and implementation*

### The Essential Role of Political Leadership

The city's political leadership plays a critical role in this process. Without strong support from elected officials, a planning director may have a steep uphill battle creating a supportive environment for planning among different departments and agencies. Only where mayors or city managers actively support planning as a central theme of their administrations is it likely that city departments and agencies, as well as independent authorities and corporations, will participate in joint planning processes or allow their actions to be guided by plans.

► **DAN KILDEE: LEADERSHIP FOR CITIES IN TRANSITION**

Creating a climate for positive change in cities that have experienced significant population loss requires effective leadership. Between 1997 and 2009, Dan Kildee was treasurer for Genesee County, Michigan. Prior to being elected treasurer he served as a county commissioner for 12 years. After creating the state's first land bank, the Genesee County Land Bank Authority (GCLBA), in 2002, he received national recognition for taking advantage of Michigan's reformed tax-foreclosure law to transform GCLBA into an active community-development tool for managing vacant and abandoned properties in and around Flint. Kildee is currently president and CEO of the Center for Community Progress, which he cofounded.

According to Kildee, his most significant accomplishment as treasurer was changing a system that was focused on liquidating assets into a system that put vacant and abandoned homes on a rational path toward demolition or reuse. Thanks to Kildee's work, vacant properties in Flint are less likely to suffer further neglect in the hands of investors. Soon after the formation of the land bank, Kildee realized that demolishing abandoned housing not only improved the aesthetics of blighted neighborhoods but also reduced the supply of housing that was competing with other properties. He says, "It was not just a question of rationalizing supply and demand but repatterning the city in a way that made the successful or sustainable neighborhoods the kind of higher-density neighborhoods that people really wanted."

In Kildee's view, policy change cannot happen without leadership, but this leadership does not necessarily need to come from elected officials. "Leadership is often manifest[ed] by someone who is willing to point out a reality that is not currently being considered and to create some disequilibrium or anxiety, which makes people uncomfortable and forces them to deal with questions that otherwise they wouldn't have to deal with." Additionally, Kildee cautions leaders against falling into the trap of promising growth and expansion as a placeholder for progress or prosperity. He sees a lot of potential for planners to help change the conversation. "Local political leaders need planners to pursue a broader set of objectives than just expansion and growth and to actually think about how planning supports quality of place and the quality of life for the people who live there," says Kildee.

While he concedes that there are significant technical challenges facing cities in transition, Kildee thinks adaptive change is essential. "The technical tools are in a constant state of change; one thing that is harder to change is the way people approach their work and their willingness to change the way they do their work."

Looking at the big picture, Kildee believes states have the most authority to set the tone for substantive change because they govern land use, infrastructure development, and public investment. Still, he sees an important role for the federal government: "We ought to have a federal government that creates not just incentives for better land-use planning or better sustainable-development systems but penalties for not adhering to those principles." ◄

While some mayors have backgrounds that predispose them to support planning efforts, most do not. Planners need to encourage newly elected mayors to see planning as important and provide the leadership needed to foster alignment of city agencies around planning and strategic goals. The same is true of city council members; it is important to have at least a few council members who strongly support planning and will advocate on behalf of strategic approaches.

Planners should seek out opportunities to educate and inform their elected officials even before they take office by creating educational forums for emerging civic leaders and by encouraging others to develop orientation programs for newly elected officeholders. Leadership in this effort can come from outside city government—through a local university, a respected "good government" organization, or a local APA chapter. Planners should build ties with such organizations to foster a culture of planning throughout their communities.

### Internal Organization and Coordination

Successful strategies for planning in city hall begin with internal organization and coordination. A city may house its planning functions in different ways. Planning may operate as a separate, stand-alone department, with the director reporting directly to the mayor or city manager or to the city planning commission. This structure is most commonly found in large cities, such as Baltimore or Philadelphia. While it can provide a high profile for planning activities, it may make operational coordination between planning and departments responsible for implementing plans more difficult.

Alternatively, the planning function may be located within a larger department administering multiple community development functions including housing, economic development, neighborhood revitalization, and code enforcement. This structure is more commonly found in smaller cities where the planning staff is usually small as well. While this structure facilitates coordination between planning and other functions within the same department, it may hinder coordination beyond the department because of the reduced stature and visibility of the planning function.

As an alternative or in addition to the planning function housed in a dedicated department, some cities have established planning functions within the office of the local chief executive. These entities, often called the mayor's office of strategic planning or mayor's office of sustainability, are generally designed to address "big picture" planning issues, while the planning department or division carries out the more routine work of planning, such as reviewing development applications. Typically, these offices contain only a small staff, but with mayoral support they can be effective advocates for a strong planning agenda. They tend to be short lived, however, reflecting the priorities of a particular mayor and often not outliving the tenure of the mayor who creates them.

In many respects the relationship between planning and other city agencies—rather than the place of planning in the city's organizational chart—ultimately determines whether plans become reality or sit on a shelf. Even where the will to work together and coordinate efforts around a strategic plan exists, systems need to be developed to ensure that people will work together and that decisions will be made in a timely fashion.

Successful outcomes may be furthered through interdepartmental reorganization. Some cities, for example, have incorporated key property regulatory functions such as code enforcement into a department that includes planning, housing, and community development to better integrate city operations, investments, and regulations involving land use and property. Another function that can offer valuable synergies if combined with planning and community development is responsibility for the city's vacant land and building inventory. The tasks involved can be managed effectively through use of well-designed information systems and management protocols. Controlling the inventory, moreover, gives the community development department a valuable tool to carry out its planning strategies.

Reorganization makes sense only where there is a clear, organic relationship among the different functions, as is the case with property-related activities. Beyond reorganization, effective planning requires interdepartmental or interagency coordination. One approach is to create task forces or working groups around specific subjects or issues; thus, when Philadelphia embarked on an ambitious effort to address its vast and complex vacant property problems, the city managing director's office created a series of working groups focused on information systems, property acquisition, and property disposition.

It is rare for planning or community development directors to convince their peers to engage in a process that subordinates at least some of their individual prerogatives to common goals. In fact, for such a process to be successful, it usually not only has to begin at the top but needs ongoing management from that level. For example, Mayor Frank Jackson of Cleveland appointed a chief of regional development to oversee the city's departments of economic development, community development, city planning, building and housing, port control, and equal opportunity.

Mechanisms for maintaining coordination can take the form of regular reporting to the mayor, city manager, or respected individual in the mayor's office; regular meetings of a coordinating committee or equivalent with the mayor or city manager; or meetings of the working groups, chaired by the city manager or a key deputy. In the last case, a logical role for the planner is to be the organizing force behind the process, working with the manager's office to define agendas and serving as the rapporteur from the meetings.

### The Scope of the Planner's Role

The planner often has only limited scope to influence the many city departments whose activities will determine whether or not a plan is carried out. In most cities the senior planning professional is not a member of the mayor's or city manager's cabinet and has little authority over implementation. But rather than simply carrying out narrowly prescribed duties without much concern for outcomes, planners working in bureaucratic environments should become advocates for planning, seizing opportunities to translate the planning agenda into action.

Planners may find kindred spirits in other departments and create informal networks through which coordination can take place. Alternatively, there may

### THE EXPANDING ROLE OF PHILANTHROPY

Municipal revenue and staff shortages mean many cities in transition have trouble implementing programs, and some even have trouble spending existing grants. Consequently, foundations, many of which have roots in legacy cities, are increasingly looking for opportunities to help build capacity in those cities. They can supplement existing governmental capacity by supporting training and the delivery of outside expertise, such as strengths, weaknesses, opportunities, and threats (SWOT) teams, consultants, and fellowships that bring in talented people. For example, the CUREx Fellowship program in New Orleans brought in young professionals to help rebuild the city's organizational infrastructure after Hurricane Katrina, and the Ford Foundation supports the Detroit Revitalization Fellows at Wayne State University. In late 2011, the Obama administration announced that the Rockefeller Foundation would be providing funding to the federal government to deploy fellows to six cities in transition through the Strong Cities, Strong Communities initiative.

According to Don Chen, senior program officer for metropolitan programs at the Ford Foundation, "we see more and more local governments on the verge of bankruptcy." Chen also observes that cities that remain solvent are providing fewer municipal services. In his view, deferred maintenance on public infrastructure has become a barrier to job growth and economic prosperity, and it seems conditions will get worse before they get better. For this reason, the Ford Foundation is now trying to identify innovative programs for infrastructure financing, such as an infrastructure banking pilot program in Los Angeles, as models for other projects at the regional, state, or even federal levels.

Chen cautions that while foundations can never meet all community demands, they can make a difference in helping cities in transition rebuild their local government capacities. Because rebuilding city capacity is a relatively new area for foundation activity, he notes, "We are constantly learning and refining our approaches to these initiatives." Moving forward, foundations will be carefully evaluating the impacts from these capacity-building grant-making strategies. ◀

be organizations outside city hall that will advocate for planning, including CDCs, councils of neighborhood associations, business organizations, and others. The Philadelphia Association of CDCs played important roles in encouraging the city to pursue an aggressive strategic approach to vacant properties and supporting the work of key staff in the city administration. Planners must be careful, of course, to operate within the bounds of what is considered acceptable by their superiors. In some cases that may be the subject of explicit protocols, but in others it may be a matter of unwritten practices and customs.

## FINDING RESOURCES FOR PLANNING

Finding the funds to support planning is a constant struggle in cities in transition. With flat or shrinking revenue bases and competing demands for public resources, cities are often reluctant to spend much for planning activities. In 2011 the City of San Diego abolished the planning department, cutting the number of positions by two-thirds and putting the remaining staff in a division within the city's department of development services. Cincinnati abolished its planning department in 2003, citing reasons beyond fiscal constraints, though it was reestablished in 2007.

With shrinking city revenues and widespread layoffs, planners are in the difficult position of competing with firefighters and police officers for resources. As a result, finding outside support for planning positions or specific activities has become increasingly important. Some cities support part of their planning staff with CDBG funds, up to 20 percent of which can be used for this purpose. Other potential sources of outside funding are "one-shot" funds or grants allocated on an annual basis or for a specified time frame, which may be more appropriate for specific activities or projects rather than ongoing positions. However, a resourceful planning director may be able to maintain staff by moving them from project to project as old grants end and new resources become available. The two most important sources of funds for planning are the federal government and foundations.

The federal government has supported planning intermittently since 1954, when Congress created the Section 701 planning grant program to cover costs associated with preparing comprehensive plans. More recently, the Federal Partnership for Sustainable Communities offered competitive grants for regional planning activities that integrate housing, land use, economic development, transportation, and infrastructure. Other federal grant programs in recent years have supported economic development, transportation, and infrastructure planning.

Foundations are another major source of planning support for cities in transition. The Kresge Foundation has provided Detroit with funding for its Detroit Works Project, while the Charles Stewart Mott Foundation has supported planning in its hometown of Flint. While national foundations like Ford or Rockefeller have supported some local planning activities over the years, they tend to focus on efforts that fit in their existing areas of interest or that are of potential national impact. Local or regional foundations are usually more likely to support efforts that can improve the quality of life or economic prospects of their home city or region. Notable examples include the William Penn Foundation in Philadelphia, the Cleveland and Gund foundations in Cleveland, and the Victoria Foundation in Newark, New Jersey. The national distribution of foundation resources, however, is highly uneven. Some cities may be able to tap only modest foundation resources.

Few foundations support planning generically; instead, they often have interests in specific planning activities that connect most strongly to their missions. Foundations with strong interests in community and neighborhood development may fund neighborhood revitalization plans, while those with strong environmental missions are more likely to support sustainability plans or greening strategies. Some will make grants to local governments, while others support only nonprofit entities like CDCs. Planners need to understand each foundation's priorities and boundaries in order to tailor a proposal. In pursuing foundation support, however, planners must always be mindful not to subordinate community priorities to those of the foundation, which may not match the needs of the community.

In addition to foundations, some United Way agencies have supported local planning, as have local businesses, either directly or through a philanthropic arm. Many of these entities provide planning funds exclusively to nonprofits. This may provide additional impetus for partnerships among cities, CDCs, and others to pursue joint planning strategies.

Finally, the value of local colleges and universities, particularly those with graduate programs in city planning, architecture, or public policy, should not be underestimated. Many students have sound planning and analytical skills—particularly those who have returned to school in midcareer—and can produce work that adds significant value to a city's planning efforts. Graduate consulting groups and outreach centers such as Pratt Institute's Center for Community Development in New York City are a valuable resource for practicing planners, while student interns can expand the capacity of a city or CDC.

## BUILDING PARTNERSHIPS

The challenges facing cities in transition demand that local governments, private organizations, and individuals work together. Local governments cannot tackle these problems alone or address separate issues in isolation. The problems of cities in transition are inextricably linked with one another. While there are many good examples of collaborative policy action that show great promise and provide replicable models, inherent in our strategic policy planning framework is the broader scope and more robust approach to planning necessary to transform existing revitalization programs into true regenerative action. In this section we take a closer look at the formation and nurturing of effective planning partnerships in cities in transition.

## TACKLING POLICY ISSUES

For our purposes, policy is the body of basic principles by which government is guided. The framework of policies affecting local public action includes (1) local policies followed by city government to govern its affairs, reflected formally in city ordinances and informally in local practices and customs, and (2) federal and state laws and regulations, administrative practices, and funding priorities.

Planners should not be passive actors in the process of debating and framing the policies that will affect the futures of their communities. Not only does the planning process inherently require planners to engage in policy issues, but the American Institute of Certified Planners' code of ethics calls on them to take active roles in this area:

> We shall seek social justice by working to expand choice and opportunity for all persons, recognizing a special responsibility to plan for the needs of the disadvantaged and to promote racial and economic integration. *We shall urge the alteration of policies, institutions, and decisions that oppose such needs.* (sec. A.1(f), emphasis added)

**CLEVELAND'S VACANT AND ABANDONED PROPERTIES ACTION COMMITTEE (VAPAC)**

Cleveland's VAPAC is a collaborative public and nonprofit working group focused on addressing vacant property policy and program issues throughout the city. VAPAC provides a vehicle to share information, coordinate existing public and nonprofit programs, and devise new programs and policies to cope with vacant properties at the city and neighborhood levels. Public members include the heads of the city's building department and housing and community development department, the mayor's chief of staff, members of city council, the housing court judge, the county treasurer, and the county director of community development. Funded by the Cleveland Foundation and coordinated by the community development intermediary Neighborhood Progress, Inc. (NPI), VAPAC draws other members from the local office of Enterprise Community Partners, the Federal Reserve Bank of Cleveland, the Cuyahoga County Land Reutilization Corporation, and the First Suburbs Consortium. Faculty and students at Cleveland State University and Case Western Reserve University provide technical support. ◀

## ► CDC PARTNERSHIPS

CDCs and other community-based community development organizations connect to residents and local businesses in the areas they serve to address the needs these constituents identify for reinforcing or remaking places to improve quality of life. While new housing development (affordable, workforce, and market rate) remains the primary mission for many community-based development organizations, a growing number of CDCs in cities experiencing dramatic population loss and substantial property disinvestment are shifting their focus to vacant land stewardship, demolition of derelict structures, park improvements, and safety enhancements.

CDCs may obtain funding from city and state governments, as well as from federal sources such as CDBG, HOME, and Low Income Housing Tax Credit allocations. Foundations and banks also provide support, often funneled along with additional federal funds through intermediaries and other support organizations. In many cities, national intermediaries such as the Local Initiatives Support Corporation (LISC) and Enterprise Community Partners function as conduits of funds targeted to achieve specified goals. For instance, LISC played a significant role in the Neighborhoods in Bloom program in Richmond, Virginia, by directing funding to selected neighborhoods, overcoming the tendency to spread funding more evenly but less effectively across a city (Galster et al. 2006). Intermediaries also provide training and other types of capacity building for community-based developers. Besides intermediaries, citywide nonprofit organizations provide support to many community-based development organizations in specialized areas such as legal assistance or techniques for brownfield redevelopment.

The community development system, or industry, in a city is vital to reinventing and strengthening neighborhoods in alignment with residents' interests. Figure 9.1 shows a simple diagram of a community development system. While some cities have few CDCs and little city government and intermediary support, others such as Cleveland have dozens of neighborhood-based CDCs that are well connected with other institutions (Yin 1998, Dewar and Thomas 2012).

Several features distinguish the Cleveland system from those in many other cities. First, Cleveland's community-based development organizations receive substantial support from the city, including about 25 percent of the city's CDBG allocations starting in 2009. In contrast, CDCs in Detroit received between 6 and 8 percent of CDBG funding annually between 2006 and 2009. This funding provides a base of support that enables continuity in staffing and activities. The strong commitment of local elected officials to community development has also meant that public institutions, such as the county land bank, effectively facilitate the work of community-based developers. Second, Cleveland has a strong local intermediary, Neighborhood Progress, Inc. (NPI), founded in 1989 by foundation and corporate leaders to increase the scale and pace of neighborhood physical development. While NPI's programs have evolved over time, its substantial long-term support has strengthened many CDCs. Third, the Cleveland Housing Network (CHN), founded by leaders of neighborhood organizations in 1981, functions as a large-scale housing developer, working in partnership with CDCs to advance their neighborhood agendas. CHN operates at a scale that manages risk and allows the employment of staff with high levels of skill in affordable housing development. Fourth, substantial grants from Cleveland foundations further support the work of NPI, CHN, and individual nonprofit development organizations. Finally, the varied players in the community development system work in a culture of cooperation with almost no publicly expressed rancor.

There are a number of actions that policy makers and planners in city government can take to strengthen and reinforce local community development systems:

- Improve systems for transferring tax-reverted properties for viable reuse projects

- Improve the subrecipient system for allocating CDBG funds to CDCs

- Integrate citywide planning and neighborhood planning so that city plans build on and reinforce resident-generated directions while remaining sensitive to markets

- Work with intermediaries, corporate leaders, foundation leaders, and others to provide training and operating support to CDCs

- Reinforce a culture of working cooperatively with CDCs (Mayer and Keyes 2005).

One of the challenges in any collaborative endeavor is building a stakeholder engagement process to ensure that partnerships remain stable, even as local officials and policy priorities change with election cycles. It is always a good idea to prepare a document that defines the roles, responsibilities, and relationships of the partners. As with any ongoing relationship it is critical to have a process for bringing in new partners and for refocusing missions as priorities shift within and outside of the organization.

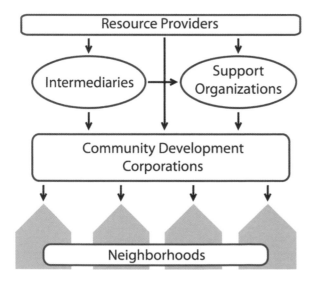

*Figure 9.1. The community development sector*

—*Margaret Dewar* ◄

While efforts to influence policy at the federal level are likely to take place through organizations such as APA or the National League of Cities, planners can be directly involved in policy efforts at the local and state levels. The latter is particularly important with respect to issues affecting cities in transition.

### Identifying Policy Issues

The first step in policy engagement is to identify and clearly define the issues at hand. While that may seem self-evident, unfortunately much policy discussion takes place without clear definitions of either the problem or the factors underlying it. Without such definitions and understanding, it is more than likely that policies that emerge from the process will fail to resolve the problem. Typically policy problems fall into two categories: policy gaps and counterproductive policies.

*Policy Gaps.* Many communities lack clear ideas of how to address many of the issues that they are facing; this is particularly true in cities in transition where the issues are complex and often fall outside the traditional purview of local government. In boom-bust cities in particular, many difficult economic and land-use challenges have fully emerged only in the past few years and have not yet been adequately recognized or addressed by local stakeholders.

Even where cities have been working for many years to address their problems, their practices may not be guided by coherent policies. How tools such as tax abatements to spur redevelopment and the disposition of publicly owned properties are used and how decisions are made have powerful implications both for cities' futures and their fiscal soundness, yet many cities lack clear guidelines, let alone well-grounded policies, to govern their use. Even smaller decisions, such as the size of a city's rental registration fee, have policy implications.

Planners are in strong positions to draw attention to critical issues because their training and ability to focus on the larger picture should enable them to spot these issues as they emerge and share information about them with policy makers and the community. They should identify areas in which the city should be developing policies and strategies to address its future and gather information on good practices in these areas. Important issues may include increased housing vacancy and abandonment, conversion of owner-occupied housing into rental housing, reuse of vacant land, manufacturing retention, affordable-housing program restructuring to reflect changes in housing market conditions, and allocation of discretionary funds. An important part of the planner's role is to encourage cities to adopt approaches and strategies that are more strongly driven by policy and better grounded in solid information and data.

*Counterproductive Policies.* While cities may lack clear policies in some areas, in others they may have policies that are inappropriate or counterproductive. Many of these policies may never have been formally discussed or adopted but have become matters of custom or responses to political pressures from constituencies. Such policies are often associated with property and land-use issues, where the tension between actions that satisfy a short-term need and those that provide the greatest long-term benefit is particularly great. Cities have been known to support development proposals without processes for considering alternatives or for analyzing the implications of those projects on housing markets or on their surroundings. For example, cities may sell properties at tax-foreclosure sales to investors to recoup unpaid taxes, even when those properties may bring in far greater returns to the city if held and reused.

## CITIES IN TRANSITION: THE ROLE OF STATE AND FEDERAL POLICY

In the past few years, long-standing arguments over the proper place of government in economic matters has intensified, with ideology often trumping sound evidence on both sides of the political aisle. Hyperbole and histrionics aside, no one really knows what perfect mix of government regulation and investment—how much or of what type—will produce the elixir our ailing economy needs. And simply waiting for the private sector to pull the rabbit out of the hat—along with millions of dollars and a lot of new jobs—is not doing the trick.

What does this mean for America's struggling cities, particularly legacy cities where the current economic downturn has only aggravated decades-long trends of job loss and neighborhood decline? What expectations should these places have for government policies that even in the best of times have often overlooked their specific circumstances and needs (Mallach 2010b). And ultimately how, with budgets as tight as they are, should planners work with public- and private-sector leaders to support the growth of innovative, sustainable, globally connected regional economies with high-quality, accessible jobs?

These are hard times in which to try to retool economies long on the wane. Wary about the durability of any recovery, businesses remain reluctant to hire, banks reluctant to lend, and consumers reluctant to purchase homes they worry will depreciate. On the public-sector side, the still weak and unpredictable economy has in turn helped create a fiscal and political environment that is contentious, constrained, and a target of deep frustration for much of the country.

But government's role in boosting regional economic competitiveness remains essential. While an innovative and flexible private sector will necessarily lead the way toward the "next" economy, public policies and investments can and must help lay the groundwork for private-sector strength, filling gaps that the pri-

*(continued on page 126)*

*(continued from page 125)*

vate sector will not and creating the conditions in which markets, places, and people can flourish.

What types of government actions should planners encourage, and from where are they most likely to come? For now, planners and their colleagues should dial down their expectations for Washington. When the new administration came into office in January 2009, hopes for a renewed federal focus on urban issues ran high—and in some ways appeared to be fulfilled. The early creation of the White House Office of Urban Affairs and programs such as the Partnership for Sustainable Communities are among several concrete ways federal leaders have demonstrated a more refined understanding of and commitment to the country's cities and metro regions.

These efforts are steps in the right direction. But the restructuring of distressed urban economies must further include a far more robust set of policies in areas as disparate as exports, energy, innovation, manufacturing, infrastructure, education, and skills training—and much of that work is still nascent at best.

This is not to say that state and local stakeholders should not work to enlist the support of the federal government for their initiatives or advocate for federal policies that align with their interests. But given the political gridlock inside the Beltway, planners and economic developers might invest more of their energies closer to home by helping state and metro leaders develop and execute policy innovations that will propel their regions'—and ultimately the nation's—economies forward. Such innovations need not wait for new, hard-to-come-by sources of funding. In fact, the smartest states and localities will use the fiscal crisis as a "glass half full" moment to push through needed reforms, while being more strategic about how to invest scarce resources.

To this end, planners working in distressed communities should ally with private, public, and philanthropic leaders around a few key policy areas that will help set the right platform for economic prosperity. Such efforts should transcend the bounds of traditional urban policy, which have tended toward narrow interventions focused on housing, neighborhood-scale revitalization, or city distress management. They must instead incorporate a broader, more systemic focus on maximizing regional assets necessary to improving local economies. Here's how:

*Match goals, resources, and delivery systems to the metropolitan geography of the economy.* In order for any urban policy agenda to have real impact, local, regional, and state leaders and stakeholders must be organized to successfully carry it out. In practice this means pushing state and local governments to more effectively administer programs and services that correspond with the metropolitan geography of the economy, as well as building the capacity of political, business, and community leaders to create and sustain collaborative, cross-sector networks within and across existing municipal boundaries.

Planners and economic developers, for their parts, should work with regional leaders to build broad, diverse coalitions of innovative thinkers and stakeholders—from major corporations to small business owners, environmental advocates to university presidents—who can together develop a competitive vision for their region, pick a few big bets around which to focus early efforts, and design a strategy plan to get things done.

States should be enlisted to support such efforts by offering incentives for local coordination and planning for state-funded projects. The planning community should also encourage state government to better coordinate economic development, infrastructure, workforce, and other economy-building programs across state agencies and to target state resources in ways that minimize interlocal competition and maximize metropolitan competitiveness.

*Build on existing regional economic strengths and connect them to the global economy.* Cities in transition are up against economic forces that are often too powerful to be overcome by tax incentives or other programs aimed primarily at financing high-profile real estate projects or luring businesses from other communities. What is needed instead is a better brand of economic development that focuses on nurturing the creation and growth of innovative, productive, and global-oriented industries and jobs.

To this end, planners and economic developers at the local and state levels must undertake ongoing, rigorous analysis of the types and locations of existing or potential regional niches and clusters, and then realign resources to foster innovation and entrepreneurship in those areas. They also need to develop a clearer understanding of their metros' export capacities and work with existing public and private export promotion offices to enhance firms' abilities to identify and successfully tap international markets (Muro and Fikri 2011, Katz and Estrate 2011).

*Reform land-use policies for economic and fiscal growth.* Finally, cities in transition need to be able to more readily convert vacant and underutilized properties from burdens to key assets for business growth, job creation, and neighborhood revitalization. Unfortunately, many states' weak and antiquated laws on tax foreclosure, land banking, code enforcement, and other topics can make this a time-consuming, complicated, and expensive process.

Planners and economic developers need to advocate for the overhaul of state laws and practices that undercut their communities' abilities to repurpose vacant land and buildings for future growth and regeneration. Policy reforms should give localities greater power to use tax foreclosure as a means by which to gain control of problem properties; grant them more flexible authority to use code enforcement and nuisance abatement to help eliminate blight and stabilize neighborhoods; and better allow them to hold, manage, and dispose of properties in ways that are sensitive to market realities and that support specific long-term economic development goals.

*—Jennifer S. Vey*

## Changing Local Policies

Local policies are defined and expressed through a variety of means. The central vehicle for expressing city government policies is the code of ordinances. While ordinances are operational documents in that they set forth what the city will do rather than why, they are based on policy—implicit or explicit—and should be drafted to reflect policies that have been adopted after careful consideration. Policy and procedure documents developed within city government as guides for action are also important. For matters with significant implications for the future, such as tax abatement or vacant land disposition, the city should have written policies and procedures formally approved by the mayor or city manager and by city council.

Comprehensive plans and strategic policy framework plans, as well as other planning documents such as neighborhood revitalization plans and the consolidated plan prepared for HUD, should have well-defined policy goals and strategies. These should be clearly reflected in the specific action proposals or fund allocations in the plan and should serve as guides for local government practice in areas affecting planning outcomes.

Planners should identify areas where city policies and practices are working against long- or short-term interests and bring them, along with alternative strategies, to the attention of elected officials and other key policy makers. This may be an uphill battle. Not only may the planner's ability to influence policy be limited, but even a patently counterproductive policy may have some rationale for its continued existence. Balancing this year's budget may take precedence in many minds over a potential but uncertain long-term return.

## Changing State Policies

Both policy gaps and counterproductive policies can be found at state as well as the local level. Under the U.S. system of government, cities are creatures of the state. While some states give more leeway to local governments or to certain cities designated as "home rule cities," local officials still largely depend on state government to define the parameters within which they operate and the manners in which they must carry out their responsibilities. State laws define how cities can regulate land use within their boundaries, the scope of their planning powers, and the extent and manner in which cities can use financial tools such as tax abatement, tax increment financing, tax foreclosure, or industrial development bonds.

Many policy gaps exist concerning the tools that the state provides its local governments, which define the scope of actions local governments are legally permitted to take. For example, some states permit cities to use what is known as "spot blight" eminent domain (i.e., the ability to use eminent domain to take scattered blighting properties for reuse, rather than only properties in designated areas for which redevelopment plans have been adopted). Similarly, some states permit vacant property receivership to enable deteriorated properties to be restored to productive use. Both are valuable tools for revitalization; most states, however, do not provide cities or nonprofits with the legal authority to exercise them.

Even more important, state policies may often establish ground rules or prescribe practices that are counterproductive from a long-term policy standpoint. State laws governing tax foreclosure, for example, may make it difficult or impossible for cities to gain control of tax-delinquent properties, forcing them to sell the properties to investors. Not only does this practice often yield less return to the city than if it could retain control of the properties, but it often contributes to a revolving door of repeated tax delinquency and abandonment. In many states policies governing such matters as taxation and transportation or economic development funding may work against urban redevelopment and revitalization, fostering counterproductive competition between cities and townships in a metropolitan area and between metropolitan areas within a state.

Knowledgeable city planners can play important roles in influencing state policies by lending their time and expertise to organizations and coalitions working on state policy issues. In many states strong coalitions have emerged that have fostered important changes either to state legislation or state administrative practices affecting cities and neighborhoods. The Housing Alliance of Pennsylvania spearheaded a coalition that has led to major legislative actions dealing with blighted properties, while in New Jersey the Housing and Community Development Network—a statewide CDC association—has taken the lead in getting legislation dealing with abandoned properties, foreclosure, and neighborhood revitalization enacted.

APA chapters engage in policy advocacy in their states, but planners by themselves rarely have the influence that state organizations such as municipal leagues, and in some cases CDC associations, environmental groups, or smart growth advocates, may have. APA chapters should join larger coalitions advocating for changes in state policies and practices and should facilitate bringing their members' expertise to bear on those issues.

Some victories are more easily won than others. Though many state coalitions have been successful in obtaining stronger tools to fight blight, changing other policies can be far more difficult if there are any entities with compelling interests in seeing such policies retained. The disparities in taxation and local finance between cities and townships in Ohio, for example, undermine the economic competitiveness of older cities within their regions but are perceived by the townships as clearly being in their interest. Any change to that system will be a major struggle.

## CONCLUSION

The challenges of the planner's job in a city in transition go beyond the conventional planning tasks of framing plans and strategies and adapting planning tools to address the challenges of those cities. The nature of those tasks—and the extent to which they require engagement by others in government, the private sector, and the larger community—demands that planners play active roles in building the environment for planning inside and outside city hall, building partnerships with other stakeholders, and addressing policy changes needed to turn planning strategies into effective action. Planners must navigate the political and bureaucratic straits of cities where competition for scarce resources can create intense political conflict; build relationships with a diverse body of individuals and organizations; and be the voice for long-term, strategic thinking in settings where regular crises make it a constant challenge to think beyond the day-to-day struggles of survival.

# CHAPTER 10

# Conclusion

 Planning practice in cities in transition is a different kind of planning. It draws on the body of traditional planning tools but adapts it to address the economic difficulties and complex land-use problems that these cities face. Fundamentally these cities must shift directions, and a more strategic approach to planning can help enable this change. The planner's role in cities in transition is, more than anything else, to foster that change: to work with public agencies, private organizations, and the community to frame strategies, recalibrate planning tools, and harness resources that can help cities in transition change their trajectories and find paths toward regeneration.

This new twist on planning demands creative approaches that have more to do with strategy, policy, market building, community organizing, and resource allocation than with conventional planning models. Cities in transition can no longer rely on classic development-driven planning and economic development models but must forge new strategies that facilitate more sustainable growth. These realities demand new skills from the planner: the ability to coordinate and integrate multiple actors, plans, and strategies; the ability to link planning, strategy, and implementation; a thoroughgoing sensitivity to both market dynamics and to the strains present in economically and racially diverse and often fractured communities; the skills to analyze and interpret the economic and social implications of development and resource-allocation decisions; and, above all, the ability to act as a change agent in a complex, fluid environment.

The environment for planning in cities in transition is not only complex but challenging. Both public and private resources are severely limited. Market demand is often weak, with few developers actively seeking to build new housing and nonresidential buildings or to restore old vacant properties. The decline of civic infrastructure—nonprofits, community and neighborhood groups—makes it especially difficult for new planning strategies to gain traction, especially in neighborhoods with decades of disinvestment where distrust is often high and confidence in local government remains low. Moreover, public revenues continue to decline in many cities as competition for the few available dollars becomes fierce. Professional and technical capacity is often in short supply, even more so following widespread local government downsizing in recent years, and small planning staffs are often spread too thin to permit reflection or strategic planning. Pressures to choose alternatives that provide short-term cash or improvement over those that offer greater long-term benefit are intense. Cumulatively these challenges give rise to many competing interests and agendas within city government, among private and nonprofit stakeholders, and across diverse factions of neighborhoods and residents. Planners have to skillfully navigate these competing pressures while building consensus for plans that offer the greatest long-term gains with the limited resources available.

Given the difficulties of being a planner in a city in transition, one might ask why anyone would choose such a job. There are many reasons. In cities in transition all of the issues that planners study—land use, transportation, neighborhood planning, social and economic issues, and policy formation— come to life. Moreover, in contrast to more prosperous cities where developers and other private interests often call the shots, the public sector—and by extension the planner—in a city in transition is in a far stronger position to chart the course of the city's future. Even more important, planners working in these cities can be key participants in efforts to rebuild communities— economically, socially, and physically—that have been undermined by economic forces beyond their control.

As the many examples in this report show, much of the work being done in cities in transition is at the cutting edge of planning practice. This includes many initiatives being pursued in legacy cities, such as the Youngstown 2010 plan, Detroit's Lower Eastside Action Plan, Re-imagining a More Sustainable Cleveland, and Dayton's Green and Gold Investment Strategy. Creative problem-property strategies are also being initiated in smaller gateway cities like Allentown, Pennsylvania, and first suburbs like Orange, New Jersey, as described in the Appendix. While there are few similar planning initiatives emerging yet from boom-bust cities, where the traumatic changes of recent years are still being absorbed and assimilated, creative planners in cities like Las Vegas are already thinking through how new economic realities will affect their cities' futures and how to change their planning practices to respond to these realities.

These initiatives and planning efforts are all quite recent; the oldest one cited in this report, the Youngstown 2010 plan, was completed in 2005. Most date from only the past two or three years, if even that. While it is far too early to draw many lessons from the experiences of these cities, we strongly suggest that planners think about these cities less in terms of grand master plans in the tradition of Daniel Burnham and more in terms of "strategic incrementalism": the ability to move forward incrementally, seizing opportunities as they emerge, but always working within the framework of a clear overall strategy of change. This, in different variations, is the approach being pursued in Cleveland and Dayton. In contrast, looking at Youngstown's experience, the 2010 plan may have changed attitudes, but its effect on the city's on-the-ground reality has been far more limited. Reflecting this perspective, much of this report is not about how to construct a plan in the traditional sense but about how to adapt traditional tools and align existing policies, programs, and resources (e.g., economic development, vacant property reuse, neighborhood revitalization, and more) so that they become part of a broader, strategic approach for regenerating the city.

*Investments in public infrastructure facilitate revitalization in Baltimore.*

Joseph Schilling

For planners who are interested in helping to shape the future of America's cities, cities in transition are truly where the action is—arguably the most interesting and challenging work that a practicing planner can find in this country. It is difficult, but it is work that reflects the highest ideals and values of the planning profession.

# Case Studies

The following case studies of Detroit; Orange, New Jersey; Allentown, Pennsylvania; and Rialto, California, highlight how four different types of cities in transition (legacy, gateway, first suburbs, and boom-bust) are working to address the challenges of neighborhood decline, vacant properties, and problem properties. Some similarities appear, such as the reliance on resources from the U.S. Department of Housing and Urban Development's Neighborhood Stabilization Program for housing rehabilitation in Allentown, Orange, and Rialto. All focus on neighborhood preservation and housing rehabilitation as major priorities. Three of the examples were driven by community-based development corporations (CDAD in Detroit, HANDS in Orange, Civic Stone in Rialto), while Allentown illustrates strategies within city hall for revamping code enforcement and nuisance abatement processes.

### DETROIT: TESTING A COLLABORATIVE, COMMUNITY-DRIVEN STRATEGIC PLAN FOR RECONFIGURING VACANT LAND

The city of Detroit exemplifies the challenges confronting legacy cities. Given its size and dramatic population loss, the scale and complexity of its challenges seem daunting even when compared with other shrinking cities like Cleveland, Buffalo, Flint, and Youngstown. Over the past several years, citizens and city officials have started to change the conversations about and trajectory of Detroit, but they must still acknowledge and confront a long history of political turmoil, failed policies, and community distrust.

This case study describes a promising community-driven approach orchestrated by the city's community-development trade association, Community Development Advocates of Detroit (CDAD). Before Detroit Works, a citywide planning initiative led by the mayor's office, CDAD worked on its own strategic land-use framework (2010) acknowledging the city's diverse landscape, which ranges from tree-lined residential blocks to acres of vacant land. CDAD tested the framework by using a four-stage collaborative process in Detroit's Lower Eastside and Springwells Village neighborhoods. By engaging residents in honest conversations about what their communities should look like, CDAD achieved great success in developing a common vision, a common language, and a common lens.

#### Housing Vacancy Challenge

Detroit's vacancy problem is well-known. Although there are many theories as to how the city arrived at its current predicament, the statistics are undeniable: Detroit has roughly 40 square miles of vacant land. Forty years of recession and the collapse of the manufacturing base have wreaked havoc on neighborhood stability, causing the city to lose population at the alarming rate of 65 people per day since 2000.

*Vacant land in Detroit*

The city's vacancy problem speaks for itself, but it also throws a lesser-known fact into sharp relief: Detroit is huge. It covers 139 square miles; the footprints of Manhattan, San Francisco, and Boston together all fit within the city's boundaries. This land mass contains enough expensive public infrastructure to support an estimated 2.5 million people—for a city whose population peaked at 1.8 million in 1950.

Detroit's economic woes were compounded by the bursting of the housing bubble in 2007. As the number of foreclosures skyrocketed and prices plummeted, the city's housing market all but disappeared. The 2010 census count of 713,777 solidified a point that was rarely spoken before: Detroit has an abundance of land without the housing market to fill it.

This hard truth was most apparent to the community development industry. In 2009, CDAD formed a task force to address the crisis. This task force brought together community leaders, development professionals, and government representatives in an effort to change a community development industry that could no longer count on housing as a source of dependable revenue.

## Changing the Conversation

The result was CDAD's "Strategic Framework for Neighborhood Revitalization," a white paper published in February 2010 directly confronting the fact that Detroit might never again be a city of two million people. It outlined 10 theoretical neighborhood types, depicting aspirational visions of what each could become in the future, and provided a new definition of what a stabilized neighborhood could look like.

The CDAD strategic framework addresses a gamut of land-use types—including traditional residential uses, extremely low-density residential uses, mixed use development, light industrial zones, and natural preserves—all packaged within a vocabulary designed to be easily understood by Detroit residents. Table A.1 briefly outlines each of these typologies.

*Table A.1. The CDAD strategic framework typologies and the "taglines" created by residents to help remember which is which*

| Land-Use Type | "Tagline" |
|---|---|
| Traditional Residential | Tree-lined blocks with neighbors on every lot |
| Spacious Residential | Big yards with fewer neighbors |
| Urban Homestead | Quiet, self-reliant living with access to Detroit's cultural amenities |
| Naturescape | Managed landscapes showcasing Detroit's natural assets |
| Green Thoroughfare | Green, well-lit traveling corridors for walking, wheeling, and driving |
| Village Hub | Convenient and walkable shopping and living |
| Shopping Hub | Drive-to shopping |
| City Hub | Center of city commerce with residential living opportunities |
| Green Venture Zone | Blue and green job zones enhancing the quality of life |
| Industry | Heavy production job zones |

## A Tempest Brews

The notion of "shrinking" Detroit is not new. Former city ombudsman Marie Farrell-Donaldson famously proposed "mothballing" certain areas of the city in 1993. In 2008, the American Institute of Architects' Sustainable Design Assistance Team published a visionary report for Detroit depicting "urban villages" surrounded by green space. These ideas spurred conversation about shrinking the city, but when published they met with ridicule and understandable suspicion from residents who had all-too-recent memories of disastrous urban renewal projects.

Shortly after the publication of CDAD's strategic framework, a series of events took place that did not bode well for any efforts to reconfigure the land-use pattern in Detroit.

On February 24, 2010, prompted by the release of a citywide residential parcel survey, Mayor Dave Bing announced his plans to rightsize Detroit. Citing the need to balance the enormity of vacant land and the city's $300 million budget deficit, Bing said that the city administration "can't support every neighborhood in the city" and that relocation programs would be imminent, thereby creating "winners and losers."

This prompted a firestorm, with community activists railing against the ever-present specter of eminent domain, which now seemed very real. *The Michigan Citizen*, which proclaims itself "America's most progressive community newspaper," unleashed a series of articles deriding the mayor, calling any effort to shrink Detroit "a modern-day trail of tears" whose goal was to abet a "land grab" for "special interests." Other progressive newspapers followed suit. The backlash against the mayor's words only solidified CDAD's belief that the most effective way to discuss vacant-land reuse was through facilitated neighborhood-level conversations hosted by local partners.

There were other misconceptions around the notion of shrinking the city. Many Detroiters mistakenly thought that shrinking the city meant redrawing the municipal boundaries. Eastside residents asked if they would be absorbed into nearby Grosse Pointe, or—much worse—be forced to form a separate municipality entirely. The concept of urban farming, hailed for years as a possible new source of revenue, was also of concern to residents. Because many Detroiters can trace a lineage rooted in migration from the agrarian South, the idea triggered mixed reactions. Some feared that they would be forced to farm. One community resident stood up at a public meeting and succinctly declared, "My family used to be farmers. We came up here to get away from farming. I'll be damned if I'm going back to it."

Amid this tempest, CDAD engaged residents in participatory planning conversations about reconfiguring land in Detroit. While many residents feared being forced from their homes, CDAD proposed a menu of options that promised "a future for every part of the city." However, in order for the CDAD strategic framework to be successful, CDAD had to field-test it and establish a replicable process that would allow any community to create its own neighborhood plan.

## The Lower Eastside Action Plan

CDAD partnered with local CDCs to establish two pilot projects in two very different areas of the city. One pilot was located in the Springwells Village neighborhood of southwest Detroit. A vibrant immigrant community, Springwells Village boasts the most active commercial corridor in Detroit. The other pilot, launched on the far east side of Detroit with a coalition of eight CDCs, was dubbed the Lower Eastside Action Plan (LEAP).

Perhaps nowhere were the fear and misconception around shrinking the city felt more strongly than the Lower Eastside, a neighborhood encompassing the largest agglomeration of vacant land in Detroit. Local CDCs needed an effective way to facilitate conversations about alternative land use. The CDAD strategic framework provided an unprecedented vehicle for residents, planners, and community leaders to discuss how to turn the current land-use challenges into assets.

The LEAP process provided the Lower Eastside community with three important elements—a common vision, a common language, and a common lens—that many communities in Detroit currently lack.

*A Common Vision.* While bold ideas are necessary to reimagine Detroit, history has shown that real change is best achieved through incremental action on the part of many actors. Large-scale interventions such as one-shot "catalytic" developments have proved to be ineffective in creating lasting change in Detroit neighborhoods and, perhaps more insidiously, have squandered finite resources.

During the housing bubble of the early 2000s, the amount of vacant land on the east side made it attractive to public- and private-sector development, but the relics of half-completed basements from numerous false-start developments that now litter the area had created much uncertainty about the viability of future investment. Community development organizations needed a cohesive vision for the area and a coordinated strategy to achieve it. The LEAP process provided them with a mutually agreed-upon, community-generated map that ensures an efficient use of resources in the years to come. This coordinated action requires the local CDCs to take on new roles such as land management and urban agriculture. CDAD is currently working with LEAP partners and others to assess the emerging needs of CDCs as they take on these new roles.

*A Common Language.* Because the Lower Eastside must pioneer land-use and neighborhood-stabilization strategies to cope with an unprecedented level of vacant land, community organizations needed to create a new vocabulary to communicate these ideas and facilitate dialogue with residents. More than anything else, the CDAD strategic framework provides building blocks for conversation. The 10 typologies are theoretical constructs that quickly allow a layperson to understand sophisticated planning concepts. Included in each neighborhood type is a set of technical implications, such as a continuum of density levels, suggested adjacent uses, industry emission standards, transportation options, and economic development strategies. Packaging these technical planning issues into concise future-oriented visions allows a facilitator to elicit technical feedback without the conversation feeling esoteric. It also provides a common platform from which to share best practices with practitioners in other areas of the city.

*A Common Lens.* Past government efforts to target investment in particular neighborhoods had seemed random or nonscientific, creating mistrust among many community organizations. Many community activists had questioned the rigor of and rationale behind city-sponsored programs such as Mayor Kwame Kilpatrick's 2007 Next Detroit Neighborhood Initiative and a hodgepodge of other philanthropic targeting initiatives. Throughout 2009 and 2010 there was an outcry from the community development industry to make the process of targeting investment more transparent and based on data rather than anecdotal perception surrounding neighborhoods.

This is why CDAD partnered with Data Driven Detroit (D3), a regional data collection, storage, and analysis firm, to create a system of indicators for the strategic framework typologies. The resultant three analyses looked at Detroit's residential, commercial, and industrial parcels through the lens of CDAD's typologies. D3's residential analysis presents a spectrum of residential health ranging from areas currently most similar to Traditional Residential Zones to areas that are currently most like Naturescapes or Green Venture Zones. Likely candidates for Spacious Residential Zones and Urban Homesteads score near the middle of the spectrum. Framing the analysis this way allows residents to think about the future direction of their neighborhood within the context of its current condition. This analysis allowed Lower Eastside residents to compare their neighborhoods with the rest of the city in a way never done before. This recognition of the area's extraordinary vacancy issues prompted residents who might otherwise advocate only for infill housing to be more open to alternative strategies of neighborhood stabilization.

*Part of Data Driven Detroit's residential analysis*

Data Driven Detroit

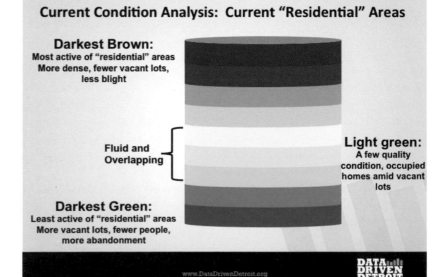

**Current Condition Analysis: Current "Residential" Areas**

**Darkest Brown:**
Most active of "residential" areas
More dense, fewer vacant lots,
less blight

**Fluid and Overlapping**

**Light green:**
A few quality condition, occupied homes amid vacant lots

**Darkest Green:**
Least active of "residential" areas
More vacant lots, fewer people,
more abandonment

www.DataDrivenDetroit.org

**DATA DRIVEN DETROIT**

## The CDAD Process

CDAD is now compiling its final toolkit to help CDCs citywide embark on participatory planning processes of their own. The toolkit includes a recommended process forged from lessons learned from both of the pilots. The process is broken down into four phases:

*Phase 1: Data.* The primary objective of Phase 1 is to present data analyses to neighborhood residents and ask them to identify any inaccuracies using their expert on-the-ground knowledge. Additionally, stakeholders are asked during the first community meeting to regularly attend future meetings and form a stakeholder advisory group (SAG). The SAG ensures consistent decision making throughout the process and forms a corps of increasingly informed residents who are able to convey decisions to their neighbors. This body of informed neighbors helps to instill trust that recommendations are made with ample community input. By vetting D3's analyses with the SAG, LEAP fostered early ownership of the process and built trust with residents, ensuring that future decisions would be made with accurate data.

D3's analyses compiled data at the census-block level, providing a precise scale of measurement needed to reflect the chiaroscuro that exists in Detroit neighborhoods—where stable streets can be directly adjacent to severely distressed ones. It allowed residents to stitch together multiple typologies into a single neighborhood to create flexible and customized neighborhood plans.

*Phase 2: Deliberate.* During this phase, residents break out into small groups and, through facilitated discussions with local partners, create a shared vision for their neighborhood 10 years into the future. LEAP's Steering Committee, made up of resident representatives, CDC leaders, and technical advisors, thought that 10 years struck a balance between idealistic long-range planning and realistic, feasible actions.

In 1997, Mayor Dennis Archer's Community Reinvestment Strategy (CRS) planning process had asked Detroit residents to create neighborhood plans for themselves. Although CRS is often touted by community groups for its level of community engagement, it is criticized for creating plans without considering available resources for implementation because it asked residents "What do you want?" as opposed to "What can we achieve?" The CDAD strategic framework process seeks to avoid this misstep.

To create a feasible vision, the Springwells Village pilot used a visioning exercise using LEGO bricks to represent chunks of "resources." Residents then spent resources using a custom-made slide rule that calculated the expenditure needed to get from a current condition to a desired future direction. LEAP went through an iterative process over the course of several meetings in which residents provided feedback about desires that were then flagged for feasibility by technical consultants. LEAP's Steering Committee developed the final version of the 10-year vision statement.

*Participants in a visioning exercise, allocating "resources" with LEGO bricks*

Joseph Schilling

***Phase 3: Decide.*** Once consensus is reached on the future vision of the neighborhood, residents then participate in further facilitated small-group discussions to decide on the priority areas that should receive immediate action. Springwells Village did this through another LEGO brick exercise in which residents identified census blocks that should be prioritized over the next five years, while LEAP created a subcommittee that identified six action projects for immediate fund-raising and implementation. The six projects included working with wealthy businessman John Hantz to find a location for his 500-acre commercial farm, assisting local nonprofit The Greening of Detroit with the reforestation of multiple sites, identifying dense residential areas for stabilization, and creating business-relocation incentives to encourage active commercial nodes at key intersections.

***Phase 4: Do.*** The last phase of the CDAD process involves working with community residents to identify specific intervention steps within the prioritized areas that culminate in an actionable work plan. Springwells Village did this through small-group facilitated discussions using a matrix of suggested interventions for the typologies. The Springwells Village host CDC, Urban Neighborhood Initiatives (UNI), is now working with other local partners to present the intervention priorities to funders and the City of Detroit, which has selected the neighborhood as one of Mayor Bing's Detroit Works short-term demonstration areas.

Partners at the LEAP table are discussing how best to continue momentum as they seek funding to implement future projects. LEAP is also currently advocating for the city's planning and development department to "adopt" their 10-year vision. LEAP, UNI, and CDAD are fashioning policy recommendations and design guidelines for each of the typologies that one day could translate into zoning overlay language. Toward this end, CDAD is working with an urban-agriculture work group convened by the city's planning commission to discuss rewriting the city's zoning codes.

CDAD seeks to build a culture of grassroots planning in Detroit that will continue long into the future. LEAP has already launched a second phase of planning in an additional area on the east side (dubbed "LEAP Phase II") to be completed in the summer of 2012. CDAD hopes communities that complete the strategic framework process will reconvene after five years to evaluate progress and recalibrate their vision and interventions as necessary.

### Residents and Alternative Land Use

Because of the Lower Eastside's unique landscape, several surveys taken of SAG members offer useful insight into resident reactions to alternative land-use concepts:

***Strategic Density.*** The range of uses offered by CDAD's strategic framework can provide a unique competitive advantage, turning Detroit's excess vacant land into an asset. For instance, a city with half of its footprint currently zoned for single-family housing, once the bedrock of the mid-20th-century middle-class lifestyle, now has the opportunity to offer a greater variety of housing forms to a wider customer base. Such housing choices could include dense mixed use lofts or low-density living that might normally be found in more rural settings.

Many Detroiters still think a suburban-style housing unit is a desirable residential form and therefore showed some preference for Spacious Residential Zones. Side-lot adoption is thought to be an effective way to stabilize neighborhoods and encourage larger lot sizes. This is in slight contrast to survey results indicating Lower Eastside residents have a real desire for walkability—69 percent of respondents said that walkability was very important to them and that walking was their preferred mode of travel. This result was echoed anecdotally in southwest Detroit, where Springwells Village residents also expressed a strong desire for larger lots but wanted to walk to commercial amenities.

Lower Eastside residents were split over the desirability of low-density living. When asked where residents would like to see Urban Homesteads, the top two answers were "I want to live on an Urban Homestead" (36 percent of respondents) and "more than 5 blocks away" (27 percent). Those residents who desired low-density living saw the surrounding natural landscape, coupled with the proximity to Detroit's cultural assets, as a reason to stay in the city.

***Nonpolluting Light Industrial Areas.*** The vacant land of Detroit's east side offers new economic development opportunities such as industries centered on urban agriculture, fish farms, and food processing centers. LEAP area residents deemed Green Venture Zones desirable, as long as they provide a significant amount of jobs and the exported product benefits the community first. Community benefits were a slightly higher priority for residents than the number of jobs created. Of the types of Green Venture Zones discussed, including commercial agriculture, tree farms, hydroponic farms, and biodiesel crops, residents clearly preferred food production.

***Low-Maintenance Natural Landscapes.*** The CDAD strategic framework encourages awareness of environmental sustainability and promotes healthier lifestyles for residents. Deliberate planning for natural areas can mitigate problems with stormwater runoff and promote a larger tree canopy. The creation of Naturescapes and Green Thoroughfares can provide residents with opportunities to enjoy passive recreation such as walking trails and greenways.

Survey respondents desired natural areas with passive recreation as long as they did not pose safety hazards for nearby residents. Predictably, with the Lower Eastside's proximity to the Detroit River, residents preferred to see Naturescapes that contributed to wetlands restoration and mitigated stormwater runoff. Along Detroit's eastern coastline, there are more than 100 acres of riverfront parks, only some of which receive regular maintenance. LEAP area residents identified parks they wanted to remain as such and those they wanted to transform into wetland Naturescapes.

### The Role of the Neighborhood Planner and Vacant Land

As postindustrial cities continue to face uncertainty about the future of their neighborhoods, critical decisions around vacant land will most likely occur in neighborhoods made up of low-income citizens. Engaging these residents on the issue of land use will rise to unprecedented importance. Although the CDAD pilots were drastically different from each other, they exhibit both the importance of the neighborhood planner's role as facilitator and the community's ability to comment, and ultimately decide, on technical planning issues in a meaningful way.

For community organizations to engage with their communities, it is necessary for them—in partnership with the neighborhood planner—to demystify the planning profession. Empowering low-income communities is necessary to overcome their distrust of government and their general feelings of disenfranchisement over land-use planning decisions. The technical expert's role then changes from making decisions to crafting tools to let community residents make their own decisions. The latter role is far more difficult.

*—Sam Butler*

**ALLENTOWN, PENNSYLVANIA: LEVERAGING CODE ENFORCEMENT WITH STRATEGIC ACQUISITION TO ADDRESS PROBLEM PROPERTIES**

Many small, older industrial cities in the Northeast and Midwest regions have dramatically lost population over the past 60 years. Pennsylvania cities with at least 30,000 residents in 2010 collectively lost more than 1 million residents between 1950 and 2010, representing nearly one-third of their combined population (Table A.2). As a gateway city for Hispanic immigrants, Allentown, now Pennsylvania's third-most populous city, is an exception. Thanks to population increases, Allentown's housing stock is largely occupied, and the city does not face serious abandonment issues. Still, property conditions and values in the city's central neighborhoods have continued to decline.

Though Allentown has experienced disinvestment similar to that in other postindustrial cities, the decline occurred there well after it did elsewhere. While many northeastern and midwestern cities hit low points in the 1970s, Allentown did not lose its last downtown department store until well into the 1990s, the same decade that Bethlehem Steel's primary production plant in the area closed. Reflecting the loss of the nation's second-largest steel producer, the number of area manufacturing jobs began to fall precipitously during the 1990s.

Though Allentown seemed poised to go the way of legacy cities like Buffalo and Pittsburgh, an influx of Hispanic residents in the 1990s began to offset the losses (Figure A.1). The city's demographic shift over the last 30 years has been dramatic. According to the Census Bureau, the city's share of residents identifying as Hispanic has roughly doubled each decade since 1980: from 5 percent in 1980 to 12 percent in 1990, then to 24 percent in 2000 and 42 percent in 2010 (Figure A.2). By that year nearly one-third (31 percent) of residents spoke Spanish at home.

As is typical of gateway cities, Allentown's population growth was not paralleled by economic growth. The area's manufacturing sector crumbled through the 1990s, although it did increase slightly in the 2000s. In 2009, three out of every four working Allentown residents (77 percent) traveled to jobs outside the city.

**The Redevelopment Authority Responds**

From 2007 to early 2011, I ran the Redevelopment Authority of the City of Allentown (RACA). Although geographically focused on the city, RACA is a creature of the state, formed in 1956 under the Pennsylvania Urban Redevelopment Law of 1945. As the law stresses, a redevelopment authority "shall in no way be deemed to be an instrumentality

*Table A.2.* Population trends in Pennsylvania cities over 30,000 population

Source: U.S. Census

| Location | 1950 Population | 2010 Population | Change | Percent of Change |
|---|---|---|---|---|
| Allentown | 106,756 | 118,032 | 11,276 | 11 |
| Altoona | 77,177 | 46,320 | −30,857 | −40 |
| Bethlehem | 66,340 | 74,982 | 8,642 | 13 |
| Chester | 66,039 | 33,972 | −32,067 | −49 |
| Erie | 130,803 | 101,786 | −29,017 | −22 |
| Harrisburg | 89,544 | 49,528 | −40,016 | −45 |
| Lancaster | 63,774 | 59,322 | −4,452 | −7 |
| Philadelphia | 2,071,605 | 1,526,006 | −545,599 | −26 |
| Pittsburgh | 676,806 | 305,704 | −371,102 | −55 |
| Reading | 109,320 | 88,082 | −21,238 | −19 |
| Scranton | 125,536 | 76,089 | −49,447 | −39 |
| Wilkes-Barre | 76,826 | 41,498 | −35,328 | −46 |
| York | 59,953 | 43,718 | −16,235 | −27 |
| **Combined** | **3,720,479** | **2,565,039** | **−1,155,440** | **−31** |

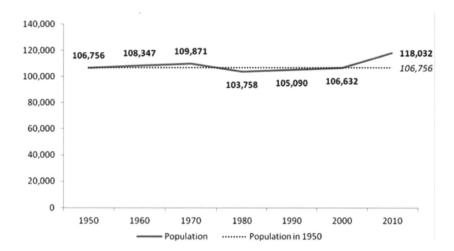

*Figure A.1.* Total population of Allentown, 1950–2010

of [a] city . . . or engaged in the performance of a municipal function." As executive director, for example, I reported not to the mayor but instead to a five-person board, which the mayor appointed. RACA did, however, work closely with city staff to make sure that it used its special powers (the ability to condemn problem properties, which the city did not have) to complement city-sponsored efforts.

Since its founding, RACA's mission has been to prevent and eliminate blight in Allentown; in practice, the authority has typically focused its efforts in the city's oldest neighborhoods adjacent to downtown. On the one hand, this is a relatively easy job; the city's stable population has resulted in a very low level of property abandonment. Just 2.5 percent of all housing units were identified as vacant by the 2000 and 2010 censuses, and code inspections suggest that only half of these were truly blighted. For comparison, 2010 vacancy rates for Reading, Pennsylvania, and Philadelphia were 4.7 percent and 4.3 percent, respectively.

While Allentown did not have many vacant and abandoned properties, it did have many problem properties for a number of reasons: (1) weak housing demand and low property values (roughly half of all owner units in center-city Allentown are valued below $80,000 according to the 2006–2010 American Community Survey estimates); (2) low resident incomes (27 percent of all residents and 43 percent of all Hispanic residents lived below the poverty line in 2010); and (3) declining home ownership rates (down from 53 percent to 48 percent citywide and from 41 percent to just 33 percent in center-city Allentown between 2000 and 2010). This is further exacerbated by the fact that many single-family homes have been converted into multifamily buildings since World War II, which puts additional strain on these properties.

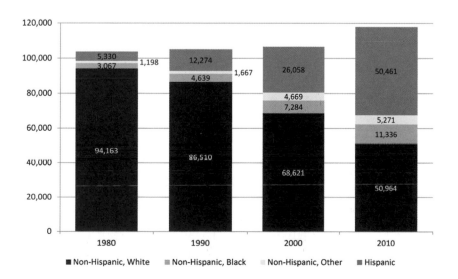

*Figure A.2.* Racial and ethnic breakdown in Allentown, 1980–2010

*Source:* U.S. Census

### Neighborhood Preservation as Redevelopment Strategy

Shortly after Mayor Ed Pawlowski took office in January 2006, it became clear to both city officials and regional stakeholders that Allentown's downtown housing stock, while potentially a real resource, was instead one of the region's biggest liabilities. With support from Lehigh County and the Century Fund, a local foundation, the city hired John Kromer of the University of Pennsylvania's Fels Institute of Government as a consultant to figure out how to best address this liability. Kromer's report was completed in October 2007 and helped chart the course for RACA during my tenure there. Unlike traditional plans, *A Housing Strategy for Allentown's Downtown Neighborhoods* was an asset-management strategy; it saw Allentown's center-city neighborhoods "as an economic asset that can and should generate significant added value to the city and region" as long as their housing was effectively managed. To do so required, among other things, taking an aggressive approach to code enforcement, reinvigorating the city's blighted-property review process, and supporting the rehabilitation of existing buildings by CDCs and urban homesteaders.

Allentown's Bureau of Building Standards and Safety (BBSS) was already inspecting all rental properties on a roughly five-year cycle and conducting systematic inspections of owner-occupied properties on a neighborhood-by-neighborhood basis, completing a neighborhood over the course of two or three years. Based on the report's recommendations, the city added a buyer-notification inspection program to its arsenal, requiring that all for-sale properties also be inspected and that either sellers complete necessary repairs or buyers agree to do so before closing could take place.

### Code Enforcement and Blight-Abatement Strategies

This multipronged approach to code enforcement was a strong first line of defense against excessive disinvestment in city properties. Kromer had criticized the city for not making "full use of its eminent domain powers to acquire problem properties for subsequent development and occupancy" and had recommended strengthening and streamlining the process. To add teeth to these efforts, RACA, working closely with staff from BBSS and the city's Department of Community and Economic Development, reformed its blighted-property review process.

*A problem property in Allentown, Pennsylvania*

Joseph Schilling

Under Pennsylvania's Urban Redevelopment Law of 1945, RACA can acquire individual properties, amicably or by eminent domain, that meet the state's definition of blight. In the blighted-property review process, RACA staff and city housing inspectors generate a list of blighted properties, inform owners of their buildings' inclusion in the process, twice present testimony on the problem conditions at these properties before the Blighted Property Review Committee, and get approval to proceed with condemnation against properties in poor condition from the planning commission, city council, and the redevelopment authority board. The law stipulates the steps in the process and establishes minimum time periods between certain steps, giving owners 60 days to appeal a "determination of blight" and the planning commission 30 days to determine an appropriate reuse for each property prior to condemnation. Beyond that, though, the pace of the process is largely up to the locality's discretion.

Prior to the review and revision of the process, RACA had introduced new lists of blighted properties to the process annually from 2001 to 2006. By 2007, though, only the lists started in 2001 and 2002 had been fully retired (meaning all properties on them were either fully brought into compliance by their owners or acquired by RACA). As a result, the process was largely an empty threat; owners who received letters indicating that a property of theirs was included in the process had no reason to believe that it would ever be taken, even if they failed to address the problem conditions. This, in turn, left code inspectors with little beyond additional citations to hold over the heads of uncooperative owners.

### Reforming the Blight-Abatement Process

We did two things to improve the blighted-property review process: (1) We organized all of the steps in the process onto an annual calendar so that staff within city hall and owners in the community would know what to expect from the process at different points in the year, and so we could be sure that properties referred to the process by inspectors in January would be ready to condemn (if they remained blighted) by December; and (2) we retired all of the existing lists, officially removing properties that were improved and proceeding with the condemnation of those that were not, to make clear that we planned to follow through.

To pick properties for the new lists, we sought recommendations from individual inspectors, who nominated longtime problem properties in their caseloads. We also took advantage of data from the city's code inspections. Any property found to be unfit for human habitation (a violation that required that the property be vacated and therefore eligible for the blighted-property review process) was flagged as such in the city's internal information system. We ran reports on these properties and compiled a database of all "unfit" properties showing when they received their violations and if and when their violations were corrected. We added properties with "unfit" violations at least one year old to the inspectors' nominations.

These two sources typically generated a list of properties far longer than could be targeted in a given year. To whittle the list down in a strategic way, we prioritized problem properties on otherwise healthy blocks, which included some properties in need of demolition but far more that would be good candidates for rehabilitation, and focused on areas where the city's systematic inspections and corresponding city-sponsored loans and grants for interior and facade improvements were concentrated. By our third year, though, the owners of all properties qualifying for inclusion in the process received warning letters before the official work of the Blighted Property Review Committee began. This alone was enough to produce improvements to many of these properties. Not counting those just receiving warning letters, RACA reached 159 properties through the blighted-property review process from 2007 through 2010: 73 properties were made code compliant by longtime or new owners; 54 were acquired by RACA (primarily using CDBG funds); and 32 remain active in the process, either undergoing improvement or awaiting condemnation.

### Coordinating Code Enforcement and Blight Remediation with Neighborhood Stabilization

These reforms to the blighted-property review process came in the midst of the Great Recession and what turned out to be the beginnings of the foreclosure crisis in Allentown.

Unlike many other cities where foreclosures increased sharply in 2007 and 2008, Allentown saw its number of foreclosures remain fairly low before starting to increase in late 2009 and early 2010. Allentown's earliest properties in foreclosure were not those that home owners had stretched to afford but rather marginal rental properties owned by amateur investors who had gotten in over their heads during the boom.

Allentown was awarded roughly $2.1 million through the first round of Neighborhood Stabilization Program (NSP) funding; the funds were distributed in late 2008, and the city had from February 2009 through August 2010 to allocate those dollars. RACA, the entity acquiring properties with NSP funds, prepared for this funding by monitoring the city's foreclosure trends closely, compiling databases of all properties eligible for sheriff's sale as well as those already in bank ownership, and mapping the locations of these properties to identify any foreclosure "hot spots."

*An NSP-funded rehab property in Allentown*

Joseph Schilling

RACA focused on blighted buildings for several reasons: (1) our blighted-property inventory and the staff time dedicated to our blighted-property workload were both increasing; (2) the earliest wave of foreclosures looked a lot like our blighted properties (in fact, many candidates for the blighted-property program started popping up on sheriff's sale lists and REO sales); and (3) it made the most sense for RACA to tackle the worst foreclosures—those buildings least likely to be attractive to responsible private buyers and most likely to act as a drag on the market by remaining vacant for a long time.

This enabled RACA to more holistically address the city's problem properties. In all, NSP funds supported the BBSS's demolition of four severely distressed buildings and aquistion of 18 additional properties, nearly all of which were either already targeted for the blighted-property review process or had code violations serious enough to be eligible for it. On average, these properties had sat vacant and abandoned for two years. Acquiring them amicably (and quickly) diverted them from the blighted-property review process— leaving more room there for other properties, particularly those whose owners would be more likely to bring them into compliance when threatened with condemnation.

Kromer's report had stressed that "supporters of Allentown neighborhoods need to do more to offset" the recent influx of investment owners into the city's downtown neighborhoods and "restore a better balance between homeowners and rental housing." To do so, he proposed helping nonprofit and for-profit developers transform deteriorated or converted properties into quality affordable home ownership opportunities and also reviving the City's Homesteading Program. Between 2007 and 2011, RACA played a key role in Allentown's response to these two recommendations. Drawing from our NSP-funded and blighted-property review process acquisitions, RACA made 38 distressed properties available to for-profit and nonprofit developers at a nominal cost to be transformed into single-family owner-occupied housing. Several of these were rehabilitated through local community-development corporations' first-time home-buyer programs. Prior to their rehabilitation, these properties collectively included 67 units, 29 of which were removed through their conversion to single-family homes.

RACA also worked closely with the BBSS on two additional disposition strategies. First, it helped the city update its defunct Homesteading Program. In the new version of the program, RACA sold properties to homesteaders for one dollar. The amount of financing that homesteaders could borrow from private lenders would be put toward rehabilitation, which would be closely coordinated and overseen by city rehabilitation specialists. RACA made 14 properties available to the Homesteading Program to help jump-start the new initiative. Second, RACA enlisted the rehabilitation specialists to oversee the restoration of two larger apartment buildings along the Seventh Street commercial corridor (one of the city's Main Street districts) that it had acquired with NSP funds. Once completed, they would be sold to generate funds for similar future "in-house" rehabilitation projects.

### Results and Reflections

In early 2009 John Kromer returned to Allentown to review how far the city had come in implementing the recommendations outlined in his original study, and he produced a progress report that April. In the introduction he congratulated city and RACA staff on achieving "remarkable successes within a short period," praising the newly instituted presales inspections, BBSS's increased collection of outstanding fees and penalties and ongoing inspections of all rental properties, and the changes to the blighted-property review process. He concluded that "these actions, taken together, create a foundation for lasting, long-term gains and improve the prospects for attracting investment that will strengthen the economy of Allentown's central business district and neighborhoods."

That foundation was to be especially important as the recession began to unfold. Despite all of our work—deploying an aggressive code-enforcement program, using the threat of eminent domain to help inspectors get compliance, using spot condemnations to acquire longtime problem properties, and then teaming with partners to either rehabilitate or demolish them—the broader economy has taken its toll on Allentown's downtown housing market. Between December 2006 and December 2011, sales prices in center-city Allentown fell by nearly half, from a median value close to $100,000 to one just above $50,000—a loss far sharper than that felt citywide (Figure A.3). The number of foreclosures has also remained stubbornly high; according to RealtyTrac, center city's

*Figure A.3.* Median sales price in center-city Allentown, 2006–2011

Source: Trulia.com

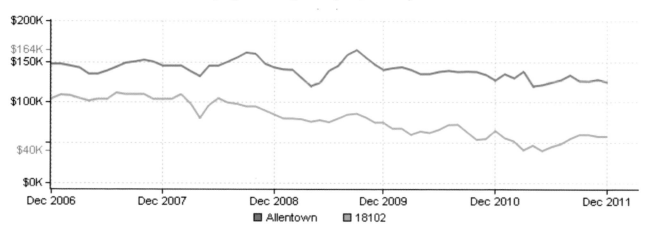

current foreclosure rate, 0.26 percent, is well above both the city's (0.16 percent) and the nation's (0.17 percent).

What Allentown and particularly its oldest neighborhoods desperately need to weather the downturn is more of the aggressive antiblight strategies initiated as the recession began. But this is just one argument in the planning debate that plays out time and again in cities across the country. To "remake" themselves, should cities focus on their downtown or their neighborhoods? Should they emphasize economic development or community development? Should they subsidize industrial complexes or festival marketplaces? Should they attract more office workers or residents of the "creative class"? Should they pursue dramatic changes or stick to incremental changes? Cities would love to do it all, but in most cases—particularly in smaller cities that lack the economic, philanthropic, and institutional advantages of larger ones—limited resources require picking and choosing.

### Back to the Future or Backsliding?

Unfortunately, Allentown's quest for a "big fix" to its economic distress is pulling it farther away from the neighborhood preservation approaches of a few years ago. Instead, Allentown has set its sights on a trophy project to bring about its revival: a downtown hockey arena that has diverted resources and staff time away from neighborhood issues and blight-remediation activities. This is a case of thoughtful planning losing out to politics—of the patience for and faith in long-term, incremental changes that act subtly to change residents' and owners' investment choices losing out to the need to attract substantial attention with high-profile projects, even if those projects face long odds of leading to long-term gains for the city. The research is clear that sports arenas neither spur substantial economic development nor translate into broader neighborhood improvements; it is unlikely that Allentown's planned arena will be different. As a result, it is likely that, when the city does return to the principles and programs outlined and lauded in Kromer's reports, the task will be a much harder one, as it will have to confront higher levels of property abandonment and problematic conditions in a larger share of the city's stock.

*—Karen Beck Pooley*

## ORANGE, NEW JERSEY: ENGAGING THE NONPROFIT AND PUBLIC SECTORS IN COMBATING PROBLEM PROPERTIES

With 30,134 residents in 2.2 square miles, the City of Orange Township, New Jersey, is a dense and diverse inner-ring suburb of Newark. By the second half of the 19th century, this city in Newark's agricultural hinterland had transformed into a thriving industrial city (known as the hat-making capital of the world), thanks to its proximity to rivers, canals, rail corridors, and highways—but by 1960 the city had lost its last hat manufacturer and was struggling to retain its industrial base. During the era of urban renewal the city felt the stings of white flight and disinvestment; between 1950 and 1990 it lost more than 20 percent of its population. By 1994, one in 10 houses in Orange was vacant or abandoned. In order to reverse the decline and attract new investment, the city needed to address these problem properties.

*A foreclosed home in Orange, New Jersey*

Source: reodev.com

### A Strategy for Rehabilitation

Poorly maintained vacant and abandoned properties attract illegal activity, threaten public safety, strain municipal budgets, and depress neighboring property values. According to Wayne Meyer, former housing director of the local CDC Housing and Neighborhood Development Services (HANDS), efforts to rehabilitate many of the worst properties in Orange were frustrated by title problems tied to tax delinquency. When the city sold tax liens to generate revenue, out-of-state investors often purchased the liens with no intention of rehabilitating the properties. Each year the properties acquired additional liens, and the prospects for redevelopment grew dimmer.

When HANDS started working in Orange in 1986 its primary focus was on building new housing on vacant sites. By the mid-1990s it was clear that vacant and abandoned buildings were undermining the progress HANDS had made. Meyer, who is now president of New Jersey Community Capital (NJCC), a statewide community-development financial institution, says the CDC came to the conclusion that "without a healthy housing market, stabilization would be impossible" and shifted its focus to acquiring and rehabilitating problematic vacant properties. HANDS cleared and acquired title to some of the worst properties in the city, and it went on to rehabilitate a number of scattered sites.

Having worked for 20 years as a private real estate attorney, Meyer joined HANDS in 2000, boosting its capacity for clearing title and acquiring problem properties. His approach to clearing title involved building relationships with the mangers of financial pools that purchased third-party liens. HANDS was often able to purchase liens eligible for foreclosure at a deep discount and then clear title by foreclosing on the property and paying off other priority liens (Meyer 2008).

Soon after Meyer's arrival, the city and HANDS convened the Orange Community Problem Property Task Force, a coalition of block clubs and neighborhood leaders, to craft a plan for acquiring and rehabilitating more than 170 vacant properties (Ableidinger 2002). Between 2000 and 2007, HANDS and its community partners made tremendous progress toward ridding Orange of the toughest vacant properties. According to Meyer, the total number of vacant homes dropped more than 70 percent during this period.

Meyer attributes some of this success to HANDS' efforts to reform state housing program rules. Eligible cities and CDCs in New Jersey can now access funding to use on a pool of prospective properties in a troubled neighborhood before establishing site control. Before this change, prospective redevelopers struggled to hold onto properties while waiting for state subsidies to flow. Thanks to an advocacy effort led by the Housing and Community Development Network of New Jersey (HCDNNJ), the state legislature adopted the Abandoned Properties Rehabilitation Act in January 2004, which created new tools that municipalities and CDCs could use to accelerate action on problem properties. The act enabled municipalities to organize special tax sales, in which they could choose a redeveloper and the eventual reuse of a property, and to use spot-blight eminent domain to acquire vacant properties outside of designated redevelopment areas.

In order to use the new tools, municipalities first had to adopt an abandoned property ordinance, which enables a designated public officer to compile an official list of abandoned properties as defined under the act. In May 2004 Orange became one of the first cities in New Jersey to adopt an abandoned properties ordinance (General Ordinances, sec. 67-14). This law requires owners to defend claims of abandonment by submitting a plan for reuse along with a bond for 125 percent of estimated rehabilitation costs. If owners or mortgage and lien holders do not meet this requirement, the city can take ownership of the property or assign its rights to another entity.

According to Meyer, by 2007 the major work of neighborhood stabilization in Orange seemed to be complete. Then the foreclosure crisis hit. "For the first time in eight years we had an uptick in vacant properties," says Meyer.

### Orange's Comprehensive Strategy for Vacant and Abandoned Properties

Since taking over as Orange's director of planning and development in July 2008, Valerie Jackson has spearheaded the city's efforts to stabilize neighborhoods hit hardest by vacant and abandoned properties and foreclosures. When Mayor Eldridge Hawkins Jr. took office in the summer of 2008, he created the Quality of Life Task Force to address problem properties. The task force included representatives from the Property Division of Planning and Economic Development, public works, fire, and police, as well as a health officer from community services. Hawkins charged Jackson with leading the new task force to identify the worst properties in the city, develop a case-management approach for dealing with these properties, and formulate a comprehensive strategy for addressing and preventing future vacancies and abandonment. The task force meets biweekly to discuss strategies for improving code enforcement and removing blighting influences. Jackson uses the inventory created by the Property Maintenance Division, police department, and fire department, as well as HANDS' annual survey, to identify properties to nominate for the official abandoned properties list.

"For the properties that we thought were the worst and needed demolition, I began sending letters to the owners and to any lien holders requesting that they correct problems or demolish the structures," says Jackson. "When we started, we had a list of about 160 vacant properties, and since July 2008 we have demolished or facilitated the demolition of over 25 properties."

*A demolition spurred by the work of Orange's Quality of Life Task Force*

City of Orange Township, New Jersey

According to Jackson, the city's strategies for addressing abandoned properties include prevention, management, and redevelopment. The bulk of the vacant and abandoned properties were in Orange's designated redevelopment areas, which has facilitated their reuse. The city has also been able to tap into Neighborhood Stabilization Program (NSP) funding to secure, acquire, and demolish properties in areas with high numbers of vacant and abandoned properties resulting from foreclosures.

The Quality of Life Task Force also worked on strengthening the city's existing vacant-housing registration ordinance to take advantage of New Jersey's Creditor Responsibility Act (CRA). The CRA authorizes municipalities to hold lenders accountable for maintenance during the foreclosure process even before they take title at the sheriff's sale. As Jackson explains, the ordinance requires owners or responsible parties "to register their properties, ensure the properties are secured, and identify a local company to maintain the properties on a regular basis." Registration fees escalate annually based on the number of years the properties are vacant, and if owners fail to secure and maintain their properties, the city can place liens on those properties to recover costs (General Ordinances, chap. 192).

"We've found that the banks are very good at registering their properties," says Jackson. After she learned that roughly 70 percent of the city's current inventory of vacant and abandoned properties were owned or serviced by one large national bank, Jackson began working with the bank's asset manager to arrange for a single local company to take over maintenance on the bank's portfolio of properties. Jackson says, "This is an important step because right now different people within the bank register and manage different properties."

The city has not held a property auction since the creation of the Quality of Life Task Force. "I've been strategic about turning properties over to developers," says Jackson. "This keeps them out of the hands of speculators and flippers."

Since the onset of the foreclosure crisis, the city has partnered with HCDNNJ, NJCC, HANDS, the Orange Housing Development Corporation (a nonprofit arm of the local housing authority), developers, and others to create strategies for acquisition, demolition, new construction, and rehabilitation of these properties. Jackson meets regularly with these stakeholders to discuss NSP-funded reconstruction and rehabilitation projects in the Central Orange Redevelopment Area (an area with single- and multifamily homes in the heart of the city) and the Central Valley Redevelopment Area (a former industrial and manufacturing area). Thanks to HANDS, the Central Valley area is now a burgeoning arts district, and the city has officially designated it as such.

NJCC was also able to negotiate a bulk purchase of 48 mortgages that had been entangled in a case of real estate fraud and investor bankruptcy. The CDC is managing the properties while it clears title and waits to implement a redevelopment strategy. As a testimony to the initiative's success, it inspired the creation of a new public-purpose subsidiary of NJCC, the Community Asset Preservation Corporation, to acquire and maintain properties in foreclosure while simultaneously assisting home owners at risk of losing their homes.

### Challenges on the Horizon

As Meyer sees it, the immediate challenge for neighborhood stabilization in Orange is a lack of capital. State funding sources are shrinking, and banks are doing less lending to nonprofit developers. "The old model of community development is under challenge," says Meyer. "CDCs can no longer depend on deep subsidies."

When Jackson meets with community groups in the city's south ward, she emphasizes the importance of shared responsibility. Because funding is insufficient to match the scale of the problem, Jackson encourages neighbors to help out with property maintenance, using property-value protection as a selling point for the extra effort.

### Looking Ahead

According to Meyer, a successful comprehensive neighborhood-stabilization strategy requires knowledge of both neighborhood conditions and problem properties. Good data are increasingly important as community-development entities learn to work with smaller subsidies.

Jackson notes that "being the public officer [under New Jersey's nuisance abatement law] and director of planning and economic development with responsibility for the property maintenance division enables me to have a broad and strategic view of the system." She adds, "I've been in a unique position to look across the system, not only at code enforcement, to develop and enhance ordinances, change the way we do work, and prevent properties from becoming vacant and abandoned. The work being done in Orange led to our participation in the Center for Community Progress's Leadership Institute at Harvard University in 2011. We are continuing to work with Community Progress, the Housing and Community Development Network, NJCC, and others to further develop our strategies."

*—David Morley,* AICP

## RIALTO, CALIFORNIA: MINIMIZING RISK IN A BOOM-BUST CITY

The sprawling boomburbs of the Sun Belt bear witness to the tremendous postwar demographic and geographic shifts in the United States. There were 54 suburban cities with populations over 100,000 that experienced double-digit growth in each decade between 1970 and 2000, and only one of these was located in the traditional industrial heartland (Lang and LeFurgy 2007). The greater Los Angeles area alone is home to 19 boomburbs, seven of which are located in the Inland Empire of Riverside and San Bernardino counties.

The Inland Empire was among the regions hardest hit by the Great Recession. Between March 2007 and July 2009 there were approximately 140,000 foreclosures in Riverside and San Bernardino counties (Santschi 2009). These foreclosures affected not only the boomburbs of Corona, Fontana, Moreno Valley, Ontario, Rancho Cucamonga, Riverside, and San Bernardino but also the "baby boomburbs" (i.e., high-growth cities with populations of at least 50,000 in 2000) of Chino, Hemet, and Rialto.

*Foreclosed housing in the Inland Empire*

© iStockphoto/GYI NSEA

### The Surprising Struggles of a Baby Boomburb

Between 1970 and 2010, the population of the City of Rialto in San Bernardino County swelled from 28,370 to 99,171. During this same period, the city experienced a dramatic demographic shift: in 1970 only 31 percent of residents were Hispanic or Latino, but by 2010 that proportion had grown to almost 67 percent. This shift is consistent with Lang and LeFurgy's finding that boomburbs are often surprisingly diverse, in contrast to the relative homogeneity of many suburban communities.

In fact, the land-use, housing, and economic analyses presented in Rialto's 2010 general plan reinforce the facts that few boomburbs are uniformly affluent and many struggle with high unemployment, overcrowding, and a lack of affordable housing—characteristics more commonly associated with traditional urban centers. For example, Interstate highways 10 and 210 divide Rialto into rough thirds, and foreclosures are heavily concentrated in the lower-income neighborhoods located between the two expressways (Rialto 2010). As in many legacy cities, the city's general plan attributes Rialto's foreclosure problems to widespread predatory-lending practices in low-income neighborhoods.

According to the Bureau of Labor Statistics (2011), unemployment in San Bernardino County has been above 11 percent since January 2009, peaking at 14.9 percent in July 2010. During this same period, Rialto's unemployment rate has been even higher than the county's, with a July 2010 peak of 18.8 percent. Furthermore, the lack of jobs in the Inland Empire often means that workers accept wages that are 10 to 15 percent lower than those for comparable positions in the coastal counties of greater Los Angeles (City of Rialto Redevelopment Agency 2008).

According to the latest Comprehensive Housing Affordability Strategy (CHAS) from the U.S. Department of Housing and Urban Development (HUD), 39 percent of all households in Rialto are low, very low, or extremely low income, making less than 80 percent of the area median household income. Perhaps even more jarring, though, is the prevalence of housing problems. Almost 79 percent of low, very low, and extremely low income households in Rialto live in overcrowded units with more than one person per room, substandard units without kitchens or plumbing, or units where housing costs exceed 30 percent of household income (HUD 2012a).

### Being Realistic about Capacity

In response to the still growing foreclosure crisis, representatives from multiple cities, counties, nonprofits, and banks in the Inland Empire began meeting regularly in 2007 to share ideas. However, few participants were prepared for the depth of the recession, and the meetings stalled out without producing a coordinated response (Searfoss 2011).

Regional talks resumed after the creation of the Neighborhood Stabilization Program (NSP) through the Housing and Economic Recovery Act in August 2008. The first round of NSP funding (NSP-1) provided grants to Community Development Block Grant (CDBG) entitlement cities to acquire and demolish or rehabilitate foreclosed or abandoned homes. The 12 eligible cities of the Inland Empire gathered with a representative from HUD's Los Angeles office to explore options including pooling acquisition money or forming a new regional nonprofit to administer the program. While these meetings failed to generate a comprehensive regional strategy, they did lead to increased information sharing (Searfoss 2011).

The targeting guidelines for NSP-1 stipulated that recipients must spend all funds in block groups where more than half of the households earn less than 120 percent of the area median income. By this criterion, almost half of Rialto qualified as a target area. In addition, the distribution of distressed properties was relatively even throughout the low-income areas of the city (HUD 2012b).

Local government capacity in many boomburbs has failed to keep pace with population growth (Lang and LeFurgy 2007). For example, according to the organization chart for Rialto's Development Services Department, the city has only two staff planners. As a comparison, the City of Champaign, Illinois, whose 2010 population was about 80 percent of Rialto's, lists seven professional planners on its planning department website. In many cases cities with small staffs depend on private partners to lighten the load of public finance and management (Lang and LeFurgy 2007). Accordingly, Rialto contracted with CivicStone, an experienced nonprofit affordable-housing consulting group, to administer the city's NSP-1 program once it became apparent that the Inland Empire communities were not going to pursue a coordinated NSP-implementation strategy (Searfoss 2011).

CivicStone's program for Rialto minimized the city's exposure to risk. The goal was to acquire, rehabilitate, and resell distressed single-family homes scattered over a wide area of the city (HUD 2012c). According to an interview conducted by the National Community Stabilization Trust (NCST) with CivicStone president Adam Eliason, the scale of the problem in Rialto meant that NSP money would be insufficient to revitalize distressed neighborhoods. Recognizing that the city's NSP-1 money would not stretch very far if it paid for all acquisition, rehabilitation, and resale costs, Rialto embraced CivicStone's suggestion to use the funds to spark interest among private developers (NCST 2010). The city, through its redevelopment authority, would use its NSP-1 funds to purchase distressed properties and to provide a financial incentive to developers willing to take the lead in rehabbing and reselling those properties. The city's rehabilitation standards act as a quality-control measure to ensure that program houses will be of higher quality than properties offered by investors looking to make a quick return on their investment (Searfoss 2011).

In exchange for assuming more risk, developers receive a relatively large payment ($16,000) once their rehabbed homes sell. According to Eliason, this flat-fee approach encourages developers to pursue as many properties as possible rather than limit their efforts to properties with the highest potential resale value (NCST 2010). After the city identifies potential acquisitions, CivicStone administers a competitive bidding process among interested developers, who project the level of subsidy they will require to complete the rehabilitation. In addition to the $16,000 fee, the city offers a subsidy of up to $10,000 per house to offset rehabilitation costs (Searfoss 2011).

CivicStone's program design for Rialto also incentivizes developer participation by providing a relief valve for worst-case scenarios. If a developer completes a rehab but is unable to resell the house, the city assumes the financial responsibility for the sale. While the developer pays for rehabilitation and resale costs, those costs are expected to come out of the developer's rehabilitation subsidy and developer fee. The developer is never expected to pay out of pocket for an unsold home (NCST 2010). Rialto trusts that its stringent rehabilitation standards will produce homes that can compete well in the marketplace. Because the city has provided clear rehabilitation requirements and program guidelines, developers are free to focus on the financial feasibility of a particular project (Searfoss 2011).

### Putting the Focus on Customer Service

Because Rialto is depending on private developers for the bulk of its program implementation, attention to customer service is essential. The city's Development Services Department includes both housing and building functions, which makes it easier for staff to address developer concerns in a coordinated fashion. As a result, the city is often able to respond to scope-of-work changes within the same day. This gives Rialto's NSP program a competitive advantage over other programs in the region that put less emphasis on communication (Searfoss 2011).

### Outcomes and Outlook

Two lessons from Rialto's NSP-1 experience are that cities need to be realistic about their capacity and that prioritizing customer service will increase the likelihood of success.

Unlike many other NSP-1 cities, Rialto's developer-partner approach allowed it to obligate all of its funds before the November 2010 deadline. As of February 2011 the program had already enabled the rehabilitation of 40 single-family homes, and only one of these projects required additional assistance from the city to help with the resale (Searfoss 2011).

In a May 2011 report on NSP-1 experiences, NCST highlighted Rialto's program as one of three particularly noteworthy examples of successful implementation, alongside programs in Denver and Phoenix. In addition to this acknowledgment, Rialto's program was singled out by the Southern California Association of Governments (SCAG) for an honorable mention in its 2011 Compass Blueprint Recognition Awards, which honor projects that demonstrate excellence and achievement in livability, mobility, prosperity, and sustainability. SCAG affirmed the city's simple victory, writing, "In 2011, the City of Rialto still faces a number of abandoned homes. However, there is a greater stability of neighborhoods compared to 2008 for the residents of Rialto" (SCAG 2011).

The biggest challenge facing the city now may be the dissolution of its redevelopment agency, effective February 1, 2012, in response to a California Supreme Court ruling upholding the state legislature's right to abolish all redevelopment agencies in the state. Rialto's redevelopment agency had been the city's lead on CDBG and NSP administration. For now, this leaves the fate of the city's redevelopment efforts in the hands of administrative staff assigned to the city's Recreation and Community Services Department. Based on reports submitted to HUD, the city has had little success in obligating its NSP-2 and NSP-3 funds. While the original program achieved its initial mission, there are still large numbers of distressed properties in Rialto, so its work has only begun.

*—David Morley, AICP*

# Resources

**PRACTITIONER INTERVIEWS**

In our research and writing for this report, we gathered insights through a series of practitioner interviews to enhance and amplify our menu of strategies. The complete set of interviews, including those that are excerpted herein, are available at www.vacantproperty research.com and www.communityprogress.net.

Charles Bartsch, U.S. Environmental Protection Agency, Washington, D.C.

Kaid Benfield, Natural Resources Defense Council, Washington, D.C.

Ian Beniston and Phil Kidd, Youngstown Neighborhood Development Corporation and Mahoning Valley Organizing Collaborative, Youngstown, Ohio

Teresa Brice, Phoenix Office of Local Initiatives Support Corporation, Phoenix, Arizona

Robert Brown, AICP, City of Cleveland, Ohio

Don Chen, Ford Foundation, New York, New York

Michael Clarke and Anthony Armstrong, Buffalo Office of Local Initiatives Support Corporation, Buffalo, New York

Deeohn Ferris, Sustainable Community Development Group, Washington, D.C.

Frank Ford, Neighborhood Progress, Cleveland, Ohio

John Gower and Tony Kroeger, City of Dayton, Ohio

Christina Kelly, Genesee County Land Bank Authority, Flint, Michigan

Dan Kildee, Center for Community Progress, Washington, D.C.

Samina Raja, University at Buffalo, the State University of New York, Buffalo, New York

Bobbi Reichtell, Neighborhood Progress, Cleveland, Ohio

**FURTHER READING**

Alexander, Frank. 2011. *Land Banks and Land Banking*. Washington, D.C.: Center for Community Progress. Available at www.communityprogress.net/land-bank-book-resources-105.php.

American Institute of Architects' Sustainable Development Assessment Team (SDAT). 2008. *Leaner, Greener Detroit*. Washington, D.C.: American Institute of Architects. Available at www.aia.org/aiaucmp/groups/aia/documents/pdf/aiab080216.pdf.

Ash, Christopher, et al. 2009. "Growing Stronger: A Plan for the Future of Detroit's Community Development Corporation System." Ann Arbor: University of Michigan, Urban and Regional Planning Program. Available at http://sitemaker.umich.edu/urpoutreachreports/capacity_building__b_/da.data/000000000000000000000000 000000000000002946211/ReportFile/growingstrongerred.pdf.

Beauregard, Robert A. 2006. *When America Became Suburban*. Minneapolis: University of Minnesota Press.

Berkooz, Corry Buckwalter. 2010. "Repurposing Detroit." *Planning*, November.

Bonham, Blaine, Jr., Gerri Spilka, and Daryl Rastorfer. 2002. *Old Cities/Green Cities: Communities Transform Unmanaged Land*. Planning Advisory Service Report nos. 506/507. Chicago: American Planning Association.

Brookings Institution. N.d. "Restoring Prosperity." Available at www.brookings.edu/metro/Restoring-Prosperity-Series.aspx.

Buffalo (New York), City of. 2006. *Buffalo's Comprehensive Plan: Queen City in the 21st Century*. Available at http://128.205.118.147/pub/pdf/BCP10-06.pdf.

Cleveland (Ohio), City of, City Planning Commission. 2002. *Connecting Cleveland: 2020 Citywide Plan*. Available at http://planning.city.cleveland.oh.us/cwp/contents.html.

———. 2012. *8 Ideas for Vacant Land Re-use in Cleveland.* Available at http://planning.city .cleveland.oh.us/ftp/8IdeasForVacantLandReuseCleveland.pdf.

Colson, N. Edward, Seok-Joon Hwang, and Susumu Imai. 2003. "The Benefits of Owner-Occupation in Neighborhoods." *Journal of Housing Research* 14(1): 21–48.

DiPasquale, Denise, and Edward Glaeser. 1999. "Incentives and Social Capital: Are Home-owners Better Citizens?" *Journal of Urban Economics* 45(2): 354–84.

Fainstein, Susan S. 2010. *The Just City.* Ithaca, N.Y.: Cornell University Press.

Fels Research and Consulting Group. 2007. *A Housing Strategy for Allentown's Downtown Neighborhoods.* Philadelphia: University of Pennsylvania Fels Institute of Government. Available at https://www.fels.upenn.edu/sites/www.fels.upenn.edu/files/A_Housing _Strategy_for_Allentown_0.pdf.

Flournoy, Rebecca, and Sarah Treuhaft. 2005. *Healthy Food, Healthy Communities: Improving Access and Opportunities through Food Retailing.* Oakland, Calif.: PolicyLink. Available at http://policylink.info/Research/HealthyFood.

Fullilove, Mindy Thompson. 2004. *Root Shock: How Tearing Up City Neighborhoods Hurts America, and What We Can Do about It.* New York: One Word/Ballantine Books.

Gallagher, John. 2010. *Reimagining Detroit: Opportunities for Redefining an American City.* Detroit: Wayne State University Press.

Glaeser, Edward, and Jesse Shapiro. 2001. "City Growth and the 2000 Census: Which Places Grew and Why?" Washington, D.C.: Brookings Institution. Available at www.brookings .edu/reports/2001/05demographics_glaeser.aspx.

Greenstein, Rosalind, and Yesim Sungu-Eryilmaz, eds. 2004. *Recycling the City: The Use and Reuse of Urban Land.* Cambridge, Mass.: Lincoln Institute of Land Policy.

Hodgson, Kimberley, Marcia Caton Campbell, and Martin Bailkey. 2011. *Urban Agriculture: Growing Healthy, Sustainable Places.* Planning Advisory Service Report no. 563. Chicago: American Planning Association.

Hollander, Justin B. 2011. *Sunburnt Cities: The Great Recession, Depopulation, and Urban Planning in the American Sunbelt.* New York: Routledge.

———. 2011. "Surprising Facts from the Census." *Planning*, March.

Hollander, Justin B., and Jeremy Németh. 2011. "The Bounds of Smart Decline: A Foundational Theory for Planning Shrinking Cities." *Housing Policy Debate* 21(3): 349–67.

Hollander, Justin B., Karina Pallagst, Terry Schwarz, and Frank Popper. 2009. "Planning Shrinking Cities." *Progress in Planning* 72(4): 223–32.

Hollander, Justin B., and Stephen Pantalone. 2011. "The Relaxed Zoning Overlay: A Tool for Addressing the Property Vacancy Cycle." *Zoning Practice.* September.

Immergluck, Dan. 2008. "Community Response to the Foreclosure Crisis: Thoughts on Local Interventions." Federal Reserve Bank of Atlanta: Community Affairs discussion paper. Available at www.frbatlanta.org/filelegacydocs/dp_0108.pdf.

Krohe Jr., James. 2011. "The Incredible Shrinking City." *Planning*, November.

Kromer, John. 2000. *Neighborhood Recovery: Reinvestment Policy for the New Hometown.* New Brunswick, N.J.: Rutgers University Press.

———. 2010. *Fixing Broken Cities: The Implementation of Urban Development Strategies.* New York: Routledge.

LaCroix, Catherine J. 2011. "Urban Green Uses: The New Renewal." *Planning & Environmental Law* 63(5): 3–13.

Linneman, P. D., and W. Rybczynski. 1999. "How to Save Our Shrinking Cities." *Public Interest* 135: 30–44.

Mallach, Alan. 2010. *Meeting the Challenge of Distressed Property Investors in America's Neighborhoods.* New York: Local Initiatives Support Corporation. Available at www.lisc.org /docs/publications/102010_Distressed_Property_Investors.pdf.

Mallach, Alan, ed. 2012. *Rebuilding Legacy Cities: New Directions for the Industrial Heartland.* New York: American Assembly.

Mallach, Alan, and Jennifer S. Vey. 2011. "Recapturing Land for Economic and Fiscal Growth." Project on State and Metropolitan Innovation, no. 5. Washington D.C.: Brookings Institution. Available at www.brookings.edu/papers/2011/0503_land_value_mallach_vey.aspx.

National Association of Realtors. 2010. "Social Benefits of Homeownership and Stable Housing." Washington, D.C.: National Association of Realtors. Available at www.realtor.org/Research.nsf/files/05%20Social%20Benefits%20of%20Stable%20Housing.pdf/$FILE/05%20Social%20Benefits%20of%20Stable%20Housing.pdf.

New Jersey, State of, Department of Community Affairs. 2012. "New Jersey Neighborhood Revitalization Tax Credit (NRTC)." Available at www.nj.gov/dca/divisions/dhcr/offices/nrtc.html.

Oswalt, P. 2005, 2006. *Shrinking Cities. Vols. 1 and 2: International Research.* Ostfildern, Germany: Hatje Cantz Verlag.

Popper, Deborah, and Frank Popper. 2002. "Small Can Be Beautiful." *Planning*, February.

Power, Anne, Jörg Plöger, and Astrid Winkler. 2010. *Phoenix Cities: The Fall and Rise of Great Industrial Cities.* Portland, Oreg.: Policy Press.

Rohe, William M., and Michael A. Stegman. 1994. "The Impact of Home Ownership on the Self-Esteem, Perceived Control and Life Satisfaction of Low-Income People." *Journal of the American Planning Association*, 60(2): 173–84.

Rohe, William, and L. S. Stewart. 1996. "Home Ownership and Neighborhood Stability." *Housing Policy Debate* 7(1): 37–81. Available at http://content.knowledgeplex.org/kp2/img/cache/kp/1373.pdf.

Rohe, William, Shannon Van Zandt, and George McCarthy. 2001. "The Social Benefits and Costs of Homeownership: A Critical Assessment of the Research." Low-Income Homeownership Working Paper Series. Cambridge, Mass.: Harvard University, Joint Center for Housing Studies. Available at www.jchs.harvard.edu/research/publications/social-benefits-and-costs-homeownership-critical-assessment-research.

Rossi, Peter H., and Eleanor Weber. 1996. "The Social Benefits of Homeownership: Empirical Evidence from National Surveys." *Housing Policy Debate* 7(1): 1–35. Available at http://content.knowledgeplex.org/kp2/img/cache/kp/1374.pdf.

Schilling, Joseph, and Jonathan Logan. 2008. "Greening the Rust Belt: A Green Infrastructure Model for Right Sizing America's Shrinking Cities." *Journal of the American Planning Association* 74(4): 451–66.

Schilling, Joseph, and Rakish Vasudevan. 2012. "The Promise of Sustainability Planning for Regenerating Older Industrial Cities." In *Cities after Abandonment*, ed. Margaret Dewar and June Thomas. Philadelphia: University of Pennsylvania Press.

Steinbach, Carol. 2005. *Reaching New Heights.* Washington, D.C.: National Congress for Community Economic Development. Available at www.ncced.org/documents/NCCEDCensus2005FINALReport.pdf.

Sustainable Cities Institute. 2012. "Urban Sustainability Directors Network." Available at www.sustainablecitiesinstitute.org/usdn.

Teaford, Jon C. 1993. *Cities of the Heartland: The Rise and Fall of the Industrial Midwest.* Bloomington: Indiana University Press.

Treuhaft, Sarah, Angela G. Blackwell, and Manuel Pastor. 2011. "America's Tomorrow—Equity Is the Superior Growth Model." Oakland, Calif.: PolicyLink. Available at www.policylink.org/site/c.lkIXLbMNJrE/b.7843037/k.B35B/Equity_Summit_2011.htm.

Urban Institute. 2012. "National Neighborhood Indicators Partnership." Available at www.neighborhoodindicators.org.

Youngstown (Ohio), City of. 2012. "Youngstown 2010." Available at www.cityofyoungstownoh.com/about_youngstown/youngstown_2010.

Youngstown Neighborhood Development Corporation. 2012. "Idora." Available at www .yndc.org/neighborhoods/idora.

———. 2012. "Lots of Green." Available at www.yndc.org/programs/lots-green.

## WEBSITES

CEOs for Cities: www.ceosforcities.org

Community Development Advocates of Detroit (CDAD): http://cdad-online.org/wp

Data Driven Detroit (D3): http://datadrivendetroit.org

Detroit Works Project: http://detroitworksproject.com/for-detroit-to-work-we-need-action-today

Enterprise Community Partners: www.enterprisecommunity.com

Genesee County Land Bank Authority: www.thelandbank.org

Growth Through Energy and Community Health: http://gtechstrategies.org

Housing and Neighborhood Development Services: www.handsinc.org

LEAP Detroit: https://sites.google.com/site/leapdetroit

LiveBaltimore: www.livebaltimore.com

Local Initiatives Support Corporation: www.lisc.org

Lower Eastside Action Plan Detroit: https://sites.google.com/site/leapdetroit

Mahoning Valley Organizing Collaborative: www.mvorganizing.org

National Community Stabilization Trust: www.stabilizationtrust.com

NeighborWorks America: www.nw.org/network/index.asp

Northeast Ohio Community and Neighborhood Data for Organizing (NEO CANDO): http://neocando.case.edu/cando/index.jsp

Redevelopment Authority of the City of Allentown: www.allentownpa.gov/Government /AuthoritiesBoardsCommissions/RedevelopmentAuthority/tabid/215/Default .aspx

Rocky Mountain Land Use Institute: www.law.du.edu/index.php/rmlui

## BLOGS

*Flint Expatriates:* A blog for former residents of Flint, Michigan. The author, Gordon Young, is a freelance journalist who grew up in Flint. His posts use different types of media to visually display Flint's not-too-distant past as well as its current state, all while providing a bit of history and commentary. www.flintexpats.com

*Burgh Diaspora:* The blog's author, Jim Russell, a geographer, focuses on Rust Belt diaspora economics and cities. http://burghdiaspora.blogspot.com

*Great Lakes Urban Exchange:* A blog dedicated to connecting various stakeholders with a passion for a Rust Belt renaissance and providing a platform for individuals to share stories and ideas. www.gluespace.org

*Rust Wire: A Voice for Change in the Industrial Midwest:* A site that looks to bring together constructive stories about postindustrial cities throughout the Rust Belt, highlighting both the challenges and assets these cities maintain. http://rustwire.com

*Nullspace: On Matters Pertaining to the Province and Government of Westsylvania:* A blog dedicated to issues of and related to government in western Pennsylvania. The author, Chris Briem, is a urban planning professor at the University of Pittsburgh. http:// nullspace2.blogspot.com

*Detroitblog: Stories from the Motor City:* This blog created by a Detroit newspaper journalist under the pen name John Carlisle features content on Detroit's unique places, spaces, and people, all mixed with a little bit of history. www.detroitblog.org

# References

American Community Survey. 2012. Five-year Summary File, 2006–2010. Washington, D.C.: U.S. Census Bureau. Available at www2.census.gov/acs2010_5yr/summaryfile.

Barry, Brian. 2005. *Why Social Justice Matters*. Malden, U.K.: Polity Press.

Beauregard, Robert. 2011. "Federal Policy and Postwar Urban Decline: A Case of Government Complicity?" *Housing Policy Debate* 12:1.

Benfield, Kaid. 2009. "They Are Stardust. They Are Golden. But Are They Right about 'Shrinking Cities'?" NRDC Switchboard, July 2. Available at http://switchboard.nrdc .org/blogs/kbenfield/they_are_stardust_they_are_gol.html.

Berke, Philip, David Godschalk, Edward Kaiser, and Stuart Chapin Jr. 2006. *Urban Land Use Planning, 5th ed.* Champaign, Ill.: University of Illinois Press.

Beswick, Carol-Ann, and Sasha Tsenkova. 2002. "Overview of Regeneration Policies." Pp. 9–17 in Tsenkova 2002.

Billitteri, Thomas J. 2010. "Blighted Cities: Is Demolishing Parts of Cities the Way to Save Them?" *CQ Researcher* 20(40): 941–64.

Birch, David L. 1971. "Toward a Stage Theory of Urban Growth." *Journal of the American Institute of Planners* 37(2): 78–87.

Bontje, Marco. 2004. "Facing the Challenges of Shrinking Cities in East Germany: Leipzig." *GeoJournal* 61: 13–21.

Bracker, J. 1980. "The Historical Development of the Strategic Management Concept." *The Academy of Management Review* 5(2): 219–24.

Brickman, Johanna. 2009/2010. "EcoDistricts: An Opportunity for a More Comprehensive Approach to Sustainable Design." *Trim Tab*, winter: 27–32. Available at https://ilbi.org /resources/competitions/livingcity/articles/Ecodistricts_TrimTabWinter2010.pdf.

Bryson, John. 2004. *Strategic Planning for Public and Nonprofit Organizations: A Guide to Strengthening and Sustaining Organizational Achievement.* 3rd ed. San Francisco: John Wiley and Sons.

Bureau of Labor Statistics. 2011. "Local Area Unemployment Statistics." Available at www.bls.gov/lau.

Burkholder, Susan, Mark Chupp, and Philip Star. 2003. *Principles of Neighborhood Planning for Community Development.* Cleveland: Cleveland State University Center for Neighborhood Development. Available at http://urban.csuohio.edu/cnd/principlesnpcd.pdf.

Cleveland Urban Design Collaborative and Neighborhood Progress. 2011. "Re-imagining Cleveland: Ideas to Action Resource Book." Available at http://reimaginingcleveland .org/files/2011/03/IdeastoActionResourceBook.pdf.

Community Development Futures Task Force. 2010. "Neighborhood Revitalization Strategic Framework." Detroit: Community Development Advocates of Detroit. Available at https://sites.google.com/site/leapdetroit/documents/CDADTypologyDescriptions .pdf.

CoreLogic. 2011. "New CoreLogic Data Shows 23 Percent of Borrowers Underwater with $750 Billion Dollars of Negative Equity." March 8. Available at http://www.corelogic .com/about-us/news/new-corelogic-data-shows-23-percent-of-borrowers-underwater- with-$750-billion-dollars-of-negative-equity.aspx.

Danielson, Michael. 1976. *The Politics of Exclusion*. New York: Columbia University Press.

Davis, Todd. 2012. "The GE EPIS Center: A Recipe for Brownfield Redevelopment Success." *Brownfield Renewal*, Web exclusive. Available at www.brownfieldrenewal.com/news -the_ge_epis_center___a_recipe_for_brownfield_redevelopment_success-173.html.

Dayton (Ohio), City of. 2003. *CitiPlan Dayton: The 20/20 Vision*. Available at www.cityofdayton .org/departments/pcd/Documents/CitiPlan2020PDF.pdf.

Dewar, Margaret. 2006. "Tax-Reverted Land: Lessons from Cleveland and Detroit." *Journal of the American Planning Association* 72(7): 167–80.

Dewar, Margaret, and June Thomas, eds. 2012. *Cities after Abandonment*. Philadelphia: University of Pennsylvania Press.

Dubb, Steve, and Deborah B. Warren. 2010. "The Evergreen Cooperative Business Network of Cleveland, Ohio." Pp. 54–58 in *Growing a Green Economy for All: From Green Jobs to Green Ownership*. College Park, Md.: Democracy Collaborative at University of Maryland. Available at www.community-wealth.org/_pdfs/news/recent-articles/07-10 /report-warren-dubb.pdf.

East Baltimore Revitalization Initiative (EBRI). 2012. "Status Report: Progress Towards Realizing the Vision of Responsible Redevelopment in East Baltimore." Available at www.eastbaltimorerevitalization.org/status-report/.

Econsult Corporation, Penn Institute for Urban Research, and May 8 Consulting. 2010. *Vacant Land Management in Philadelphia: The Costs of the Current System and the Benefits of Reform*. Philadelphia: Econsult. Available at www.econsult.com/projectreports /VacantLandFullReportForWeb.pdf.

Frater, Mark, Colleen M. Gilson, and Ronald J. H. O'Leary. 2009. "The City of Cleveland Code Enforcement Partnership." June. Available at www.communityprogress.net /filebin/pdf/CLE_CE_Partnership.pdf.

Fund for Our Economic Future. 2012. "Advance Northeast Ohio." Available at www .futurefundneo.org.

Galster, George, Peter Tatian, and John Accordino. 2006. "Targeting Investments for Neighborhood Revitalization." *Journal of American Planning Association* 72(4): 457–74.

Godschalk, David R., and William R. Anderson. 2012. *Sustaining Places: The Role of the Comprehensive Plan*. Planning Advisory Service Report no. 567. Chicago: American Planning Association.

Hack, Gary, Eugenie Birch, Paul Sedway, and Mitchell Silver, eds. 2009. *Local Planning Contemporary Principles and Practices*. Washington D.C.: ICMA Press.

Haefner, Carl, John Gannon, Terry Mushovic, Shannon Nec, and Patricia Schrieber. 2002. *Reclaiming Vacant Lots: A Philadelphia Green Guide*. Philadelphia: Pennsylvania Horticultural Society. Available at www.pennsylvaniahorticulturalsociety.org/garden /vacantmanual.html.

Hoyt, Lorlene, and André Leroux. 2007. *Voices from Forgotten Cities: Innovative Revitalization Coalitions in America's Communities*. Cambridge, Mass.: MIT School of Architecture and Planning.

Indianapolis Smart Growth Renewal District Partnership. N.d. "About Us." Available at www.smartgrowthindy.org/about/index.html.

Kaiser, Edward J., and David Godschalk. 1995. "Twentieth Century Land Use Planning: A Stalwart Family Tree." *Journal of the American Planning Association* 61(3): 365–85.

Katz, Bruce, and Emilia Istrate. 2011. "Boosting Exports, Delivering Jobs and Economic Growth." Project on State and Metropolitan Innovation, no. 2. Washington, D.C.: Brookings Institution. Available at www.brookings.edu/papers/2011/0126 _exports_katz_istrate.aspx.

Kemp, Roger L., ed. 1992. *Strategic Planning in Local Government: A Casebook*. Chicago: APA Planners Press.

Kingsley, G. Thomas, Robin Smith, and David Price. 2009. *The Impacts of Foreclosure on Families and Communities*. Report prepared for the Open Society Institute. Washington, D.C.: Urban Institute. Available at www.urban.org/UploadedPDF/411909 _impact_of_forclosures.pdf.

Kodrzycki, Yolanda. 2002. "Educational Attainment as a Constraint on Economic Growth." In *Education in the 21st Century: Meeting the Challenge of a Changing World*, ed. Yolanda Kodrzycki. Boston: Federal Reserve Bank of Boston.

Kostof, Spiro. 1992. *The City Assembled: The Elements of Urban Form Through History.* Boston: Little, Brown and Co.

Lang, Robert E., and Jennifer B. LeFurgy. 2007. *Boomburbs: The Rise of America's Accidental Cities.* Washington, D.C.: Brookings Institution.

Leonard, Jennifer, and Joseph M. Schilling. 2007. "Lessons from the Field—Strategies and Partnerships for Preventing and Reclaiming Vacant and Abandoned Properties." *Real Estate Review* 36: 31–39.

Litt, Steven. 2008. "Euclid Corridor Project Helps Drive $4 Billion in Cleveland Development." *Cleveland Plain Dealer*. February 10. Available at www.cleveland.com/arts/index.ssf/2008/02/euclid_corridor_project_helps.html.

Longworth, Richard. 2008. *Caught in the Middle: America's Heartland in the Age of Globalism.* New York: Bloomsbury Press.

Mallach, Alan. 2005. *Restoring Problem Properties: A Guide to New Jersey's Abandoned Property Tools.* Trenton, N.J.: Housing and Community Development Network of New Jersey. Available at http://data.memberclicks.com/site/hcdnnj/NJToolkitFINAL.pdf.

———. 2008. "Managing Neighborhood Change." Montclair, N.J.: National Housing Institute. Available at www.nhi.org/research/521/managing_neighborhood_change.

———. 2010a. *Bringing Buildings Back: From Abandoned Properties to Community Asset.* 2nd ed. Montclair, N.J.: National Housing Institute/Rutgers University Press.

———. 2010b. *Facing the Urban Challenge: New Directions for Federal Policy in America's Distressed Older Cities.* Washington, D.C.: Brookings Institution. Available at www.urban.org/uploadedpdf/1001392-urban-challenge.pdf.

———. 2011a. "Building Sustainable Ownership: Rethinking Public Policy toward Lower-Income Homeownership." Philadelphia: Federal Reserve Bank of Philadelphia. Available at www.philadelphiafed.org/community-development/publications/discussion-papers/discussion-paper_building-sustainable-ownership.pdf.

———. 2011b. "Demolition and Preservation in Shrinking Cities." *Building Research and Information* 39(4): 380–94.

Mallach, Alan, and Eric Scorsone. 2011. "Long-Term Stress and Systemic Failure: Taking Seriously the Fiscal Crisis of America's Older Cities." Washington, D.C.: Center for Community Progress. Available at www.communityprogress.net/long-term-stress-and-systemic-failure-resources 110.php.

Mayer, Neil, and Langley Keyes. 2005. "City Government's Role in the Community Development System." Washington, D.C.: Urban Institute. Available at www.urban.org/uploadedPDF/311218_city_government.pdf.

McGovern, Stephen J. 2006. "Philadelphia's Neighborhood Transformation Initiative: A Case Study of Mayoral Leadership, Bold Planning, and Conflict." *Housing Policy Debate* 17(3): 529–70.

McMahon, Ed. 2011. "Zoning at 85." *Urban Land Institute blog*. November 21. Available at http://urbanland.uli.org/Articles/2011/Nov/McmahonZoning.

Michigan Municipal League. 2011. *The Economics of Place: The Value of Building Communities around People.* Ann Arbor, Mich.: Michigan Municipal League.

Miller, Barry. 2009. "Plans That Fit the Purpose." Pp. 213–28 in Hack et al. 2009.

Mishkovsky, Nadejda, and Joseph Schilling. 2005. "Creating a Regulatory Blueprint for Healthy Community Design: A Local Government Guide to Reforming Zoning and Land Development Codes." Washington, D.C.: International City/County Management Association. Available at http://bookstore.icma.org/freedocs/Active%20Living%20Code%20Reform.pdf.

Muro, Mark, and Kenan Fikri. 2011. "Job Creation on a Budget: How Regional Industry Clusters Can Add Jobs, Bolster Entrepreneurship, and Spark Innovation." Project on State and Metropolitan Innovation, no. 1. Washington, D.C.: Brookings Institution. Available at www.brookings.edu/papers/2011/0119_clusters_muro.aspx.

National Capital Planning Commission. N.d. "Southwest Ecodistrict." Available at www.ncpc.gov/ncpc/Main%28T2%29/Planning%28Tr2%29/SouthwestEcodistrict.html.

National Community Stabilization Trust (NCST). 2010. "Lessons from Rialto: An Interview with Adam Eliason, President, CivicStone Consulting." Available at www.stabilization trust.com/local_work/success_stories/rialto.

New York, State of. 2012. "Regional Economic Development Councils." Available at http:// nyworks.ny.gov.

Nivola, Pietro. 1998. "Fat City: Understanding American Urban Form from a Transatlantic Perspective." *Brookings Review* 16(4): 17–20. Available at www.brookings.edu/press /REVIEW/fa98/nivola.pdf.

Park, Chad, Mike Purcell, and John Purkis. 2009. *Integrated Community Sustainability Planning: A Guide.* Version 1.0. Ottawa, Ontario: The Natural Step. Available at www.naturalstep .org/en/canada/toolkits.

Partnership for Sustainable Communities. 2011. *Urban Farm Business Plan Handbook.* Chicago: U.S. Environmental Protection Agency Region 5. Available at www.epa.gov /brownfields/urbanag/pdf/urban_farm_business_plan.pdf.

Porter, Michael. 1997. "New Strategies for Inner-City Economic Development." *Economic Development Quarterly* 11(1): 11–27.

Portland Sustainability Institute. N.d. "EcoDistricts: Building Blocks of Sustainable Cities." Available at www.pdxinstitute.org/index.php/ecodistricts.

Rialto (Calif.), City of. 2010. General Plan. Available at www.ci.rialto.ca.us/development _4598.php.

Rialto (Calif.), City of, Redevelopment Agency. 2008. "Labor/Workforce Data." Available at www.ci.rialto.ca.us/redevelopment_1225.php.

Santschi, Darrell R. 2009. "Inland Empire Economic Development Corp.'s First Refurbished Home Nearly Ready." *Press-Enterprise* (Riverside, Calif.), August 24. Available at http:// ieerc.com/wp-content/uploads/2011/07/082409IEERC_PE.pdf.

Schatz, Laura. 2012. "Decline-Oriented Urban Governance in Youngstown, Ohio." In Dewar and Thomas 2012.

Schwarz, Terry. 2008. "The Cleveland Land Lab: Experiments for a City in Transition." Pp. 73–83 in *Cities Growing Smaller,* ed. Steve Rugare and Terry Schwarz. Kent, Ohio: Kent State University.

Searfoss, Laura. 2011. *Local Perspectives on HUD's Neighborhood Stabilization Program.* Washington, D.C.: National Community Stabilization Trust. Available at www.stabilization trust.com/static/uploads/files/NSP_local_perspectives_NCST_final_report.pdf.

Shibley, Robert G., and Bradshaw Hovey, eds. 2002. *The Lower West Side Neighborhood Stabilization Demonstration Project Housing Design Review Guidelines.* Buffalo, N.Y.: City of Buffalo Housing Design Advisory Board. Available at http://128.205.118.147/pub /pdf/westside_screenres.pdf.

Solomon, Arthur P., ed. 1980. *The Prospective City.* Cambridge, Mass.: MIT Press.

Southern California Association of Governments (SCAG). 2011. "Compass Blueprint Awards 2011." Available at www.compassblueprint.org/awards.

Trust for Public Land (TPL). 2011. "LandVote 2010—Americans Invest in Parks and Conservation." San Francisco: TPL. Available at http://cloud.tpl.org/pubs/confin -LandVote2010-rpt.pdf.

Tsenkova, Sasha, ed. 2002. *Urban Regeneration.* Calgary, Alberta: University of Calgary Faculty of Environmental Design.

Tumber, Catherine. 2011. *Small, Gritty, and Green: The Promise of America's Smaller Industrial Cities in a Low-Carbon World.* Cambridge, Mass.: MIT Press.

U.S. Department of Housing and Urban Development (HUD). 2012a. "Consolidated Planning/CHAS Data." Available at www.huduser.org/portal/datasets/cp.html.

———. 2012b. "Neighborhood Stabilization Program Data." Available at www.huduser .org/portal/datasets/nsp.html.

———. 2012c. "NSP Grantees." Available at http://hudnsphelp.info/index.cfm ?do=viewGranteeAreaResults.

Vey, Jennifer. 2007. *Restoring Prosperity: The State Role in Revitalizing America's Older Inner Cities.* Washington, D.C.: Brookings Institution. Available at www.brookings.edu/~ /media/Files/rc/reports/2007/05metropolitanpolicy_vey/20070520_oic.pdf.

Wachs, Martin. 2009. "The Systems of the City." In Hack et al. 2009.

Young, Robert F. 2011. "Planting the Living City." *Journal of the American Planning Association* 77(4): 368–81.

**American Planning Association**

*Making Great Communities Happen*

The American Planning Association provides leadership in the development of vital communities by advocating excellence in community planning, promoting education and citizen empowerment, and providing the tools and support necessary to effect positive change.

**526. Codifying New Urbanism.** Congress for the New Urbanism. May 2004. 97pp.

**527. Street Graphics and the Law.** Daniel Mandelker with Andrew Bertucci and William Ewald. August 2004. 133pp.

**528. Too Big, Boring, or Ugly: Planning and Design Tools to Combat Monotony, the Too-big House, and Teardowns.** Lane Kendig. December 2004. 103pp.

**529/530. Planning for Wildfires.** James Schwab and Stuart Meck. February 2005. 126pp.

**531. Planning for the Unexpected: Land-Use Development and Risk.** Laurie Johnson, Laura Dwelley Samant, and Suzanne Frew. February 2005. 59pp.

**532. Parking Cash Out.** Donald C. Shoup. March 2005. 119pp.

**533/534. Landslide Hazards and Planning.** James C. Schwab, Paula L. Gori, and Sanjay Jeer, Project Editors. September 2005. 209pp.

**535. The Four Supreme Court Land-Use Decisions of 2005: Separating Fact from Fiction.** August 2005. 193pp.

**536. Placemaking on a Budget: Improving Small Towns, Neighborhoods, and Downtowns Without Spending a Lot of Money.** Al Zelinka and Susan Jackson Harden. December 2005. 133pp.

**537. Meeting the Big Box Challenge: Planning, Design, and Regulatory Strategies.** Jennifer Evans-Cowley. March 2006. 69pp.

**538. Project Rating/Recognition Programs for Supporting Smart Growth Forms of Development.** Douglas R. Porter and Matthew R. Cuddy. May 2006. 51pp.

**539/540. Integrating Planning and Public Health: Tools and Strategies To Create Healthy Places.** Marya Morris, General Editor. August 2006. 144pp.

**541. An Economic Development Toolbox: Strategies and Methods.** Terry Moore, Stuart Meck, and James Ebenhoh. October 2006. 80pp.

**542. Planning Issues for On-site and Decentralized Wastewater Treatment.** Wayne M. Feiden and Eric S. Winkler. November 2006. 61pp.

**543/544. Planning Active Communities.** Marya Morris, General Editor. December 2006. 116pp.

**545. Planned Unit Developments.** Daniel R. Mandelker. March 2007. 140pp.

**546/547. The Land Use/Transportation Connection.** Terry Moore and Paul Thorsnes, with Bruce Appleyard. June 2007. 440pp.

**548. Zoning as a Barrier to Multifamily Housing Development.** Garrett Knaap, Stuart Meck, Terry Moore, and Robert Parker. July 2007. 80pp.

**549/550. Fair and Healthy Land Use: Environmental Justice and Planning.** Craig Anthony Arnold. October 2007. 168pp.

**551. From Recreation to Re-creation: New Directions in Parks and Open Space System Planning.** Megan Lewis, General Editor. January 2008. 132pp.

**552. Great Places in America: Great Streets and Neighborhoods, 2007 Designees.** April 2008. 84pp.

**553. Planners and the Census: Census 2010, ACS, Factfinder, and Understanding Growth.** Christopher Williamson. July 2008. 132pp.

**554. A Planners Guide to Community and Regional Food Planning: Transforming Food Environments, Facilitating Healthy Eating.** Samina Raja, Branden Born, and Jessica Kozlowski Russell. August 2008. 112pp.

**555. Planning the Urban Forest: Ecology, Economy, and Community Development.** James C. Schwab, General Editor. January 2009. 160pp.

**556. Smart Codes: Model Land-Development Regulations.** Marya Morris, General Editor. April 2009. 260pp.

**557. Transportation Infrastructure: The Challenges of Rebuilding America.** Marlon G. Boarnet, Editor. July 2009. 128pp.

**558. Planning for a New Energy and Climate Future.** Scott Shuford, Suzanne Rynne, and Jan Mueller. February 2010. 160pp.

**559. Complete Streets: Best Policy and Implementation Practices.** Barbara McCann and Suzanne Rynne, Editors. March 2010. 144pp.

**560. Hazard Mitigation: Integrating Best Practices into Planning.** James C. Schwab, Editor. May 2010. 152 pp.

**561. Fiscal Impact Analysis: Methodologies for Planners.** L. Carson Bise II. September 2010. 68pp.

**562. Planners and Planes: Airports and Land-Use Compatibility.** Susan M. Schalk, with Stephanie A. D. Ward. November 2010. 72pp.

**563. Urban Agriculture: Growing Healthy, Sustainable Places.** Kimberley Hodgson, Marcia Caton Campbell, and Martin Bailkey. January 2011. 148pp.

**564. E-Government (revised edition).** Jennifer Evans-Cowley and Joseph Kitchen. April 2011. 108pp.

**565. Assessing Sustainability: A Guide for Local Governments.** Wayne M. Feiden, with Elisabeth Hamin. July 2011. 108pp.

**566. Planning for Wind Energy.** Suzanne Rynne, Larry Flowers, Eric Lantz, and Erica Heller, Editors. November 2011. 140pp.

**567. Sustaining Places: The Role of the Comprehensive Plan.** David R. Godschalk and William R. Anderson. January 2012. 104pp.

**568. Cities in Transition: A Guide for Practicing Planners.** Joseph Schilling and Alan Mallach. April 2012. 168pp.